WALL OF FAME

As public education declined and many Americans despaired of their children's future, Pulitzer Prize-winning journalist Jonathan Freedman volunteered as a writing mentor in some of California's toughest inner-city schools. He discovered a program called AVID that gave him hope. In this work of creative non-fiction, Mr. Freedman interweaves the lives of AVID's founder, Mary Catherine Swanson, and six of her original AVID students over a 20-year period, from 1980 to 2000. With powerful personalities, explosive conflicts, and compelling action, *Wall of Fame* portrays the dramatic story of how one teacher in one classroom created a pragmatic program that has propelled thousands of students to college. This story of determination, courage, and hope inspires a new generation of teachers, students, and parents to fight for change from the bottom up.

"Jonathan Freedman tells a moving and inspirational story of real reform in education—the 'radical' remedy of believing in kids of every background and challenging them to reach their potential."

—Robert J. Caldwell, Editor
San Diego Union Tribune's "Insight" Section

"If you are skeptical about all school-reform efforts, read *Wall of Fame.* It is a compelling story that educators throughout the nation need to hear. It describes AVID and its founder, Mary Catherine Swanson, and how a program to help disadvantaged students prepare for college is helping reform secondary schools across America. At a time when interest and concern about schools is at an all-time high, AVID is a great success story that demonstrates thoughtful school reform can make a difference for kids."

—Gary K. Hart
California Secretary for Education

"For thoughtfulness, fairness, and an unslakable drive to be a solution-oriented journalist, I admire few reporters more than Jonathan Freedman."

—Colman McCarthy
©1999, *The Washington Post*
Reprinted with permission.

"A powerful tribute to the difference one dedicated, caring, organized teacher can make on the lives of thousands of students for generations to come. A must-read for educators who really want to break the cycle of failing kids, failing schools!"

—Dr. Mary G. Jarvis
1996 National Principal of the Year

"Real life, real education—a story that demonstrates the power of teaching, learning, and commitment. Never have I read a book that so clearly communicates that success can be taught. This book offers concrete tools and strategies to guide all students and teachers to be their best. It answers the often-asked question, 'Why teach?' Because you change lives!"

—Sandra McBrayer
1994 National Teacher of the Year

"Jonathan Freedman has captured the essence of a true educational reformer. . . . Mary Catherine Swanson inspires all of us . . . to follow our hearts, but use our minds to tackle seemingly intractable problems in education. . . . As a high-school principal who supported one of the earlier AVID programs in my school, I can honestly say AVID helped us change teaching practices schoolwide and alter students' lives forever."

—Dr. Doris Alvarez
1997 National Principal of the Year

"A moving account of AVID's . . . uniquely effective record of educational reform. Amid the chorus of voices talking about improved student achievement, here is a program that actually walks the walk. This book is especially meaningful to me as President of San Diego State University, as many AVID graduates have enrolled and graduated from our university."

—Dr. Stephen L. Weber
President, San Diego State University

"Wall of Fame is not a memorial to a tragic war, but a living tribute to children who overcame prejudice, fear, and violence to become the first in their families to go to college. A powerful metaphor for a new generation determined to succeed by the rigorous standards of the twenty-first century."

—Dr. Gerry House
1999 National Superintendent of the Year

Other Books by Jonathan Freedman

FROM CRADLE TO GRAVE:
The Human Face of Poverty in America
Athaneum Publishers, New York 1993

COLLECTED ESSAYS:
Pulitzer Prize-Winning Editorials on Immigration Reform
Copley Newspapers 1987

THE MAN WHO'D BOUNCE THE WORLD
Turtle Island Press 1979

WALL OF FAME

One Teacher, One Class, and the Power

to Save Schools and Transform Lives

WALL OF FAME

JONATHAN B. FREEDMAN

AVID ACADEMIC PRESS
IN COLLABORATION WITH
SAN DIEGO STATE UNIVERSITY PRESS

First Edition

ISBN 0-9700773-0-0
Library of Congress Card Number: 00-103264

AVID Academic Press
in Collaboration with San Diego State University Press
website addresses: www.avidcenter.org
www-rohan.sdsu.edu/dept/press/

Production Services: The Page Group, Inc.
San Diego, California
Cover design: Máximo Escobedo
Cover photograph of Javier Escobedo: Máximo Escobedo
Typeface: Ehrhardt MT

To

Isabelle, Madigan, Nick, and Genevieve:

the four chambers of my heart.

It is the visions of our students—

their courage, determination, and triumphs—

that awakens our most cherished memories.

It is the visions of youth at its most impressionable,

when teachers and students gather nectar,

that causes flowers to bloom,

weaving garlands of their most wondrous lives.

—Mary Catherine Swanson

INTRODUCTION

HARD HOPE

― HARD HOPE ―

In the fall of 1997, I crossed the line from documenting "the human face of poverty in America" to work as a writing mentor with kids in inner-city schools. I had won a Pulitzer Prize a decade earlier for editorials advocating humane reform of America's immigration laws, including an historic 1986 "amnesty" that enabled over 2 million undocumented immigrants to become legal residents of the United States. I spent my moral capital writing a book, *From Cradle to Grave,* which showed how people at every stage of life could overcome incredible obstacles, grow, and thrive. But as the gap between rich and poor widened in the 1990s, I spiraled downward into despair about the future of America's children. I wanted to stop writing about the problem and become, in some small way, a part of the solution. Using writing as a tool, I sought to kindle the flames of hope in children. In fact, I was searching for hope for myself, my children's generation, and America's future.

While my own teenage daughter and son went to suburban public schools, I offered my skills as an itinerant writing mentor— "Have Pen, Will Travel"—in 5 inner-city schools, working with 700 children, ages 10 to 18. These children spoke a dozen languages and had grown up in violent neighborhoods ranging from the gang turf of Southeast San Diego to the killing fields of Asia, Africa, and Central America. Dozens of student refugees had experienced unspeakable horrors of mass killings, hunger, and cannibalism; hundreds of neighborhood kids had witnessed drive-by shootings, rape, drug use, and gang fights; and a third of my students had suffered physical or sexual abuse. In one class, two 11-year-old students had been orphaned by gang violence. Yet they were children who wrote about their pets, loved to eat cookies, and dreamed of going to Disneyland.

The high schools where I taught were not Disneylands. The dilapidated buildings, armored with steel gates, were guarded by police. Classes were held in scabrous "portable" schoolrooms, where poor working conditions lowered teacher morale. As the school district raised standards, the low-income schools where I taught were put on academic probation and threatened with closure if their principals did not improve test scores. Yet the schools lacked the resources to cope with their students' needs for shelter, nutrition, and stability. Teachers were overwhelmed and felt put down and abandoned. Kids were so anxious about their security—emotional, social, sexual—that they could not focus on classroom learning. Politicians were demanding higher standards and accountability, but the chain of command transformed these high goals into mean regulations, punitively enforced or blatantly ignored. Everybody blamed everybody else: Administrators blamed teachers, teachers blamed students, students blamed families, families blamed the system, the system blamed society, society blamed race, race blamed history, history blamed human nature. . . . Nobody accepted responsibility.

Yet two classrooms I visited seemed altogether different: student morale was high, teachers were dynamic, study was rigorous, learning was exciting. In these classrooms, I saw kids take responsibility for completing assignments, tutors help them prepare for tests, students help each other, and the teachers support and cheer them on to go to college. On the wall of Mr. Visconti's classroom at Crawford High School, students had painted an arresting mural. At the top, in foot-high letters, a brash, graffiti-style sign proclaimed:

WALL OF FAME

Beneath it, stenciled in gritty black letters, ran a long list of students, followed by the dates of their graduation, and the universities they were attending. I counted dozens of names, many of which I could not pronounce, and I was amazed that they were attending some of the finest public universities in California. How was this feat accomplished? In this low-income high school, only a small fraction of the students attended college, yet in this particular class every student over the last three years had gone on to a four-year university. Furthermore, some of these graduates, now enrolled in local colleges, returned to tutor their younger peers twice a week.

As I observed the class, I began to see that it was not limited to one academic discipline. Instead, the students seemed to be working on all of their classes at the same time. The subject matter of this class was *the students themselves*. These kids took responsibility for themselves; teachers took responsibility for their students. They all seemed to work together and to genuinely care about each other.

I remember one student who raised his hand continually to ask questions. He spoke slowly and with great formality, yet his pronunciation was difficult to understand. He seemed to sing vowels like a tribal storyteller from the heart of Africa. His vocabulary had been developed by reading, not watching television. His name was Buay Tang, and only a few years ago he had escaped, with his brother, from civil war and starvation in the Sudan. An orphan at age 10, Buay had lived in squalid refugee camps and did not arrive in America until he was 13, speaking no English. Yet three years later he was studying advanced mathematics and chemistry. How was this possible? What had enabled him to succeed?

Intrigued by this class, appropriately called AVID, or Advancement Via Individual Determination, I asked permission to come back, and I kept on coming back, week after week, for an entire school year. In June, all 28 AVID students were accepted to four-year colleges. Was this an anomaly?

I discovered that 93 percent of the students in this nationwide AVID program gained admission to colleges and universities; 89 percent were still enrolled two years later. This enrollment rate was 75 percent higher than the national average; retention was 56 percent higher. What was the secret of this program?

To seek answers, I called upon Mary Catherine Swanson, the former high-school English teacher who created the first AVID classroom in 1980. Since its inception, she told me, AVID had spread to more than 1,000 schools in 16 states and was now serving more than 50,000 students. If this program was so successful, I wondered, why was it not better known?

In 1998, I approached Mrs. Swanson with a proposal to write a book about the people in her program. Against the backdrop of one teacher's struggle to change public education, the book would follow the lives of six students in her original class and several students currently enrolled in AVID classes. It would strive to be a vivid human portrayal of the changes, for better or worse, in people's lives—not a dry analysis of the program. I did not know where the book would lead, but I asked for her cooperation and support.

Mrs. Swanson agreed to be interviewed in depth and gave me access to AVID classes around the country. Thus began a series of weekly interviews with Mrs. Swanson and a two-year journey to explore AVID programs in California, Colorado, and Virginia. To stay directly involved with kids, I volunteered as a writing mentor in a middle-school AVID classroom.

In order to support this journey, the Charles A. Dana Foundation generously provided funding. *Wall of Fame* is published by AVID Academic Press in collaboration with San Diego State University Press. As the author, I insisted on artistic control. Mrs. Swanson read the manuscript to check for errors in fact, not meaning or style. The collaborative effort reflects my personal involvement and AVID's philosophy of responsibility and respect. By disclosing these relationships at the beginning, I hope readers will reach their own conclusions at the end. What I offer is my personal viewpoint of a subject that I care so passionately about that I chose to get involved. What is lost in dispassionate objectivity may be found in depth of perception arising from participation.

For more scholarly perspectives on AVID, I suggest the reader consult *Constructing School Success* by University of California San Diego Professor Hugh Mehan, et al. (Cambridge University Press); *Altered Destinies* by Professor Gene I. Maeroff of Columbia Teacher's College (St. Martin's Press); and numerous research reports, journal studies, and newspaper articles that have been written by others about AVID.

This is a work of creative non-fiction. I have condensed large blocks of time, limited the number of characters, and dramatized turning points. It is impossible to portray all of Mrs. Swanson's 200 original AVID students, much less the tens of thousands who now participate in AVID programs. The stories I have selected, I believe, reflect this larger picture. When possible, I have interviewed the subjects about whom I write, but some have lost contact with Mrs. Swanson.

While the struggles and success stories of AVID students are well documented, interpretations of what happened are indelibly colored by personal opinions. Therefore, in order to protect the privacy of those who do not share my sensibilities, I have changed the names and identities of those who appear here, except for Mrs. Swanson, her immediate family, and those who gave express written permission for their names to be used. Occasionally, I have created composites. For those readers who find themselves here in some fashion, I can only say this: The characters in this book are not real but emblematic, possessing virtues and flaws common to all humanity. Being a public-school teacher in today's classrooms is an uncommonly difficult task, but there is no more important mission than educating children to cross boundaries.

This is a book about crossing boundaries on many levels. Mary Catherine Swanson crossed boundaries to help students overcome obstacles, and she is unique in having also crossed the boundary from classroom teacher to become a national leader in education reform. AVID students crossed class and ethnic boundaries to take advanced classes and, in so doing, challenged themselves to surpass their own limits. As a journalist, I had to cross perceptual boundaries in order to discover that students can learn *if given the support.* The final boundary is the shibboleth that public schools cannot prepare today's students for the real challenges of our time. If the Wall of Fame, celebrating students like Buay Tang, signifies anything to me, it is an eloquent defense of public education as the foundation of our pluralistic democracy.

Midway through my journey, Mrs. Swanson invited me to share my personal observations with 2,000 AVID teachers who attended the 1999 Summer Institute in San Diego, California. Mary Catherine was in the audience, along with some of her original students and recent AVID students. Sitting with her were the most important people in her life: her father, husband, son, and a former county superintendent who had given AVID a secure home.

"Today is the last Friday the thirteenth of the millennium," I gulped. "Am I nervous?" The audience erupted in laughter. "I am a writer, not a teacher," I confided. "Yet my own life changed when I crossed the line between writing about social injustice—and helping kids cross boundaries." I told about my year as a writing mentor in inner-city schools, asking kids from the most hopeless neighborhoods to pen essays, answering the most difficult questions facing any human being: *Where do I come from? Who am I? Where am I going?*

"I wanted them to discover a future—hope," I said, pausing, "and that's how I discovered AVID."

Mary Catherine Swanson sat with her family, obviously uncomfortable with being the focus of attention, even though her prodigious efforts had brought together the threads of two generations, spun in far-flung corners of the globe, woven with the hues of all complexions into a fabric of human relationships called AVID. The students in that room were living examples of how education could change lives, and the lessons their teachers had learned could prepare a new generation for the challenges of the twenty-first century.

But how did one young teacher in one small classroom defy the education hierarchy; inspire, cajole, and prod disadvantaged students to determine their own destinies; and revolutionize public schools?

This is the AVID story—the 20-year learning adventure of Mary Catherine and her students.

PART ONE

ZERO AT THE BONE

1980

— ZERO AT THE —
BONE

The seeds of AVID were sown during the idealistic autumn of the "American Century," when public schools were assigned what was arguably the most difficult task facing this country: to wipe racism off America's slate and teach children equality. A new generation of educators and students would succeed, civil-rights advocates believed, where generations of bigoted adults and segregated schools had failed to end a separate and unequal society. Social reformers sought to give a new generation an equal chance to reach the American Dream, beginning with a good education. Desegregation of schools, they argued, would finally end America's legacy of slavery and prejudice. A century after the Civil War, integration would bring healing to America.

Instead, school desegregation would cause a backlash that deepened wounds of fear and prejudice. In 1954, the U.S. Supreme Court ruled in *Brown, et al. v. the Board of Education of Topeka, Kansas, et al.* that segregated schools violated students' Constitutional rights. Over the next four decades, public schools would become the focal point of America's bitter racial, cultural, and economic conflicts. By the year 2000, California schools, which had been optimistically built on earthquake faults during the 1950s, would sit astride some of the deepest racial and cultural fault lines in America.

San Diego lies at the southernmost end of California's geological and cultural fault lines. This sprawling suburban metropolis on the southwest corner of the continental United States is at a crossroads where the Mexican border intersects the Pacific Rim. In World War II, San Diego was known as "Dago," a predominantly Navy town. As the economy diversified in the 1960s and 1970s, San Diegans laid back in the sand and sipped margaritas while "Sun Diego" grew like crazy. By the 1980s, it had become the sixth-largest city in the United States. Mayor Pete Wilson called it "America's Finest City."

But beneath the feel-good veneer, San Diego mirrored the problems of middle America, with the added seasonings of Mexican salsa, African-American barbecue, Vietnamese soy, Thai curry, and Ethiopian spice. Like many American cities that were *not* flash points of race riots, San Diego's schools were "de facto" segregated and unequal, by neighborhood—not law. Interstate Highway 8, which brought migrants from the East Coast and the South to the Pacific, became a rough dividing line between affluence and poverty. North of I-8 were white suburban communities of Clairemont and La Jolla, where excellent high schools sent a large proportion of graduates to college. South of the interstate, inner-city neighborhoods grew in the shadows of downtown and graffiti-scarred schools excelled in sports, not academics. African Americans lived in proximity to Hispanic Americans and recent Mexican immigrants, while refugees poured in from U.S. military interventions, tribal wars, genocides, and catastrophes in Indochina, Central America, and Africa.

In 1978, a federal judge ordered the San Diego Unified School District to draw up a voluntary plan to end segregation of its public schools. Although the judge never ordered forced busing of individual students, the school bus would become the vehicle for transporting thousands of children across the dividing line. Minority parents were attracted by the "magnet schools" north of I-8 that offered auto shop, business, and marketing programs. These programs often turned out to be remedial classes with low expectations that isolated minorities in an instructional ghetto within a school.

By the spring of 1980, the shock waves of San Diego's new court-ordered desegregation program reached Clairemont High. This white middle-class school, located on a bluff above the Rose Canyon earthquake fault and overlooking Mission Bay, was acclaimed for academic excellence. Many students grew up in 1960s-style tract homes that had been built especially for aerospace workers who designed the *Atlas* missile at a nearby facility. The loyal faculty, many of whom had taught at Clairemont since its opening in 1959, took pride in Clairemont's reputation. A large proportion of students took college-level honors classes, and top students went on to the University of California and Ivy League colleges. This middle-income school was academically competitive with the best public and private schools like La Jolla High, but it was routinely trounced on the football field by inner-city schools like Lincoln High.

Eleven miles north, the University of California at San Diego (UCSD) was becoming a national leader in biology, engineering, and other high-tech fields. The university supported biotech industries, attracting population growth that, in turn, spawned the construction of a brand-new University City High School campus in a white professional neighborhood.

By the spring term of the 1979–80 school year, Clairemont's faculty knew that most of their affluent white students would move to University City High. They also knew that 500 students from the poorest urban neighborhoods, most of them Hispanic or African American, would arrive via buses in the fall. Between the spring and fall, Clairemont's student population would change from 95 percent white to 38 percent minority.

Some of Clairemont's aging white faculty members had believed they would coast to retirement, lecturing to the same kind of students with their same old notes. Viewing change as a threat, they now seethed with resentment, confusion, and fear. Many felt betrayed that "their" school was being overwhelmed by "those kids" from the ghetto. Teachers who esteemed their students' high test scores as a measure of their professional status felt personally affronted. Some hoped to follow their most affluent students to University City High, which some Clairemont teachers had helped design. Others felt hopelessly trapped. How could a school distinguished for educating middle-class students at the highest academic levels teach minority and poor children who scored at the lower middle and bottom?

Two of Clairemont's teachers, however, saw this tempestuous change not as a threat but as a challenge.

Mary Catherine Swanson and Jim Grove, her mentor of ten years, liked to talk after school about the purpose of public education and their calling as teachers. They believed that the education of *all* students, not just the best and brightest, was fundamental to the survival of American democracy. A teacher's job was to help her students learn, period. Although it sounded simple, it contrasted with the notion among some Clairemont faculty members that a teacher's job was to cover specific *subject matter*, usually as quickly as possible. From this elitist perspective, if the lazy spawn of welfare mothers, illegal immigrants, and other undesirables didn't get it the first time, let them fail—or go back to Mexico. Mary Catherine and Jim found such cynicism and bigotry abhorrent. Although their teaching styles differed as much as their generations, they shared a common belief in advancement through individual determination.

Mary Catherine taught children at both the top and the bottom of the Clairemont student body of 2,400. Her honors classes challenged students to develop analytical skills and to write complex essays. Indeed, many of her students went on to the University of California at Berkeley or other prestigious universities. On the lower end, some of her students in the "developmental reading program" were still sounding out words at age 16. She prodded them to finish their rote exercises quickly and read popular paperbacks of their own choosing. This got them reading for pleasure, improving their skills dramatically and stimulating their curiosity to learn.

The musty smell of the aging school, with rain-stained acoustic ceiling tiles, was a daily reminder of the sweat and toil that made adolescent learning a uniquely human endeavor. This gritty struggle with its setbacks and triumphs deeply attracted Mary Catherine to share her students' fears, hopes, and dreams. She wanted not only to expand their *minds,* but to open up possibilities for their *lives.* Each new morning, Mary Catherine came back to Clairemont, flung open the windows, and breathed in the breeze from the sea. Every morning, she gazed with wonder at the liquid ambar trees that turned colors with the seasons.

These beautiful trees, also known as sweet gum, fascinated her. They are not native to San Diego's mild climate, where many trees stay green all year. The liquid ambar's colorful pageantry of the seasons is a rare phenomenon in San Diego. For Mary Catherine, these deciduous trees with their colorful leaves clearly marked the transitions of the school year.

Jim Grove led Clairemont's highly acclaimed "Seminar" class of 15 students, whose minimum IQ scores were at least 145. Grove had taught high-school and community-college classes for 25 years and had been Mary Catherine's friend for the last 10. Mary Catherine found Jim to be wise and introspective, constantly seeking ways to teach kids effectively. He did not suffer fools lightly and challenged his students with rigor, demanding that "surfer dudes and dudettes" declaim passages from Chaucer's *Canterbury Tales* in Olde English. Yet he had grown up dirt poor in Texas, in and out of orphanages, and had empathy for bright children traumatized by unstable homes. Jim was committed to *meeting kids' needs* and knew how to motivate those particularly smart but socially inept kids on whom other teachers had given up.

Mary Catherine greatly admired Jim and shared his high calling for the profession of teaching. She loved their long talks in September afternoons as the sun melted into the sea, and Jim conjured up green flashes of insight. But in the gloomy February mornings of 1980, she wondered if her successful days at Clairemont were over and whether or not she should move on.

At age 36, Mary Catherine, a striking blonde, was at the peak of her career as English Department Chairwoman of Clairemont High. For 14 years, she had taught rigorous English classes; led intellectually stimulating college-level literature seminars; and sent stellar graduates to Harvard, Stanford, and Berkeley. In 1980, Mary Catherine was invited to join the faculty of a brand-new school, University City High, located in a planned community rising east of La Jolla. This was an exciting prospect, for she had been consulted on the design and curriculum of the new school, and its modern architecture and advanced classes embodied her belief in excellence.

"If you come to University City High, you can create the English Department from the ground up," the new principal told her.

"With interdisciplinary studies and a whole new curriculum!" she dreamed aloud.

The principal nodded as she ticked off progressive ideas on her academic wish list. "I'll need an answer soon," he said.

Back at Clairemont, she mentioned the offer to colleagues lunching outdoors in the sun.

"Yes, you can go to University City or stay at Clairemont and greet the hordes off the bus," a cynical history teacher commented. Hungry seagulls wheeled above the dingy green courtyard, a shadow passed overhead and wary teachers, knowing what came next, ducked the falling matter. The tired teacher turned to Mary Catherine. "If I were you, I'd take the opportunity to get out of this school before it becomes a zoo."

Colleagues laughed at the thinly veiled reference to the minority students who were going to be bused there that fall from the inner city of East San Diego to Clairemont. Mary Catherine's back stiffened beneath her crimson blouse. Why couldn't she take those kids off the bus and put them in advanced classes? Did cynical teachers think blacks and Hispanics couldn't handle it? Wasn't helping students what public-school teaching was all about?

Yet the opportunity to a create an interdisciplinary curriculum at University City High sent her thoughts soaring above the spattered pavement to new academic heights. Could she pass up this wonderful offer?

Mary Catherine now faced the defining choice of her teaching career. This decision would test her resolve and reveal her true character.

As a banker's wife and mother of a son, she lived in an affluent white community of one-acre homesites tended by Mexican gardeners. Her spacious, two-story home was an hour's commute north from Clairemont High. She had never had occasion to visit the low-income neighborhoods of Southeast San Diego or Barrio Logan. Could she effectively teach students bused in from inner-city neighborhoods and barrios whose accents and experiences were foreign and whose academic records were mediocre to poor? How could an academically demanding teacher from a "lily-white" family best *meet the needs* of children of color, whose parents might not speak English or had only a minimal education? Should she stay with what some of her colleagues feared was a "sinking ship" at Clairemont or follow her privileged students to a brave new school?

Mary Catherine's choice would have to be made before the end of the school year, when the liquid ambar trees turned color once more.

On the commute home each night, Mary Catherine's thoughts turned from school to her challenges as wife and mother. When she turned into the leafy lanes of the San Diego suburb of Olivenhain, Mary Catherine once again would become absorbed in the lives of her devoted husband of 14 years, Tom, and their beloved eight-year-old son, Tommy.

Mary Catherine Jacobs and Tom Swanson had grown up in the same small town of Kingsburg, California. The Jacobs family of four was small by Kingsburg's standards, and they were the only people with the surname Jacobs in town. Born in the hopeful aftermath of World War II, Mary Catherine was the daughter of Ed and Corrine Jacobs. Ed was publisher and editor of the *Kingsburg Recorder*, the town's newspaper, and was an alumnus of the Columbia Graduate School of Journalism in New York. He took his bride, Corrine, to California in 1940, bought the *Kingsburg Recorder* at age 26, and ran it all his life. Mary Catherine's paternal grandfather was a former college professor and president of a midwestern college. From the time she knew how to read, it was expected that she would do well in school and go to college.

"What grades did you get?" her daddy would tease her. "Zero, zero, zero, zero?"

"No, Daddy. A, A, A, A!" she would exclaim with pride.

Her father was always there for her when she was sick. As a child, she was plagued with stomach upsets. From age 3 to 12, she threw up regularly. Doctors gave her a thousand tests, but never came up with a medical diagnosis. She would vomit so violently that she would dehydrate. Then her father would take her to the hospital and sit with her, the long night through, while the IV filled with glucose would drip down a tube through a needle stuck in her thigh—her forearms were too skinny to support the needle. Her mother never came. Perhaps, in retrospect, the vomiting was the result of emotional tension between mother and daughter, Mary Catherine now speculates. But her father was loyal and loving. At Columbia School of Journalism during the 1930s, he had penned not only news articles, but poems and short stories. And in the 1950s he made up stories starring "The Mighty Midget," a superhero who gave his daughter the courage to dream that, with determination, she could overcome the worst things a child could imagine. Then, after agonizing hours of waiting for the glucose bag to empty into his daughter's swollen thigh, he would "accidentally" knock it over, apologizing to the nurses—and rescue his daughter. Early the next morning, sleepless and red-eyed, he would go to work without complaint—a legacy of compassionate determination he would hand down to his daughter. Half a century later, she would consider it a privilege, not a duty, to take care of her father in old age.

A photograph of Mary Catherine's elementary school reveals a dozen blonde girls wearing Swedish pinafores with white handkerchiefs. She wore a Swedish folk costume, but was not Swedish, which gave her a slight sense of what it meant to be excluded. Later, in high school, the stubborn father and his daughter engaged in heated debates about everything from predestination and free will to the right of civil-rights workers to occupy segregated lunch counters in the South.

Mary Catherine was popular, an A student, a cheerleader, and the co-valedictorian of her high-school graduation class. Inwardly, she felt like an outsider, yearning for a world beyond Kingsburg. Mary Catherine went away to college at San Francisco State University, where she studied journalism. She also took English classes at UC Berkeley and dreamed of following her father's footsteps into newspapering.

In contrast, Tom's Swedish immigrant family was large, and he seemed to be related to everybody. There were more Swansons in Kingsburg than you could shake a stick at. After high school, Tom went to the University of California at Davis, where he studied economics. The two kept in touch, across the widening gap between conservative Central California and the upheaval of Berkeley in the 1960s.

Mary Catherine undertook a strenuous double-major program and graduated in three years. She wrote columns that were published in the San Francisco State *Gator* newspaper. She took unpopular stands, as did her father in his courageous newspaper editorials, which were frequently published as columns in the *Los Angeles Times*. Everyone in Kingsburg knew what Ed Jacobs stood for, especially when he was a lone voice upholding high principles in a small town. Like father, like daughter. In the rebellious 1960s, Mary Catherine was a contrarian voice arguing for respect for law *and* social justice. She advocated that old-fashioned "square" values were the best way to subvert an unjust, corrupt system. Her controversial views were not popular with radicals, nor, for opposite reasons, with her father.

In her final year, she debated between choosing a career in journalism or teaching. Sometimes she dreamed of going to her father's alma mater and fighting her way into the male-dominated world of journalism. But she also loved literature and the passionate academic world of ideas, and she often dreamed of becoming an English teacher.

In October 1965, Mary Catherine won a prestigious scholarship. She called Tom Swanson, whom she'd been dating on and off for six years.

"Tom, I got a Woodrow Wilson Fellowship to the Columbia School of Journalism!" she exclaimed.

He congratulated her, but his voice was low. "Columbia's in New York City, right?"

"Yes, right on Broadway at 116th Street, in the media capital of the world!"

"And you'd be there for two years?" He paused. She answered yes, wondering at his lack of enthusiasm. Tom's voice grew determined. "I'd like to come to San Francisco and see you."

Tom didn't have a car. He begged his brother to loan him his beat-up Volvo, and his brother agreed on the condition that Tom loan him money. With only a few dollars for gas, Tom rushed south. He'd never driven this kind of stick shift before, but made it safely to Mary Catherine's apartment on Junipero Serra Boulevard.

Her flat was above a bar. She shared the ancient walkup with two roommates, and it was furnished on a thrift-store budget. Tom sat beside her on the avocado-green couch, the broken springs jabbing them as they looked at each other. It was four o'clock in the afternoon, and the fog was rolling in.

"I don't want you to go to New York. Once you see the bright lights, I don't think you'll ever come back," Tom said. "I want us to get married."

Mary Catherine leaned back as far away as she could, trying not to seem impolite. She had suspected he might propose, but had dreamed he'd take her to the top of Coit Tower overlooking San

Francisco Bay and beg for her hand on bended knee. Instead, he sat on the edge of the couch, and she looked at his sun-tanned face, his eyes steady, though his knees were knocking. There was nothing phony about Tom, and if there was one word that described his combination of humility, determination, and pride, it was *integrity*. Her mind told her to choose Columbia, but her heart had already made her choice, based on qualities that she most valued and that shone through Tom's eyes.

"It's a huge decision, but I think you're probably right," she said with unruffled simplicity.

"Come with me to Davis! There's a huge party at my fraternity tomorrow, and we'll announce it there!" he cried. They packed up and took off, heading for the Golden Gate Bridge. Approaching the toll booth, Tom nervously ground the gears, lurching to a halt. He fumbled for coins and missed the toll keeper's palm, dropping a quarter on the ground. As the toll keeper leaned down, Tom pumped the gas too hard. The car backfired and they rolled across the bridge, precariously suspended between shores.

When they arrived in Davis, Tom confessed that he was virtually broke. To celebrate their engagement dinner, they pulled into a drive-in and ate Frosty Freeze ice-cream cones. That night, calling home, Mary Catherine consulted the man whose opinion she most respected.

"Dad, I've got to choose between Columbia and Tom," she said. "I know how much Columbia means to you, but I told Tom yes. Before we announce our engagement, I want to know your opinion."

"It's your decision," her father said. It was the first time that he had shown her the respect of making her own judgment.

"Thank you, Dad. I want to share my life with Tom."

"Are you going to settle down and be a housewife?" her father asked bluntly.

"No, I want to become a teacher."

"Of little kiddies?"

"I have no interest in teaching elementary school, Dad. You know that. I want to teach high-school students literature and expository writing, to grapple with ideas."

"What about money?"

"Teaching is a calling," she said. "I value intellectual satisfaction over material wealth."

Mary Catherine and Tom built a good life together; she became a teacher, and he went to graduate school and then to work in a bank. Despite economic hardships in those early years, they never asked their parents for a nickel.

The birth of their son, Thomas Jacobs, in 1972 felt like a miracle to Mary Catherine. After six years as a classroom teacher, she sacrificed her profession to become a full-time mother. But after a semester of changing diapers, Mary Catherine found herself growing frustrated. She cherished Tommy beyond words, but missed the stimulation of teaching. Knowing herself, she believed she would be a better mother if she could keep alive intellectually, so she asked Tom what he thought about her returning to teaching part time.

"Whatever you want to do, I will support you," he said.

Due to the kind of fortune that sometimes made her think teaching was her destiny, she found a grandmother who was looking to take care of a child at home. Miraculously, the kindly woman lived across the street from Clairemont High, so Mary Catherine dropped Tommy off before school and took him home in the afternoon. Sometimes she brought him into her classroom to play in the company of students who doted on him. The smell of chalk dust was in his blood.

Tommy was as wonderfully unique as any normal boy of his age. The Swansons were sophisticated professionals in America's sixth-largest city, but they lived by a code of small-town values. They wanted their son to grow up with all the opportunities available to a boy in the 1970s. From the moment Tommy went to kindergarten, his parents were committed to do everything they could to give him the best education possible. They also believed in hard work, honesty, respect, and the freedom to choose one's own path.

They expected that their son would do well in school and, if and when he needed help, they would be there to encourage, challenge, and support him. A college education was Tommy's birthright. Mary Catherine wanted the same things for her students that she wanted for her son.

Jim Grove had his own story, one that Mary Catherine did not fully know. When he was seven years old, Jim and his brothers were placed in an orphanage in El Paso, Texas. His parents were alive, but their marriage was dead. With a hard-drinking father and stressed mother, Jim was bounced between warring parents, who could not always put a roof over their children's heads. Jim started working full time at the age of 14; set up a house for his brothers; and supported them; doing the cooking, cleaning, ironing, and shopping. Jim's father worked on the railroad and the lonesome whistle echoing across the desert called Jim to visit glittering cities beyond the Rio Grande. Jim dreamed of being in the movies. After all, he'd actually sung "God Bless America" on the radio. So he dragged his brothers on a train from Texas to Hollywood, where they auditioned at the Megland Kiddie School on Venice Boulevard. If they made it, the school promised them a Hollywood audition. The Grove brothers stood up on the stage and sang their hearts out.

"Those little fellas don't sound too bad," said the talent scout, "except that big skinny one." He pointed at Jim. "He's got an awful nasal twang." Jim slunk off the stage, bringing his brothers back to Texas.

Lord, how he hated school! There were so many more important things he had to contend with—like paying the bills and feeding his brothers—to waste time in the schoolhouse. He worked as a soda jerk in a drugstore to make ends meet.

When Jim discovered books, he read everything he could get his hands on. The more he learned, the more he realized what he didn't know, and his mind consumed ideas with the wild abandon of a prairie brush fire. He still had no interest in classes and was surprised when his name was called at a high-school student awards ceremony.

"Jim Grove, National Honor Society!" the principal announced. Climbing the stage to grasp the certificate and receive a handshake, Jim was stunned. As his classmates applauded, he could barely say thanks before stumbling back to his seat. That night he brought the certificate home, but Pa showed little interest in a piece of paper that wasn't a greenback. Still, the award startled Jim into thinking about a future beyond the saloon doors swinging closed behind his father. One day, Jim screwed up his courage and shared his dream aloud.

"Ma, I sure would like to go to college," Jim said.

"You'll be sorry!" she cried, shaking her finger.

"Why, Ma? Maybe I can get a scholarship."

"It's a will o' the wisp!" Angrily, she brushed the award away, along with his hopes of ever convincing her. Tears of rage welled up in his eyes, and he went back to his chores, stoically raising his little brothers. Years later, Jim would defend his mother, explaining that it wasn't that she didn't want the best for him. She just didn't think it was possible for a poor boy to go to college, and she did not want him to be disappointed.

Jim kept reading. He bought books, borrowed books, even stole books. Something compelled him to seek higher education, yet none was available in his border town. He had no more of a future than tumbleweeds blowing in the dusty vacant lots of his lost childhood.

Finally, history intervened when communists attacked South Korea. The boy from El Paso joined up to defend the Free World. After doing his part, the Korean War veteran caught the tail-end of the GI Bill—a ticket to higher education. So the boy who hated school became a teacher.

In 1959, brand-new Clairemont High School opened its doors in a space-age neighborhood of tract homes built for aerospace workers and their families. *Sputnik* had propelled America into the Space Race, and Clairemont Mesa became the manufacturing center for the *Atlas* missile program.

Jim was 30 years old, a new teacher at the birth of a new school.

"Everything in the air was for teachers," he recalled 40 years later. "We had a big support system, the best students in town. Integration was not even on the horizon. I was starry-eyed."

A large percentage of Clairemont students were the first in their families to go to college. America was creating opportunities for millions of people from humble backgrounds to join the middle class. Education was the great escalator to middle-class status, and California lavished its treasure on public education.

Jim thrived in the atmosphere of innovation. By 1964, he was chairman of the English Department at Clairemont. In 1970, he reinvented its Seminar Program. He recruited a lot of bright kids who were failing in traditional classes. His secret was a combination of traditional tough "book-learning" and flexible scheduling that enabled students to work in small groups.

Jim met Mary Catherine in 1970 and quickly saw that she was an extraordinary teacher. She followed his footsteps to become the chairwoman of the English Department.

To make the decision of whether to go or stay at Clairemont High School, Mary Catherine consulted her students, both at the top and the bottom of the performance spectrum. She never asked them specifically what to do, but rather talked with them about their own choices, hoping to hear her own voice speak from within.

The joy of teaching stellar students was to sit on a wooden folding table and discuss poetry with a budding young English scholar named Kathy. Mary Catherine would always remember Kathy's blonde hair, pulled back from her face, and her blue eyes shining with passion as she teased nuances of meaning from "A Narrow Fellow in the Grass," a poem by Emily Dickinson.

The poem was about a snake, and the phrase that intrigued Kathy described the moment when the reclusive poet encountered a serpent in the grass, feeling pierced to "zero at the bone." The lively discussion in advanced English was not enough for Kathy; she remained after class and engaged Mary Catherine in a tête-à-tête, exploring the subtle emotions evoked by the poet.

"What do you think 'zero at the bone' means?" Kathy asked, holding the poem between her thin fingers, as if to squeeze meaning out of Dickinson's enigmatic words.

"To me, it's about those surprise encounters in life that absolutely stop you dead," Mary Catherine answered thoughtfully. "You can turn around and run or you can face the danger. You have to make a conscious decision."

Kathy seemed to be weighing the words inwardly, considering a choice in her own private life. Then her eyes suddenly brightened and she cried, "Thank you, Mrs. Swanson!"

Mary Catherine never knew what Kathy had decided; she didn't have to. Sometimes, all a student needed was someone to listen. These were the deep encounters that Mary Catherine cherished most as a teacher, and the intellectual side of her complex personality wanted nothing more than to share the excitement of literary, and personal, discovery with students like Kathy.

It was dark when Mary Catherine left her classroom and walked along the grassy path. She was stopped dead by the decision in her own career. Should she follow her stellar students to University City or face the serpent in the grass?

The decision cut, *zero at the bone.*

Yet, before making her decision, Mary Catherine also heard the silent cry for help of a floundering student who clung to the lower end of the performance curve, struggling to read. Gretchen was painfully thin, with pasty skin and a look of stupor in her dull blue eyes. Though she was a junior at Clairemont High, a grade-school primer baffled her. Reading was so intensely frustrating that she would habitually scratch her scalp until it bled. None of the other students would sit near her for fear of being brushed by her bloody fingernails.

Gretchen showed signs of poor nutrition and perhaps abuse. In those days, teachers like Mary Catherine were not trained to deal with students' health or learning problems. They were hired to teach subjects, not perform social work. Yet Mary Catherine believed that, if Gretchen could learn to read, she might gain self-confidence and then begin to groom herself. But how could Mary Catherine reach this girl?

Mary Catherine filled her classroom with popular paperbacks. "If you finish your programmed materials early, you can spend the rest of class reading anything you like," she urged her students. Slowly, Gretchen began to take an interest in romantic bestsellers. As she shared a heroine's life, her eyes would lose their dull look and quicken with light. Mary Catherine met with her privately and made a deal: Whenever she saw Gretchen scratch, she would give a secret eye cue, as if to say, "You're doing it again."

By June, Gretchen made enough progress in reading to move to a regular English class. The scratching stopped. Did the eye cues enable her to fulfill the hidden potential of her IQ?

It is a great thing for a teacher to change a life in some way.

As she contemplated the achievements of her students at the top and the bottom, Mary Catherine felt a growing confidence in her ability to help both groups. But most students were somewhere in between. What about students in the middle? They tended to be invisible. They floated through school with grades of C or sank to Ds and Fs.

The top students got positive attention, while kids with bad grades and behavior problems got negative treatment. But there were very few programs to motivate kids in the middle. Students who lived with low expectations at home, she knew from bitter experience, all too often fulfilled them in school. As the looming recession of the 1980s threatened to make the rich richer and the poor poorer, this middle group hung in the balance. Yet America's success would ride on the fate of the middle class. In the new "global economy," as futurists called it, jobs that did not require a high-school education would virtually disappear. A college or graduate degree would be crucial to support a family in the high-tech twenty-first century.

Yet public schools were not raising kids *up*, but letting them *down*. This middling group of under-served students with low expectations and poor basic skills, Mary Catherine realized, would be heading by bus to Clairemont High in the fall.

Who, she wondered, *would be there to greet them?*

She pictured their frightened faces as they got off the bus at a hostile new school. They needed a teacher who would challenge and support them, she believed, with the same expectations that she had for Tommy. The privileged kids at University City High would make it without her, she admitted to herself. The eyes of students riding the bus implored her, cutting *zero at the bone*.

"I'll be there," she said out loud.

— LIQUID AMBAR —

Mary Catherine and Jim saw the future coming and dared to wonder: *How could they make integration work for their students without sacrificing excellence?*

If they were going to stay at Clairemont High and teach the new students the old way, they would fail. If they lowered academic standards, watered down the curriculum, and accepted mediocre achievement, the students would just get by—indeed, this is what many of the older faculty seemed resigned to accept, in return for keeping their jobs and pensions.

But Mary Catherine felt that giving up, or dumbing down Clairemont classes, would cheat the new students of a chance at college and a better future. How could teachers turn their backs on these children?

Yet the opposite approach might even be worse. If teachers held rigidly to strict standards, ignoring the new kids' backgrounds and lack of skills, and gave them Ds and Fs, the new students would be schooled in failure.

In their daily talks, Mary Catherine and Jim kept coming back to the same premise: A teacher's role was to *meet* students' needs. But how could academically rigorous teachers *meet* poorly prepared students just off the bus, without sacrificing their own professional integrity and commitment to excellence?

Mary Catherine would have to improve students' learning skills, boost their self-confidence, and motivate them to take responsibility. This would require a mutual commitment between teachers and students. The approach was theoretically sound, but what about their greater responsibility to educate *all* students in their classes?

Jim was adamant about maintaining the highest standards for his Seminar class and, as English Department chairwoman, Mary Catherine would not think of paring down college-prep courses; the new students would have to be prepared to meet the same standards. Both agreed: The top must not be sacrificed for the middle or bottom.

This challenge set them wondering: *Could students from opposite sides of the achievement gap meet somewhere in the middle and help one another?*

"My Seminar kids could tutor your students in algebra, English, and history," Jim offered.

"My kids have street smarts and could show your sheltered kids a thing or two," Mary Catherine responded.

"Yeah, and in the process, maybe they'd learn to communicate with each other," Jim laughed.

"And maybe they'd confront their prejudices head on and begin to see each other's virtues, as well as flaws," she added excitedly.

"If they actually help each other academically and socially, perhaps they'll learn to get on as equals," Jim countered.

"Isn't that what integration is all about?" she asked.

Jim and Mary Catherine saw advantages for both groups of "outsiders." Beneath their prejudices and fears, kids who felt isolated because of intelligence or accent or skin color yearned to be accepted.

Jim and Mary Catherine grew passionate as they circled round the incendiary issues of race, equality, and social justice—like dancers around a fire. Without realizing it, they were treading on sacred ground. The educational system was run by the superintendent of schools—invested by the board of education with the authority of a chieftain. In 1980, Superintendent Tom Goodman was nearing the end of his powerful tenure. Decisions were made at the top and sent down the chain of command to teachers at the bottom, who were supposed to implement changes, *not* instigate them.

Without fully realizing it, Jim and Mary Catherine were instigating change from the classroom up. They were proposing nothing less than teacher-based educational reforms. This was an audacious act: If it were to succeed in one school, it might be perceived as a threat to the chiefs at district headquarters, known commonly as the Ed Center. They had no idea of the immense task ahead, nor of the hostility they would unwittingly provoke from the top down.

Indeed, in the aftermath of desegregation programs decades later, question marks still hang above America's embattled public schools: Can teachers reform the system from within? If so, what would those changes look like in the classroom?

As summer vacation approached, Mary Catherine and Jim needed a plan of action for the new school year beginning that fall. This plan would have to be approved by the principal, who was under orders to implement an integration plan designed, from the top down, by the district's central office. They would have to convince him to take the risk.

Mary Catherine and Jim decided to start small with one 50-minute classroom period a day, using all the resources at their disposal: one teacher, students as tutors, a small budget, and connections with the UCSD Outreach Program.

In a new mentoring class period, Mary Catherine would prepare C students, who had little hope of going beyond high school, to take a college-prep curriculum. During the rest of the day, her students would be mainstreamed with college-bound students and would be expected to compete on a level playing field. This was unheard of. To prepare her students adequately, she would need the help of Seminar students from Jim's class to act as peer tutors. In addition, college students would be brought from UCSD to tutor her students, whose parents had never attended college. Jim's Seminar budget allowed him to take his small class on field trips to theaters and museums as far away as Los Angeles. But 15 kids couldn't fill a bus with 46 seats. Mary Catherine would fill those seats with her own students, exposing them to college campuses and cultural experiences that would ordinarily fall far outside of their scope of experience.

This innovative new program needed a name. Jim imagined an average student from a poor, chaotic background, not unlike his own—a bright kid who, despite hurts and insecurities, was avid to learn. Avid comes from the Latin *avidus,* meaning "eager for knowledge." Mary Catherine liked the connotations. If AVID was used as an acronym, what might the letters stand for?

Jim rubbed his beard. *A* could stand for *achievement,"* he suggested.

What inner qualities would be required to reach that goal? Students and teachers, Jim and Mary Catherine agreed, would need *individual determination* to overcome obstacles and strive to improve learning. By what path? *Achievement Via Individual Determination.*

"I like the way it flows," Jim said, as the words rolled easily off his tongue.

"Yes, but many programs promise achievement," Mary Catherine warned him, wrinkling her brow. "What we are proposing is to move students forward academically and socially." She closed her eyes and contemplated the ultimate goal that would make this program unique. Suddenly, her eyes flashed open. *"A* is for Advancement!"

"Advancement Via Individual Determination," Mary Catherine enunciated each word distinctly, her voice rising with excitement. "AVID—that's the name!"

Thus, AVID was born.

Hurriedly, they drafted a plan to create an experimental AVID class. Before taking their proposal to the principal, Mary Catherine tested their ideas out on the vice principal, Mr. Swarz. With his military crewcut and Barry Goldwater eyeglasses, he greeted her plans to integrate minority students into honors classes with the enthusiasm of Governor George Wallace welcoming blacks to the University of Alabama.

"The district won't accept AVID as an accredited course," Swarz declared.

"What if course credit is given on an experimental basis?" she asked.

"Clairemont teachers still won't want those bused-in kids taking up places in advanced classes," he said.

"What if we hire tutors to help them study?"

"You won't get money for tutors from *this* office," he replied derisively.

"What if we get a grant?"

"What if! What if!" he shouted. "You can't change the school system from Room 206 and, no matter how *avid* you are to erase prejudice, you can't change people's abilities by mixing them together. Human nature is human nature."

Mary Catherine glared at him. "Let's presume all your pessimistic predictions happen anyway. But if we give up before we try, nothing good will happen at all."

Swarz's objections only strengthened Mary Catherine's resolve and buttressed the AVID proposal. Still, she and Jim had no research to back up their plan, only their own hunches that it could work. With anxious resolve, they took a revised proposal to the principal. Walking down the serpentine path between the liquid ambar trees, Mary Catherine approached the moment of commitment: *zero at the bone.*

Principal Wayne Guthrie, a hearty outdoorsman with a deep voice, broad shoulders, and rugged features, ushered them into his office. "Swarz says you've got a dangerous proposal," he sighed warily.

"Not unless you consider teaching minorities how to excel in school dangerous," Mary Catherine said. She and Jim laid out their thesis. "We believe that C students bused in from low-performing schools can be integrated successfully into college-preparation classes at Clairemont, *without* sacrificing excellence."

The principal frowned. "How are you going to accomplish this miracle?" he asked skeptically.

"Recruit kids *in the middle,* not at the bottom or top," Mary Catherine explained. "Let me have these kids for two periods a day—AVID and English—five days a week, and I'll tutor and support them academically to succeed in all their other classes," she leaned forward, speaking passionately.

"What makes you think they won't fail?" Guthrie asked.

"I don't accept failure," she said. "Look, Wayne, I don't have all the answers. If something doesn't work, chuck it and try something else. It is my job to teach kids. Look at it this way. If I'm successful, you'll look really good. If I fail, you can blame *me!*"

Silently, Guthrie stared out the window, his eyes on a distant peak that rose in his own imagination. He looked weary and embattled, an educator caught in the crossfire of changes beyond his control, who had lost the capacity to care.

"If we don't do our best, who will?" she urged, leaning forward. "If we expect less from these kids, why should they bother coming here? Challenging and supporting them makes sense!"

The principal roused himself. "Frankly, I'm going to retire this spring," he said gruffly, confiding his secret for the first time. "Since I won't be here for the busing hullabaloo next fall, you've got my okay." His eyes twinkled. "Do whatever you want."

When the cheering stopped and the news finally sank in that they had been given permission, Mary Catherine faced the challenge of creating AVID out of thin air. Jim would advise and support her, but she must create the new program in her own classroom. She had to choose her first steps carefully or the unprecedented opportunity would be lost. The exhilarating sense of freedom was balanced by the weight of responsibility. Mary Catherine had enough rope to throw her kids a lifesaver—or to hang herself.

She needed to begin recruitment immediately. With summer break approaching, she dashed to set up interviews. Rather than asking the students to come to her, she went to inner-city middle schools, seeking prospective students for her first freshman class. She asked counselors for names of eighth-graders who would be coming to Clairemont High School on the bus in the fall. She looked through counseling folders for kids with C grades, few or no discipline referrals, strong attendance records, and who qualified for the free or reduced-cost lunch program. She was seeking kids who were getting average grades in regular classes, but who could do better if challenged. She asked teachers to recommend kids who had potential. She was not looking for rebels or kids with behavior problems. She wanted students who wanted to go to college, but who did not have any idea of how to get there. More than likely, their parents would not have attended college, might not have a high-school diploma, or wouldn't even speak English at home. These parents could not provide the guidance their children needed to navigate the college application process.

At the end of her search, Mary Catherine found a preliminary group of about 80 students.

These kids were then called out of class and told that a teacher wanted to speak to them about a program that would help them go to college. They were curious and a little bit intimidated by the prospect of talking to a high-school teacher. At age 13, it's difficult for kids to think ahead to the next hour, let alone the next year. College was a million miles away.

She spoke to groups of students again and again, until the faces blurred. Her pitch was a combination of pep talk and admonition:

It's an honor for ninth-graders to be asked to join AVID and prepare for college. You will be required to take college-preparation courses. You can make it, but you'll have to work hard, and it won't always be easy. You'll have college tutors who know the ropes to help you, and I will be there to support you all the way.

"Is AVID like a regular class?" asked one student.

"AVID is an elective. That means that you will have to sacrifice music, art, or shop in order to be in the AVID class. It meets five days a week. And I will also be your English teacher the first year, so you will have me for two periods a day. That way we can really get to know each other, and you can really get to know the kids in the AVID class. I will make certain that your reading and writing skills are strong."

"How long does AVID go for?" asked one girl.

"It's a four-year commitment."

"No way!" the girl muttered under her breath, provoking giggles.

"AVID is not for all of you," Mrs. Swanson said sternly. "But for those who stay with it through high school, we will be like family."

The students stared at her wide-eyed, looked down at the floor, or smiled inwardly. It was too much to absorb in one meeting, they told her years later. Many could only barely grasp the possibility being offered.

Maybe it was the energy and passion emanating from Mary Catherine, or the special attention she gave them, or maybe it was just hearing the magical word *college*. But the experience of being talked to, one on one, as if each one was an important person, was a memorable moment and one that AVID students, 18 years later, would say was a turning point in their lives.

Mary Catherine was beginning AVID even before she had set up the classroom, before she had nailed down the curriculum, or had hired the tutors. She was starting a relationship.

It was not easy to recruit kids for a course that would take a lot of work and would not give an instant pay-off. Mary Catherine was also being selective. She did not want kids to fail AVID or for AVID to fail them. She sent them home with a flyer in English and Spanish to tell their parents or guardians about the program. If they were interested, parents *and* students were to sign and return the paper. From the get-go, Mary Catherine wanted families to support their children in this major commitment. After all, college might not only open a child's horizons, but it could also change a family's expectations.

In the end, 50 kids signed up.

Mary Catherine invited the students and their parents to come to an introductory meeting at Clairemont High School in June 1980. Many students came without their parents. She spoke to them briefly to see how sincere they were.

"I wanted to see the fire in their eyes," she reflects now. "If a child really wanted to do it, I took him, whether or not his parent wanted it."

Mary Catherine chose 40 students, knowing there would be attrition over the summer, and ended up with 32 AVID students coming to Clairemont in September.

Before the students arrived in the fall, Mary Catherine had to create a support structure to help them survive academically. Her new students, on average, were about two years *below* grade level in their basic English and math skills. Some immigrants were just mastering English and were years behind! The challenge was to enroll them in advanced classes that were one or two years *above* grade level so that they would have the requisite credits for admission to college. From two years behind to two years ahead; the gap was huge.

How could students who were struggling with reading, writing, and arithmetic possibly make it in English literature and algebra classes? Mary Catherine believed that it was possible to perform this feat through purely academic means, but she totally underestimated the need for social services and emotional support for children born in *The Other America*. Nor did she anticipate the language and cultural difficulties faced by students like the boat people from Vietnam and undocumented immigrants from south of the border.

Academic rigor demanded extra attention for each student; one teacher could not possibly do it alone. In private schools, children could receive intensive attention from teachers interacting with small groups. Middle-class families were sometimes able to provide private tutors to supplement the education their children received in large public-school classes. Mary Catherine and Jim had agreed to share resources and curriculum.

But peer tutors were not enough to close the gap that divided America's poor from the educated elite. Requirements for entry to the University of California were tough even for children from privileged families, and teachers of advanced classes at Clairemont High School, she feared, would simply refuse to admit students from the busing program because they did not have the prerequisite credits.

Mary Catherine would have to find college tutors and figure out a way to pay them. The nearby campus of the University of California at San Diego was the natural place to look. For years, Mary Catherine and Jim had sent their top students to UCSD. They had developed contacts there: professors and former students. In 1980, UCSD had earned the indignity of being the campus with the lowest ethnic diversity and the highest attrition rate among minority students within the University of California system. The ivory tower perched on cliffs overlooking La Jolla was under pressure from the regents, Governor Jerry Brown, and the minority community to open the doors to students of color. Mary Catherine knew that UCSD needed to attract the same pool of students who would come to Clairemont under the court-ordered busing program, so it seemed possible that UCSD might have an interest in helping with the preparation of qualified minority students. Yet there were almost no institutional ties connecting public schools and public universities, no programs to help students from minority backgrounds to bridge the education gap between the underclass and the halls of academe. The two systems existed in largely separate worlds, as if they had no shared interests. Minority students slipped between the cracks.

Later, Mary Catherine would attempt to bring together local high-school and college teachers who dared to attempt to build such a bridge. But for now that endeavor would have to wait. The immediate need was to get college students from UCSD to tutor younger kids at Clairemont. Mary Catherine and Jim wrote up a proposal and approached UCSD's Community Outreach Program. The director of the program was sympathetic to their goal of preparing minority high-school students for the rigors of the university. He reviewed their proposal to pay tutors the same wage they earned for tutoring on the UCSD campus. He also happened to be a handwriting expert, who searched their scrawls for telling personality characteristics.

Finally, he looked up with an approving grin and declared, "I want to work with you, too."

Mary Catherine wondered whether this was due to the excellence of their proposal or the quality of their handwriting. But she was not about to quibble.

"I need the tutors this fall," she said bluntly.

"Fine," he agreed.

"There's only one problem," she admitted. "We will need money to pay them."

"Let's write a grant proposal," he suggested.

An administrator of the UCSD Outreach staff dashed off one proposal. Separately, Mary Catherine carefully submitted her own proposal to the Bank of America, requesting $7,000 to pay for tutors. Thankfully, that fall, the Bank of America grant came through. Later, unsubstantiated hearsay alleged that the UCSD proposal *also* had been granted, but the money had disappeared— along with the grant-writer—to South Africa. With the much-appreciated Bank of America grant, Mary Catherine was able to hire four of her former high-school students, then enrolled at UCSD, to tutor AVID students three times a week in math, science, and English. Hopefully, they would lead their younger peers across the opportunity gap.

— A SECOND HOME —

Mary Catherine wanted to create a classroom that felt like home. She scavenged tables and chairs from the cafeteria (white flight had left the cafeteria half empty). Out went narrow desks arranged in rows. In came wide tables, where students could face each other in discussion groups.

She found six study carrels and hauled them out onto the grass. Students airbrushed them with surfing scenes. She hoped the blue waves would have a calming effect when kids panicked over algebra formulas.

At a carpet store, she talked the manager into giving her a huge stack of floor samples. She laid the motley samples upside down on the ugly linoleum floor and randomly taped them together. Then she flipped over the "area rug" and used it to arrange a comfy reading area in the corner. The carpet was a patchwork of colors, like her students.

She convinced her friend, the school librarian, to give her two copies of every ninth-grade advanced-level textbook. That way, her students could not hide behind the excuse that they'd left their books at home. The texts would also enable tutors to refresh their knowledge on a subject and to anticipate questions. Then, a couple of used encyclopedias were rescued from oblivion. They might have been a few years out of date, but they provided access to a world of knowledge.

Mary Catherine created a career center, where kids could try on professions and see if they fit. She collected year-old college catalogues from public universities and private colleges, mascots, banners, and posters of collegians lounging by ivy-covered walls: tangible evidence of the excitement and reality of collegiate life. She wanted to create a homelike atmosphere imbued with the unspoken expectation that it is the natural order of things to study hard and go to college.

An old typewriter and battered filing cabinets that she collected for the room made it easy (before computers became commonplace in classrooms) to write reports and store notes. Few students had desks or study areas at home, so it was important that the AVID classroom be a comfortable place where they could hang out and study together.

Clairemont's colors were royal blue and orange, an unfortunate combination, artistically speaking, but highly suited to the proud Chieftains. In outrageously bright orange and blue letters, "AVID" was emblazoned on the door. The garish sign could be seen from 100 yards away, a beacon of hope in the institutional gray gloom.

Two weeks before school started, Mary Catherine came to the counseling office to register her students in honors classes.

"I'm sorry, but the algebra section is filled," Margaret Walsh, counselor for the gifted students, informed her.

"How about advanced history?"

"That's filled, too."

"And English? As department chair, I should have some say."

"They're all filled."

Mary Catherine fumed. "The whole purpose of integration is to challenge all students with academic rigor and support them to succeed! If they are shut out of honors classes, they'll be stuck in the remedial track leading to menial jobs. Why bus them across town, if only to exclude them from the best Clairemont has to offer?"

The counselor listened sympathetically, then shrugged. It was out of her hands.

"You know good and well that if they were 'gifted' students, the school would open up more honors sections for them!" Mary Catherine cried. "We have to find a way around this."

Margaret smiled slyly, lifting a key out of her drawer.

The Sunday evening before the Monday when kids were to enroll, Margaret turned the key in the lock of the back office and opened the cabinet that held the registration records. Mary Catherine sneaked into the files and placed her students' names at the top of the lists for advanced classes. Secretly, they locked up and went home.

Monday morning, students jammed into the gym for registration. They were given computer cards, which were punched as they moved from table to table, only if their names were found on the pre-registration lists. AVID students were placed first in every advanced class. Soon, the class sections filled up. Mysteriously, the "gifted" students had been shut out! Outraged parents raised a stink and, sure enough, the system responded to the demands of well-connected parents and more advanced sections were created— just as Mary Catherine had predicted.

Using guerrilla tactics to brainstorm, design, recruit, fund, decorate, and register kids for an ambitious college-preparation program in four short months, Mary Catherine had subverted the system to provide equal opportunities for her new students. She was already breaking the rules and school hadn't even begun. Later, she would pay a price for bucking the system. But in September of 1980, the experiment was just beginning.

— SIX WHO CAME — BY BUS

Before daybreak, the makeshift fleet of school buses, spewing diesel exhaust, rumbled over pot-holed avenues to the darkened street corners of an anxious city. The Voluntary Ethnic Enrollment Program, known as VEEP, launched thousands of sleepy-eyed children from warm beds to chilly bus stops. There they waited for city buses that did double duty, transporting students between rush-hour commuter routes. To accommodate this insane bus schedule, students had to awaken at 5 A.M., stand on street corners in the cold and dark, and hope to catch overcrowded buses that would bring them to school by 7 A.M. These human iron filings were attracted, by mysterious forces beyond their control, to "magnet" schools that offered special programs and to "feeder" schools, like Clairemont, that did not (with the exception of AVID). Of the 500 new students waiting for buses to Clairemont, 32 had been recruited for AVID. Six of these recruits—Clarence, Máximo, Angelina, Bernice, Joe, and Kouang—reflected, with their bright shining eyes and tense expressions, the fears and dreams of their peers in the first AVID class.

Clarence

Clarence awoke at 5:30 and got dressed in his best school clothes. His oval face and warm dark eyes gave him a gentle demeanor, but his compact body, broad shoulders, and muscular legs revealed athletic prowess. Clarence was both well-rounded in his extracurricular interests and aggressive. He had to be both, if he was going to lift himself and his family above the poverty line.

Clarence was the eldest child, and the only male in a family of four females, living in a small house in Southeast San Diego. His parents had divorced when he was two, and his father went away. His mother and grandmother, whom he called M'Dear, both worked hard to support him and his little sisters. M'Dear was the housekeeper for a doctor's family and his mother made torpedo sandwiches for sailors at the Navy base. They were the descendants of slaves and sharecroppers who had come to California for a better life.

Only once did Clarence feel the slap in the face of southern segregation, and that had been on a bus trip he had taken to Louisiana, when he wasn't allowed to use a whites-only bathroom. Back in San Diego, he grew up in sunshine, playing and laughing with his friends through the halcyon days of childhood, in a modest African American community. The streets were not always safe, but there were no drive-by shootings, no crack cocaine or gangs, when he was a boy, and he didn't know that Southeast San Diego was called a *ghetto* until he was old enough to resent that derogatory word and to argue that he never considered himself "poor."

Clarence's dad was not around to take him to baseball games, but his best friend's dad took a special interest in Clarence, cheering him at bat and on the gridiron. The doctor whose family employed M'Dear for years was also a role model for the young boy. Clarence looked up to the hardworking women who raised him. His mother and grandmother taught him respect and self-sacrifice—his mother kept driving her run-down car, rather than buy a new one, so that she could spend money to buy Christmas presents—and what they lacked in education they made up for in character.

Nobody in Clarence's family had gone to college. He attended a neighborhood elementary school where most of the kids were African American. There, he made lasting friendships with other young athletes who would remain friends, and later become rivals. In junior high school, Clarence attended an integrated school, but still kept his friends from home.

For his AVID interview, Mrs. Swanson had ushered Clarence into a small conference room and shut the door. She wanted it to be an intimate non-threatening meeting, where the young man would feel special.

"Do you want to go to college?" she asked.

"Yes, ma'am," he said politely.

"Do you feel you *can* go?"

Clarence shrugged. "It costs a lot, doesn't it? Mom and M'Dear want me to go to college, but they have a lot of bills."

"Are you willing to work hard?" she asked.

Clarence nodded, revealing a crown covered with closely cropped hair. She noticed his gentle eyes and strong chin. For his part, Clarence was taken by Mrs. Swanson's enthusiasm. She seemed like a teacher who really cared about kids.

"AVID applicants are chosen," Mrs. Swanson said, "but you must decide whether or not to choose AVID."

When Clarence walked out, his eyes were wide with excitement. That evening, he found out that Mrs. Swanson had called home to discuss AVID with his mother. She was amazed that a teacher wanted to help her son go to college. He thought about it all night long. In the morning, he decided to join AVID. Half of his friends had decided to stay in the old neighborhood; the other half were to attend Clairemont High.

The last days of summer brought the friends together for the last touch-football games, then, early on Monday morning, Clarence boarded the bus. He sat by the window, watching his old friends (and new rivals) walk to Lincoln High. Then the bus headed north on the freeway, crossing the Great Divide.

Máximo

The same morning, Máximo Escobedo stood anxiously at a bus stop in Barrio Logan, scrutinized by his neighbors. He and his seven brothers had crossed the border from Tijuana because their parents dreamed that they would go to college in America. Máximo's mother, Maria de la Luz, had received only six years of schooling. His father, Victoriano, left school at age nine.

Máximo was born in Guanajuato, "the city of the little frogs," Mexico, in 1965, when Mary Catherine was a senior at San Francisco State University. Máximo was the fourth son, coming behind Victor, Sergio, and Benjamin. After Máximo came Jaime, Javier, Gustavo, and Arturo. With eight sons to raise, Luz was not a hugging-and-kissing kind of mom; she was tough on the boys, but always loving and supportive.

When Máximo was young, the family moved to Tijuana. His father opened a small blacksmith shop. Their home was in a canyon with green hills that bloomed with yellow wildflowers in the springtime. Across a rusting fence lay the surreal and forbidding no-man's land of the U.S.–Mexico border. The Escobedos had little money, but were wealthy in faith, family, and hope for the future.

Máximo's father applied for legal immigration to the United States. After many years, their green cards arrived, and they crossed *la frontera* to the strange land called America. To their horror, they passed families, called *illegales,* running across the freeway, hunted like animals by *la migra* (immigration agents), while Americans drove by impassively. They passed the shimmering Coronado Bay Bridge and the skyscrapers of downtown San Diego. The car lurched into a run-down neighborhood where teenagers hung out on the street corners. These kids who grew up in the barrio wore baggy pants sagging low on their hips, Pendleton shirts, and tattoos, and were called *cholos*. The barrio was forbidding.

Their three-bedroom house overlooked the Interstate 15 freeway. There was no grass, only concrete, broken glass, and the hiss of traffic rushing, day and night, directly below the house. *Where are the cars all going in such a hurry?* Máximo wondered. There was little else to do except play soccer with his brothers, skinning their knees on the concrete.

The *cholos* looked down at the recent immigrants from Mexico, who looked down at the *cholos* because they spoke street Spanish. Compassionate, yet intimidated, Máximo saw them as neither fully Mexican nor American, but an angry mixture of hurt and pride.

Victoriano worked overtime at the shipyards. Luz ruled the house, where the boys slept on iron bunkbeds, four to a room. So close to the soaring heights of the Coronado Bay Bridge, they had fallen into a pit ruled by gangs, guns, pimps, and druggies.

As September approached, Mrs. Escobedo inquired about schools for her sons. She wanted all her boys to learn English, graduate from high school, and go to college. She searched for the best schools in San Diego.

So it was, in late August, that Mrs. Escobedo piled her sons in the car and drove to Clairemont High School. Speaking no English, she tried to communicate with office clerks, who spoke no Spanish. The guidance counselor took one look at Máximo, who was darkly handsome, polite, and dressed in clean clothes, and she made an instant determination that he belonged in remedial courses.

Máximo was put in Spanish One, English as a second language, physical education, shop, and geometry classes. When he protested, the counselor also put him in a class called "Public Speaking." This was a problem, since he could barely speak English.

The first day, the teacher asked the students to come before the class and introduce themselves. Máximo had no idea what was going on. Finally, his name was called, and he stood terrified, stammering out: "*Mi* name Máximo Escobedo. *Mi* mama and papa is Victoriano *y* Luz. I got *siete* brothers."

So began Máximo's immersion in English. He did so well in his classes that he came to the attention of Mary Catherine, who recruited him for AVID. He was the first in his family to have an American teacher offer to guide him toward college. His older brothers had to make it on their own, and his younger brothers were still in grade school and junior high.

Angelina

Angelina, an immigrant from Central America, was recruited by Mary Catherine. When Mary Catherine interviewed her, Angelina's eyes looked like those of a frightened deer caught in the headlights of an oncoming car. She faced the wall and spoke to the floor. She avoided all talk of her family. Her school records showed that Angelina, like Máximo, had been placed in remedial classes. Without guidance, she appeared doomed to perform poorly, get pregnant, drop out of school, and raise children on welfare.

Yet one of Angelina's teachers saw her differently. This teacher believed that Angelina was performing poorly in remedial classes not because she was unintelligent, but because she was bored by the mindless exercises.

"I have a Latina in my class," the teacher told Mrs. Swanson. "She is very bright, but doesn't know much English. I think she could benefit from AVID."

Mary Catherine respected the teacher's judgment and shared her view about the deleterious effects of remedial education on bright students. She agreed to take Angelina, even though her grades were below the C range. Yet something worried her about the girl's apparent fear of being looked at, or looking people in the eye. What was the girl hiding? Or hiding from?

Angelina's life had been far from angelic when she lived in Honduras, but she was not about to reveal her personal hell in San Diego, which had begun when her mother brought Angelina and her two younger sisters to the United States. Her mother took up with a pot-bellied trucker from South Carolina with the word *Mother* tattooed on his right deltoid and the name *Nancy* on his left. He called himself Vince and let them stay in his two-bedroom granny shack while he made trips across the country. At first he seemed nice to her mother, until she found out his name wasn't Vince and he had a wife on old Route 66—then the fights began. At night, Angelina heard dull thumps through the bedroom wall and her mother crying. The next morning, her mother's face would look like a bruised mango. Angelina pleaded for her mother to take them away, but her mother made excuses for the man who beat her. The truth was that they were penniless and her mother did not want to drag her daughters onto the streets. They lived in terror, trapped in his lair.

The three girls shared a bedroom. Late one night, "Vince" sneaked into Angelina's bed while her younger sisters slept. Angelina never cried out because she feared his violent retaliation against her mother. She allowed him to come into bed again and again because, as long as he was using *her* body, he would leave her younger sisters alone.

Angelina carried this secret with her, sitting alone on the bus. At school, she took a seat at the back of the class and faced the corner.

Bernice

Bernice changed her clothes three times before choosing a pink sweatshirt, tight jeans, and platform heels for school. She packed her school bag with essentials: nail polish, brush, comb, makeup mirror, mascara, and lipstick (which her mother promptly removed). She looked in the bathroom mirror and frowned at her complexion.

Bernice had looked forward to being in high school since she saw cheerleaders at a basketball game years before. Bernice dreamed of becoming a cheerleader, but at Clairemont they all had long, straight, sun-bleached hair and blue eyes.

She was excited by the prospect of new friendships and the fun of attending a "status" suburban school. She was just an average student and not really interested in books. But her parents had heard about AVID and wanted her to join. She said *no way,* unless her friend Tabitha went too. Tabby was a B student, but she liked to kick back and have fun. After their interviews with Mrs. Swanson, the girls came to the conclusion that AVID was simply going to be a glorified study hall. They'd sit around a table and pass notes and do their nails. Maybe they'd even meet some boys on a field trip.

So they signed up together.

The girls met at the bus stop and admired each other's hair. They sat together and sneaked looks at boys, laughing the whole way. Before the bus reached Clairemont, they made a pact. If AVID turned out to be a hard class, or if Mrs. Swanson was strict about studying, Bernice and Tabby would put that teacher in her place.

Joe

Joe slouched to the bus stop, dark hair hanging over his eyes, hiding his crooked teeth and gaunt chin. He lived in a run-down house wedged into a triangular street corner that framed his world—a slim slice of the American pie. Joe didn't know why he was bothering to care about school. At home, the TV was always on and his siblings were running around the messy, three-room, rented house. There was no peace, no quiet, no place to study.

Narrowing his eyes to block out the street, Joe dreamed of living in a new house, with big glass windows and a white picket fence. Inside, there would be high ceilings, a big living room, and a sunken family room with deep couches where he and his brothers and sisters could lounge. The family bedrooms would be on the first floor, but a spiral staircase would lead to a secret room on the second story, which was all his own. In his glass-walled turret, his water bed would revolve like the lamp in a lighthouse. There would be a private bathroom, an entertainment center, and a drafting desk where he could design super-modern homes for movie stars.

At the bus stop, Joe ran into a tattooed Vietnam veteran who lived in a shack next-door to his house.

"What you doin' up so bright and early, kid?" the wounded vet asked, leaning on crutches.

"Got to take a bus all the way to Clairemont High," Joe said.

"Not bad," the vet smiled. "What do you want to be when you grow up?"

"An architect," Joe answered.

The vet smiled sadly. "Dream on, boy. I wanted to be a basketball star."

I'll show him! Joe thought, clenching his fists. But as he gazed down the street, littered with broken bottles and shattered hopes, his hands became limp and numb, and he barely had the energy to lift himself up onto the bus. *How can I ever become anything?*

Joe had signed up for AVID. Yet now as he rode through the slums south of Interstate 8, he doubted he would ever escape. Joe was glad to be going to a new school; maybe he would make some new friends. But he lacked faith in his abilities and preferred to be a daydreamer. If Mrs. Swanson gave him tough assignments, he wasn't going to put himself out. Joe's survival strategy was to lay low and let others get attention. He was invisible.

Kouang

Kouang's arduous journey to AVID began on a small boat crammed with wretched, seasick refugees fleeing from Vietnam. He was too young to understand why they had run away in the night and boarded the stinking vessel. All he knew was that his mother grabbed him and his little sisters and pushed them up over the side. The boat was too crowded to find a place on deck, so they huddled in the bilge, filled with water that came up to his ankles. He cried for his father, but his mother shushed him and hid her tears. She did not know if her husband were dead or in a communist "re-education camp." The boat's engine rumbled and the land sank into the waves as the boat headed out to sea.

Now, three years later, Kouang waited for the bus, which was full when it arrived. The driver kept the door closed and shook his head when Kouang rapped on the glass, trying to get on. Kouang's insistent pounding finally convinced the driver to relent. Kouang climbed up the stairs and felt a push from behind, sending him hurtling down the aisle as the bus accelerated. He grabbed onto a metal seat, managing to break his fall, but his pack fell onto the floor, spilling open. Raucous laughter burst forth from the kids in the back of the bus, as he scrambled to pick up his pencils.

The slightly torn pack had been a gift from his mother. She had bought it for $2 at the thrift store and brought it to their apartment as a surprise. She was a seamstress, working days, nights, and weekends to mend things for a dry-cleaning shop. Her eyes were going bad but she was proud and did not like to take money from the county welfare agency.

Kouang listened to the students, missing a lot of words but catching the gist of what they said. They were complaining about the long wait for the bus and having to go to school, and he wondered if they knew how lucky they were to have free schooling. In Vietnam, his mother told him, he would have been working in the rice paddies or in the army, serving the communists.

He could not understand why the Americans did not realize how lucky they were. They did not appreciate their schooling, enjoy the marvel of riding on a bus, or the freedom of being able to speak out loud what they felt. He appreciated these things because he never had had them, and he appreciated his mother for making sacrifices.

Yet he knew he could not say these things without being laughed at, so he kept silent and did arithmetic calculations in his mind, seeing if he could multiply as fast as a hand calculator. He liked math because it was logical and he understood the language, unlike English, which was very hard for him to learn. *But would he make it in school?* He shivered, remembering the journey. The sea was so large and his boat had been so small.

As the bus pulled up to Clairemont High, the kids poured out and Kouang was left alone. Walking down the steps, he felt eyes staring at him and he suffered a searing flashback. They looked like pirates, but not the fanciful kind in children's books—the vicious kind who had boarded the sinking boat.

In her own nightmares, Mary Catherine could feel her students' hopes and trepidations. Tossing and turning, she obsessively struggled to help them, but could not match their names to their faces. She awoke at 4:30 A.M., laid out breakfast for Tom and Tommy, and was on the road by 5:30. She wanted to be at school at least an hour before the buses arrived so she could welcome her kids to AVID.

— THE BEGINNING —

The first AVID class entered Room 206 sheepishly, with big eyes fixed on packed bookshelves. Mrs. Swanson greeted each student with a smile, her manner friendly but businesslike. The opening day of school coincided with her thirty-sixth birthday, and this was the greatest challenge of her career. She faced a color-field of 32 interesting faces. Each had a dream to conjure, a hurt to heal, a mind to reach, a story to unfold.

"I am Mrs. Swanson," she began at 7:10 sharp. "Welcome to a pilot class called AVID—Advancement Via Individual Determination. As you can see, you are a very special group of students, and this is a very special classroom. The number-one rule here is that we always respect one another." Silence from students. "I have great expectations for this class," she continued. "By senior year, I expect each one of you to be prepared to enter a four-year university. As long as you work diligently, I will always be here to help you. We will all succeed in our goal of a college education!"

She introduced tutors from the University of California at San Diego: Debbie, a communications major; James, studying political science; Nina, a history major; and Judy, a student of urban planning.

"Tutors, would you please pass out AVID notebooks?" The two-inch ring binders had six dividers, one for each subject: English, math, biology, history, foreign language, and AVID. "Your first writing assignment is 'Why did you choose to enroll in this class, and what do you want to achieve?'" Students gaped with dazed eyes.

"Ideas, anyone?" Mrs. Swanson asked. No one volunteered. "Today and tomorrow, we are going to evaluate your skills in language and math. Once we see your strengths and weaknesses, we can work together to improve your skills." Kouang stared at the skills test as if facing a firing squad. Clarence squirmed. Angelina hid her face.

In 1980, it was unusual for a teacher to collect individual data for each student. Mary Catherine wanted to establish a starting line and measure progress over four years. Intuitively, she realized the importance of evidence to document and defend her program. But in the beginning, the results were a shock.

"These kids are four to five years behind!" Mary Catherine exclaimed to Jim after school one day. "This fellow is reading at a fourth-grade level. How can these students possibly compete in advanced classes?" Yet both teachers believed they should look at the statistics and see human faces. Mary Catherine plotted her students' performance with dots silhouetted against national stanines. The dots looked like footprints running toward the distant ribbon of a finish line. One by one, she called all 32 students to her desk for a conference with a tutor.

"Don't be discouraged," she said. "We are going to bring up your skills to handle difficult curricula *while* you take advanced classes."

She believed that AVID should focus on remediation of basic skills and on accelerated learning. The conflict between these two teaching methods—acceleration versus remediation—split the apple core of public education. Accelerated learning stimulated minds to learn rapidly by engaging them in a race for knowledge. Remedial teaching demanded rote repetition and mindless memorization.

Mrs. Swanson favored acceleration over remediation. But the District Headquarters chose the opposite approach: remediation via rote repetition, on a multi-million-dollar budget. The district's ambitious program to raise the test scores of thousands of disadvantaged students in minority schools was labeled AGP: Achievement Goals Program. In 1978, in response to the court's desegregation ruling, a whole new curriculum was designed to teach test-taking skills through remedial techniques. Workbooks were created for all grades, and teachers acted as drill sergeants. Minority students who were bused to majority schools were exempted from AGP, giving Mary Catherine freedom to test the AVID strategy. In 1980, the AVID program was virtually unknown, a puny seven thousand-dollar David to the district's million-dollar AGP Goliath. She wasn't conscious of the competition: Her focus was solely on her students' progress.

"Today, we are going to go over your papers," Mrs. Swanson said on Friday. The class released a collective gasp.

"In front of everybody?" Bernice asked.

"There's no reason to be ashamed of making mistakes," Mrs. Swanson said. "Once we find them, we can work on solutions." She strode to an overhead projector and placed a student's writing face-down on a glass screen. A hush fell over the room as the students read silently, some moving their lips. The anonymous passage read: "I be thinking about college for along time!"

"We say 'I have been,' not 'I be,'" Mrs. Swanson corrected. "Among friends, we speak slang. But here we speak academic English—our common language in school." She turned to Máximo and Kouang. "We live in a pluralistic society and want you to preserve your languages. But here everyone must learn English so we can talk to one another and be heard, write to one another and be understood. We call this 'writing to learn.' Are there any questions?"

No one spoke. *No questions* was becoming a problem. Her students' innate curiosity was dampened by fear of sounding stupid. They would have to conquer embarrassment and develop a strong sense of personal worth in order to participate in advanced classes. "What is the most important thing about school?" she asked, provoking them to think. "What are you doing? Why are you here?"

"My parents make me," Joe answered, hiding his face. Others gave trite answers, like "It's the law" or "To be with my friends."

She kept questioning until they began to wonder for themselves why they were in school, what goals they wanted to set for the future. Other classes were about subject matter. AVID was about the students themselves. "I understand how intimidating it is to ask questions in your advanced classes, especially when you are the only AVID student," she said. "But if you don't understand the assignment and get a bad grade, *you* will be the one to suffer." The students nodded. "I am going to teach you how things work around here, the unspoken rules of the game at Clairemont High. If everyone but you knows the rules, you will make a mistake and get punished. But, if you know the rules, you have a choice either to follow them or to knowingly break them—and take the consequences."

Clarence looked at his friends from the football team. They understood the rules of sports, but had never absorbed the rules of learning.

"Let's do role-play," Mrs. Swanson said. "Bernice, pretend I'm a teacher with whom you have a problem."

Bernice played the role. "Mr. P, you just lecture a million miles an hour. How you expect us to keep up?" Students cheered her on.

Mrs. Swanson cut them off, assuming the demeanor of Mr. P. "Bernice, you accuse me of going too fast?" she barked. "I've taught U.S. history for 15 years, and I know what we have to cover every week! If you can't keep up, I suggest you drop history."

"You can't put me down!" Bernice cried.

"Talking back will only get you in trouble," Mrs. Swanson replied, back in her role as AVID teacher. "It's natural to be afraid. So, before you speak, tell yourself: I'm an important person. I'm strong. I'm going to do this!"

"That's sucking up!"

"No, it's showing that you respect yourself and want to learn the material." The class was silent, but Mrs. Swanson saw many students listening. At the back of the room, Joe stared at the floor, lost in interplanetary linoleum. "I can teach you how to be in control of yourself and your future," Mrs. Swanson promised. "The rest is up to you."

Fish sticks were the "Daily Special" in the school cafeteria. Mary Catherine pushed her cottage-cheese salad along the cafeteria line, overhearing bitter complaints from some of her colleagues. Grousing about "those minority kids" was the topic of the month in the teachers' lunch room. They complained about the loss of their peers, the added workload, the rudeness of students. These complaints revealed the depth of abandonment felt by some of the old guard.

This she understood, and she could sympathize with their confusion and hurt at the abruptness of change. But what she could not bear were the slurs against innocent children "invading" precious accelerated classes. She held her tongue and took her lunch back to the AVID room, where she preferred to eat with her tutors and students.

Mary Catherine was resented by some of her colleagues for her youth and beauty, for her power as department chairwoman, and for what seemed to be her arrogance and disdain. She tried to interest her colleagues in the English Department in new materials by placing notes in their mailboxes. After attending a district-level meeting that offered supplementary readings for English students, she spent two hours composing a report about the proceedings. "If you want to order paperback novels such as *I Know Why the Caged Bird Sings* or *Of Mice and Men*, please respond by Friday," she wrote in a memo. She placed copies in 15 mailboxes.

Friday, she went to her own mailbox and found it empty. As she walked through the faculty room on Monday, Mary Catherine overheard one English teacher whisper, "Did you see that pompous message?" Another teacher laughed. "Who does she think she is? I'm certainly not going to change what books I teach."

She had no talent for making small talk, which, in her view, wasted valuable time that she would rather spend with students.

"What will you wear to the faculty luncheon?" a colleague asked.

"I haven't thought about it," Mary Catherine responded vaguely, hurrying off to class. She was an intensely private woman with a sense of public duty. She took the business of teaching very seriously, but she could be extremely patient and kind with students.

When a former student wrote to her from college, asking for a recommendation, Mary Catherine noticed that one of her colleagues, a math teacher, had received the same request.

"I don't know who this is," he said, scowling at the letter.

"It's Pearl!" Mary Catherine laughed. "Don't you remember?"

He looked baffled.

"Let's get the yearbook and find her picture," Mary Catherine offered, guiding him gently to the shelf where yearbooks were stored.

"Why do you think I *care* who this student is?" the curmudgeon rebuked her. Mary Catherine's shock at his apathy only served to steel her determination. However, her determination made her both friends and enemies. After a battle, she was quick to forgive, to laugh and move on, and she did not hold grudges. She put her students' needs first—ahead of her colleagues'—which generally struck her fellow teachers as arrogant. In pursuing her goals, she mistakenly thought that she could go it alone.

The Clairemont faculty was divided into three groups: those who opposed integration; those who embraced the new changes; and the vast majority, who could be swayed in either direction. She needed this latter group more than she knew.

After four solid days of English, algebra, biology, history, and AVID, Clarence suited up for football practice; charged through bruising tackle drills; ran five aching laps around the high-school track; caught a late bus home; wolfed down M'Lady's delicious ham, sweet potatoes, and collard greens; helped his mama clean up the kitchen; and played with his little sisters.

"Carry me piggy-back!" cried the younger one, jumping on his back. Clarence winced with pain, but his love for his sisters was such that he could not resist bucking them like a wild mustang until they fell off. "More! More!" they cried.

"I got to study," he said, limping off.

"Shoo, your brother's got important work to do for this family," M'Lady cried, chasing them to bed. At 8:00 he sat alone at the kitchen table to study. He could barely keep his eyes open. The assignment sheet condemned him to 28 algebra problems, a biology quiz, a history paper, and two chapters of *A Separate Peace.* "And tomorrow is Friday!" he groaned. Every Friday was binder check in AVID class, where tutors went through the week's homework sheets, tests, and notes, grading on how well the students took notes.

"You can do it," Mrs. Swanson had told him, and Clarence was determined to try. Practically holding his eyelids open with pencil erasers, he finished homework by 11:00 and slid into the sheets. Stress and aching shoulders made him toss and turn until 1 A.M. At 5:30, the alarm jangled him from dreams of sleeping until noon.

In the pre-dawn gloom, he pulled out of bed and dressed in the dark.

M'Lady had already tiptoed down the stairs and carried her cleaning bag to the bus stop, where she caught the first of two transfers to the doctor's house. Mama was getting the girls up, to loud cries. She would drop them off at school and drive her beat-up Chevy across the Coronado Bridge, soaring like a rainbow over the harbor, to the North Island Navy base, where, by noon, she would fix over 300 sandwiches for hungry sailors.

Clarence shivered at the bus stop. He envied his neighborhood buddies who were fast asleep in their warm beds and would get up five minutes before school and sprint to class. Passing Lincoln High, he felt guilty for playing football for Clairemont. He'd heard rumors that some Lincoln players called him a traitor behind his back.

He pulled his collar up around his ears and shoved his hands in his pockets. It hurt to be called a traitor, but getting a better education was his best shot. He was the man of the family, and he wanted a better life for them all. *One day, I'll buy Mama a new car and a house for M'Lady*, he promised himself. Clarence dreamed of a football scholarship, recruiters coming to watch him play, a chance to start with a professional team. He knew he was too small-boned for a major career, but football was a *metaphor*—wow, the word popped into his head from AVID class—for his ambitions.

Belching diesel smoke, the bus arrived late, and Clarence lugged his pack aboard. His athlete buddies were already in their seats. They slapped him a high-five and went back to sleep. Three of them shared a table in AVID class, but right now they looked like zombies. The long hours on the bus, hard classes, after-school practice, and homework made every day seem like a cruel joke. Yet Clarence was not one to feel bitter; it wasn't in his nature. Lulled by the rocking bus, he fell asleep. At 6:55, the weary riders were shaken awake by squealing brakes as the bus lurched to a stop at Clairemont High. The line of buses caused a traffic jam. Students driving cars honked their horns at the lowly bus riders. Describing how it felt to arrive on the bus, one AVID student would later recall: "From the moment you got to school, everybody looked at you like you didn't belong. You were an infidel on hallowed earth."

Walking into his first-period class, Clarence also felt looked-down on by his biology teacher. Mr. Brundage never called on the AVID kids, seeming suspicious of their presence in an advanced science class. Clarence felt intimidated. He wanted to speak up, but he was too *shy*, a wimpy word for lacking confidence in himself. He wondered about taking these super-hard classes. How could something so good for your future feel so bad today?

The teacher passed out a mimeographed quiz. The questions made his eyes cross, like dribbling four basketballs with two hands. He made it through the multiple-choice part, then faced the final question: Describe *photosynthesis*.

Photo what? His mind went blank.

Mrs. Swanson devoted Fridays to informal group discussions, motivating students who were freaking out about problems to find ways to solve them. These first weeks were especially tough. She wanted students to engage in realistic discussions. She had no particular agenda in mind, although she hoped to stimulate hearts to open up, a risky thing for teens, especially those whose parents came from stoic religious traditions in Asia and Mexico. If she could get them to open just a crack, strong emotions would emerge. The human need to be heard would overcome fear of embarrassment. Then hearts would inspire minds to find the right words, she hoped, and express insights gained from extraordinary experiences, far beyond the scope of their sheltered middle-class peers.

Clarence yawned, consumed by the Sleep Monster. "I'm sorry," he apologized, stifling a second yawn. The droopy-eyed class nodded assent like sleep walkers in *The Night of the Living Dead*.

"What are your dreams?" Mrs. Swanson asked, hoping to spark some excitement.

"Umm," Clarence smiled. "I'd eat a Double Big Mac, then sleep until Christmas. My priorities are sleeping, eating, and playing football—in that order."

"That's all?" she inquired.

"Oh, I forgot—college!" he laughed.

Kouang listened to the other students' complaints about the bus ride, reacting with frustration and disbelief. He was wiry, with penetrating eyes that seemed to take everything in without betraying his emotions. He wore a shirt that stuck to his scrawny neck and he proudly displayed a mechanical pencil in his pocket. He was burning to say something, but his throat couldn't form the words.

Mary Catherine seized the moment. "Kouang, tell us how your family came here."

He shuddered, as if sprayed with saltwater. His lips were parched, cracked, and he didn't know how to begin. To conceal his shaking hands, he held onto the edge of the table, as if to a sinking boat, and searched for words to describe his family's escape from Vietnam. He was not telling a story but reliving it.

"My father fight communists," he began, speaking so softly that the students leaned forward to hear him. "They take him away, say he in 're-education camp.'" His eyes stared starkly. "That place no school—it torture prison! We never see him again."

The class grew silent. They had seen ghastly images of the Vietnam War on TV, but that was history. This was real, and Kouang was bearing witness.

"My mother carry baby sister on her back and hold my hand," he said. "We run away in night—take nothing, just bag of rice. When baby cry, mother afraid wake up guard and she cover baby mouth." He bit his lips. "Baby stop breathe, almost die."

Clarence looked down at the floor, then up into Kouang's eyes. They were not slanted and impassive, like the Asian stereotype, but soft and crescent-shaped, like the new moon. "We go on old fishing boat," Kouang said, holding onto an imaginary spar. "Too many people. Everybody stand on top of everybody else. Weight too heavy, water coming in, boat sinking. My sister crying and I am crying too!" They were many days at sea without fresh water or food, he explained. The sun was so hot that his skin blistered and blackened and fell off. Mary Catherine touched her white forearms, imagining charred skin peeling off in strips.

"Mother is telling us: We go to America—freedom!" Kouang

said. "But I don't know what *freedom* mean. I only want to drink and eat."

Guiltily, Máximo thought of the corn tortillas stuffed with frijoles, cheese and chicken, smothered with salsa, that his mother cooked. He and his brothers fought for second and third helpings, but this was for fun, and no matter how little money there was, his mother always provided enough for all eight brothers.

"People drink saltwater, go crazy," Kouang was saying. "Old lady die, and they throw her in sea."

The class gasped. Mrs. Swanson moved protectively to shield Kouang. "You don't have to go on."

"I want to finish," he said. One day a ship came, waving a flag, and they were pulled up the side. Sailors gave them food and water and doctors treated them, saving his sister's life. They landed in a refugee camp in Thailand and waited for months. Then a plane flew them across the Pacific to Camp Pendleton, and they were relocated to a place called East San Diego. That was three years ago. He was learning English and he hoped they understood his accent. School was very hard, but now he was in AVID. He didn't mind riding the bus, because he was going someplace, he didn't know where, but he had hope. Turning to the class, he said, "I very thank America."

"We are thankful to have you in our class," Mrs. Swanson said, putting her arm around his thin shoulders.

"Your journey makes our bus ride seem easy," Clarence said, echoing many students' thoughts. Tabitha glanced at Bernice, who was wiping away tears. Máximo sketched Kouang's profile, wishing he had the courage to stand up and tell his own story. Someone started clapping and others joined in—the sound swept across the tables, spread out like continents, moving from Latin America to Asia and back to America again.

"Kouang, I want you to write your story down, just the way you told it," Mrs. Swanson said, turning to meet the eyes of all her students. "You each have a story. If you share your journey, we will learn from each other's lives to be stronger than we can ever be alone."

— PHOTOSYNTHESIS —

Clarence looked at the D atop his biology test and hid his eyes in shame. He was not alone. Throughout the school, AVID students scored poorly on their first exams. The test results confirmed to many teachers that minorities "without prerequisite credits" did not belong in advanced classes. When students saw the red check marks and low scores, many felt the same.

"Photo whatsis?" Clarence asked himself, stumbling on the pronunciation of *photosynthesis*. His exam was slashed with check marks. He felt totally frustrated. He had actually tried to memorize the biology terms before the exam, but the definitions had vanished under pressure. *Maybe they're right. I can't do it.*

Bad news from the biology test flowed into the AVID classroom like pollution from a broken sewage pipe. Mrs. Swanson ignored the foul smell, seeing rich fertilizer for learning.

Outside, the liquid ambar trees were still in leaf, and from their beauty she found inspiration. "Photosynthesis is a difficult concept," Mrs. Swanson said, admitting that she didn't fully understand it herself. "I can't teach you biology, but I can show you how to master these concepts by working together in a group."

There were four steps to group learning, she explained: "First, write your questions." She wrote a question mark on the board. "Second, ask if someone in the group has any answers they can carefully explain. If no one does, go through the chapter together and search for answers. Now comes the important part: Don't just repeat the gobbledygook from the text. Instead, put the answer into your own words." She paused, waiting for them to absorb her experimental process. "Does everybody understand?"

The students looked more confused than ever. "Mrs. Swanson, you talk too fast," they complained.

"I'm sorry, but that is how teachers lecture," she said. "You've got to learn how to take notes. Did you take notes on what I just said?"

A few voices spoke up. She inspected their notes. Jumbled words and numbers. "Well," she sighed, "I see we have to learn how to take better notes." She did a mental double-take. *How could she teach a method of note-taking, when she didn't have one herself?*

After class, she was called aside by one of her tutors, who was a history major. "I've got a method," Nina said. "It's called Cornell notes, and it's helped me a lot." She began to explain how the method worked.

Mary Catherine listened, but didn't really understand. *A better way is to learn by doing,* she thought.

"I've got an idea!" she exclaimed. "Why don't you teach me and the class at the same time. Tomorrow, we'll set up an overhead projector. While I talk to the kids about a study method, you take Cornell notes, using a grease pencil. The kids will hear me, and they will see your notes being written on the screen. Then they can write their own Cornell notes."

On the next tutoring day, Nina drew a vertical line one-third of the way from the left margin. While she dashed notes on the right side, she left the left side blank. Then, during pauses in Mrs. Swanson's lecture, she went back and wrote topics and brief questions beside the material. The left side asked questions. The right side gave the answers.

"You can quiz yourself by covering the right side and answering the questions on the left," she demonstrated. "Then lift your right hand and see if you got the correct answer."

The class followed her direction, covering the left margin and asking each other questions.

"Or, you can do the reverse," Nina explained. "Cover the question, study the material, and see if you can pose the right question."

"Wow!" Mrs. Swanson rejoiced. "Nina, I really want to thank you for teaching us Cornell notes." She turned to the class. "In AVID, tutors become teachers; teachers, students; and students trade parts as questioners and tutors. We're becoming a community of learners."

The next day, she greeted the class with excitement. "Let's try it out. Break up into learning groups. Nina, you take the biology group."

When they had gathered around, Nina asked for questions. Joe ducked beneath the table, tying his shoelace to avoid answering.

"Shoot, what is photosynthesis?" Clarence asked.

"It's what leaves do to turn green stuff into energy."

"What is the green stuff called?" asked a girl who made a face.

"Chloroform," guessed the guy beside her, leering behind glasses.

"That's what murderers use to suffocate people!" Nina laughed. "Check out the chapter."

They dove into the text.

"I got it," cried a girl, tossing her black braids. "Chlorophyll!"

"Write it down in the right column. Now, in the left, write the question: 'How does chlorophyll work?'"

"It takes in sunlight and starts a chemical reaction."

"Good. Write the concept down. Now that we have the concept, let's turn back to the text and see how the photochemical process works." They found the chemical formula. Writing on the board, Nina explained how sunlight converts carbon dioxide and water into organic compounds, the building blocks of life. "Now look at the word *photosynthesis,*" Nina said, discovering new meaning herself. "Notice, it is a compound word, just like the process! What two words does it come from?"

"Photograph," Clarence answered.

"It has the same root. Photons are particles of light and energy. Good. What does the word *synthesis* come from?"

"Sin?" Bernice sang out, provoking laughter.

Nina waited until the laughs died away, then explained. "Synthetics are things that are made by combining other molecules. So what does *photosynthesis* mean?"

"Light up things?"

"Almost. Try again."

"Combining water and carbon dioxide through light."

"Yes!" Nina exclaimed. "Here's the answer. Photosynthesis is the process in which energy from light combines water and carbon dioxide into organic compounds. Green pigment in chlorophyll is the energy converter." Then she asked each of the students to explain the concept to someone else, using their own words.

Mary Catherine stood back, listening. Sunlight fell on the leaves of the liquid ambar trees. The room heated by the morning sun was warm as a greenhouse. Through the windows the radiant splendor of light from the liquid-moving branches dappled the faces of students. They were absorbing energy through their eyes and ears. They worked together, combining molecules of knowledge. And she saw that the tables were like leaves—the pigmented students were energy converters, synthesizing questions into concepts. The process was organic and natural.

She witnessed a Tree of Knowledge, transforming inquiry into meaning.

— BINDER CHECK —

"Binder check!" Mrs. Swanson announced to the class. "Tutors, you will check the students' binders and grade them for organization, assignments, grades, class notes."

Groans burst forth like geysers spraying sulfurous water. The acrid smell of resentments fouled the AVID room.

"Why do we have to do this stupid thing again?" Bernice protested.

Mrs. Swanson crossed her arms, answering archly, "If you have a question, raise your hand and I will decide whether to call on you."

Bernice rolled her eyes, lifting a limp forefinger, as if to test the wind. "Mrs. Swanson, for the likes of me, I don't understand why we gotta have our notes checked each week. We done it last week."

"And the week before," Mrs. Swanson added, "and you will do it every week . . . for the next four years, until note-taking comes so naturally that you'll fly right through college."

"Four more years?" Bernice wailed. The prospect of submitting her three-ring binder, filled with secret doodlings and romantic notes, to weekly inspections sparked open rebellion. She wanted to call Mrs. Swanson a *Notebook Nazi*, but feared the consequences. "We're not in kindergarten," Bernice whined.

Unperturbed, Mrs. Swanson handed Binder Grading Sheets to the tutors, who passed them out among the students. The pages had three punch holes, to be inserted in AVID binders, and looked like this:

Binder Grading Sheet   Score _____

Student's Name _____ Date _____

Tutor's Name   _____

Organization (5 points)   _____

_____ Plastic pouch: 2 pens, 2 pencils
_____ Papers in order from newest to oldest
_____ No loose paper
_____ Name, date, and subject on all papers
_____ Blank paper in the back of each section

Agenda Book (20 points)   _____

_____ Parent signature every day (10)
_____ Homework logged in agenda every day (10)

Grade Sheet (25 points, 5 points per class)   _____

Grades recorded & homework assignments recorded!
_____ English   _____ Science   _____ Math

_____ History   _____ AVID

Class Notes (50 points, 10 points per class)   _____

**The students must have notes or
a log for each subject each day!*

Reflection
These are the two things I need to improve on for the next binder check:

  1)

  2)

_____   _____

Student Signature   Parent Signature

AVID
Advancement Via Individual Determination

Binder checks had multiple purposes: to teach kids how to organize the chaos of their studies (and minds) into a coherent order, to see when their assignments were due, to plan their time, to find their notes and papers, and to make them take responsibility for their schoolwork. The points for completing each task added up to a percentage of the AVID grade. These habits of mind were fundamental to organizing the daily tasks of school. They had been inculcated in Mary Catherine by her father, and she would pass them on to her students.

But many kids were ignorant of how the education system worked. Education was not a tradition in their families and they were doomed to fail, not because they were dumb, but because they did not know simple things like when assignments were due, how to budget time, or when to ask for help. Children of college graduates were usually taught this at home. It seemed so simple: By learning the rudimentary skills, habits, and disciplines, AVID students would gain freedom to use their minds, to shape time to their needs—to soar.

Her students hated binder checks. They resented her for making them do the drudgery. They did not care that she was teaching them four principles: disciplined study, independence of thought, self-reliance, and freedom. She did not mind being unpopular. Better to be tough, even stern and demanding, than to coddle them. She did not like to be cast in the Orwellian role of "Big Teacher," but she believed it comforted children to know their limits and take responsibility. They would become masters of their fate by becoming the masters of their binders.

— LIFESPAN OF GRASS —

After two and a half grueling months, AVID students were struggling to get Cs, and some were floundering with Ds and Fs. This put a greater burden on teachers to give extra help, and a few teachers were openly rooting for AVID students to fail.

One day, Mary Catherine walked into a U.S. history class to inquire about a test that three of her students had flunked. She found the teacher sitting at her desk, paying her bills, licking postage stamps, and sealing envelopes, while the students were socializing. One of the students stood beside the desk with an outstretched palm.

"I want you to run to Del Taco and get me two beef tacos, a chicken enchilada, and hot sauce," the teacher ordered the student. "Here's money for the food. And would you mind mailing these bills for me?"

Sending a student off campus during school hours to perform a teacher's personal chores was not only improper, but illegal, and Mary Catherine couldn't resist darting an angry glance at the history teacher.

"What's the lesson today?" Mary Catherine asked.

"What? You think I want to teach students like these?" the teacher scoffed, pointing at the AVID students.

"If you don't want to teach these students, wouldn't you be happier somewhere else?" Mary Catherine retorted, storming out.

Such encounters were rare, but resentment amongst her colleagues was growing. It wasn't only the other teachers' fault, Mary Catherine admitted privately. Her teaching strategies were not working quickly enough. Originally, she had intended to divide time between acceleration and remediation, but now she found that it took every minute to help kids keep up with their classwork. There was literally no time for remedial skill learning. The individual learning plans on which she had worked so hard languished in the files.

So, in order to reach the Pike's Peak of academic excellence, the plodding wagons must jettison excess baggage and speed up the pace of study: Acceleration or Bust. In the long term, Mary Catherine believed, AVID students would catch up. But the kids' academic futures were on the line right now. So, too, was her credibility and AVID's chances of surviving. Sadly, she had seen grassroots educational programs grow and die with the fleeting lifespan of prairie grass. The skeletons of well-meaning reforms littered the trails that were supposed to lead to a college education.

Mary Catherine hunted for every piece of evidence that showed progress, no matter how small. Not only did she need to bolster the students, she needed to convince their teachers that the extra work they were putting in was going to pay off. In the beginning, signs of progress were hard to find. After combing attendance records, Mary Catherine discovered that, on average, her AVID students had only been absent half a day since school began. That was a whole day better than the attendance rate for the student body as a whole. She put this message out in teachers' mailboxes but, as usual, got no response.

Mary Catherine took a hard look at herself and realized that her efforts were putting teachers off.

"People consider AVID students a pain in the butt," Jim Grove told her bluntly.

Mary Catherine thought of Kouang's essay. He had written his story in faltering language, with many mistakes. But after she had circled errors and made suggestions, Kouang had rewritten it twice. Perseverance was his amazing strength. The essay was still far from perfect, but it rang true.

Mary Catherine began spending more time in the teachers' lounge. She endeavored to be a good listener. But when a disgruntled English teacher inveighed against immigrants "insulting the English language," she could no longer keep silent.

"They may lack English skills, but they have something important to say," Mary Catherine said. "Please listen to this student essay. It was written by a Vietnamese refugee who arrived in America three years ago. It's called 'Boat People Are People, Too.'"

She held the essay close to her chest and read Kouang's story aloud, as he wrote it, in a strong clear voice. The flight from Vietnam, the escape on the boat, the sinking ship, the hapless victims thrown overboard.

"I am so happy to come to America," Kouang concluded in his essay. "My father lost in Vietnam because of communists. My mother works very hard on sewing machine all day. She does not speak English, but she wants me to get a good education. There is only one thing I do not understand. Why do some people call us gooks? Boat people are people, too."

The teachers fell silent. The basketball coach, a Vietnam War vet, looked at the floor, his throat working.

"That's so powerful," murmured an advanced history teacher, amazed not by the student's courage and wisdom, but by his articulate expression.

"I'm amazed," said another skeptic. "Did he really write it?"

"Yes, he wrote and rewrote it, and it's still full of errors," Mary Catherine said, pulling the page away from her chest and revealing the awkward handwriting covered with red marks. "And here is his copy."

The teachers examined the third draft. Even with bifocals, some of the older instructors found the words hard to decipher. The letters resembled calligraphy, a brush painting of a bamboo forest.

What was the sentence structure? Yet, when the eye slowed, figures emerged, voices spoke to the teachers. Expressions of consternation alternated with glints of discovery as they saw beneath the rough surface of language the indomitable human spirit of a young man named Kouang. The English teacher pushed her glasses high on her forehead, admitting, "I never would have guessed such rotten grammar could mask such profound meaning."

"Every student has a story," Mary Catherine exclaimed, clasping the essay to her breast. "That's why I'm so excited about working with you to help them achieve their dreams."

One moonlit Friday in early November, Mary Catherine was awakened by a nightmare. In her surreal dream, AVID students were dressed like aborigines. While other Clairemont students were studying hard for exams, her students were building a bonfire atop a mountain in New Guinea. She implored them to crack their books. Instead, they danced feverishly in the firelight and stared hopefully at the midnight sky.

"What are you waiting for?" she asked them.

"The big bird will drop answers from the sky."

Later, she realized that the dream was based on a television documentary she'd seen. During World War II, Allied bombers, trying to supply troops in the field, had mistaken a bonfire for a flare signaling an Army landing zone, and had dropped supplies into the jungle. Aborigines had followed the parachutes and discovered battered crates spilling treasure: C-rations, canned heat, machetes, boxes that made beeping sounds. Every month at the same moon, they built fires atop the mountain, imploring the gods of the sky to send more treasures. A ritual developed around the faith in the magic of the fire to call manna from heaven. Anthropologists called it a "cargo cult." The documentary left the impression that the aborigines were still waiting.

"Why am I dreaming about cargo cults?" she wondered on the way to work.

The previous Monday morning, Mrs. Swanson had faced the AVID class alone. None of the college tutors had shown up. For one week, Nina, James, Debbie, and Judy were taking their midterm exams at UCSD and could not come to Clairemont High.

Mrs. Swanson, the professional, had no trouble tutoring English and history, but Mary Catherine, the former student, was still terrified of binomial equations.

How could she pinch hit for Judy as an algebra tutor? She believed, naively, that the students would continue to study together in the tutors' absence.

"AVID students, break up into your study groups," Mrs. Swanson directed. "Algebra and biology groups, use your notes to help each other."

The kids opened their textbooks and stared at the ceiling, as if awaiting Big Tutor to drop answers from heaven.

"Why aren't you asking each other questions?" Mrs. Swanson asked.

"I can't do my algebra, because my tutor's not here."

She went around the tables, hearing the same complaints. The tutors wrote the equations on the board. The tutors solved the problems.

Mrs. Swanson realized she had made a mistake. She had believed that it was enough to hire intelligent tutors who knew the material. She had not thought sufficiently about tutorial methods, nor given them guidelines. The tutors had wanted to please her by helping kids get the right answers. Each AVID student was required to bring in questions to the tutorial group. The tutors thought they were being good tutors by providing the correct answers. The students had become dependent on the tutors for solving homework problems. With the tutors absent, the students did not know how to study with each other, much less on their own. With the best of intentions, the tutors had convinced the students that if they only waited long enough, someone would drop the answers from the sky.

AVID had become a cargo cult.

When the four tutors returned after midterm exams, Mrs. Swanson huddled with them to analyze what had gone wrong and to brainstorm ways to improve their tutoring. There was no animosity. It was a common realization that the students had become dependent on being fed the correct answers. The tutors wanted to do a good job and, in this spirit, they discussed how to make changes.

Instead of telling the tutors what to do, Mary Catherine involved them in the inquiry and pursuit of a better methodology. She drew on their experiences, their closeness to the students, their creativity, and, finally, their enthusiasm. For their part, the tutors appreciated the trust and responsibility that this teacher was investing in them. Young though they were, and without formal training, they were being asked to cooperate in the development of a new tutoring model—a model that major "teacher-training" institutions and educational researchers had so far failed to adapt to the practical realities of a changing student population.

"Cornell notes are very important," Mrs. Swanson explained. "We know that if kids come to class with notes prepared, we have a basis for study. But this raises two questions: One, how are we going to get kids to ask good, insightful questions? Two, how do we train ourselves as tutors to ask kids good questions—questions that don't lead to preconceived answers, but that challenge them to think?"

The tutors struggled to speak, but Mrs. Swanson held up her palm.

"Don't try to answer now in the abstract," she cautioned. "Be practical and specific. Each night, I want you to go over the next sections of material in your disciplines and write out questions that will provoke your students to inquire more deeply. Then, instead of merely helping them solve the problems in the next homework assignment, challenge them to ask *why* this is important, *how* it fits into the larger picture, and *where* this knowledge can be useful in their lives."

"But what if they push me for an answer?" asked Debbie, the communications major.

"Play Sigmund Freud," Mrs. Swanson said, mimicking the father of psychoanalysis. "Answer their question with another question."

Debbie shifted in her seat, uncomfortable in the role of shrink. "Won't that just confuse things?"

"Ambiguity is reality viewed close-up," Mrs. Swanson said, leaning forward until her nose almost touched Debbie's. "Things look clear from a distance, but when you approach them you cannot escape discovering marvelous anomalies, like the lavender shadows of your lovely eyelashes falling on your cheeks." She pulled back, addressing Nina, James, and Judy. "If you can intrigue them so that they come out of their hiding places, they will be drawn into the gravitational field of the unknown. Someone once compared knowledge to the structure of an atom: The more you know, the heavier the nucleus and the greater the attraction to learn more."

Nina, the engineering/history major, raised her eyebrow and curled her lip, skeptical of scientific metaphors coming from an English teacher. She said, "Atoms can attract or repel each other, depending on their ionic charges."

"Okay, what do I know about atoms?" Mrs. Swanson laughed. "Let me give you an example in literature. We're working on the novel *A Separate Peace* by John Knowles. This is about two adolescent boys, friends and rivals, in a New England prep school before World War II. They are performing a dangerous and forbidden ritual of manhood, to climb a tree and jump into the river. Now, the antagonist, Gene, pushes Finny out of the tree. Why does he do that?"

"He's jealous?" asked James, a political science major.

"Is it possible there is another reason?" Mrs. Swanson reflected. "What is the author trying to say here?"

"There is good and evil in all human beings," answered Judy, who had family struggles at home and was putting herself through UCSD.

"What do you mean by *good?*" inquired Debbie, the communicator.

"What is the opposite of evil?" Judy retorted slyly.

"Jeopardy!" Mrs. Swanson's face flushed with the excitement of pursuit. "In great literature, human motivation is layered. When kids look for a 'right' answer, they will jump on one reason, one cause. As a tutor, we are trying to get them to consider other, perhaps contradictory, reasons, as varied as *our* motivations for helping kids in AVID. We share the pursuit of knowledge, but there is no single path and probably no absolute truth, only points of view on the mysteries of life, framed in words that transcend time and space—which explains my love of literature! Each child learns differently, and each relationship between mentor and student is unique, from the agony of butting heads to the epiphany of 'a marriage of true minds.' That is why tutoring is so exciting."

Her golden hair appeared to catch fire; her passion burned in their minds like glow bugs captured in fossilized amber. She was quite simply using the same techniques to challenge the tutors to think analytically about tutoring as she was asking students to think analytically about what they were learning. AVID principles worked the same way for tutors as for students. Mrs. Swanson created a chain of inquiry in which people at all levels—teachers, tutors, and students—were constantly asking questions. *What does this mean? How does it relate? Is there a different perspective?* Problems were raised in the spirit of finding a solution. But the solutions did not come automatically. Students, tutors, and the teacher constantly asked: *How can it be done better?*

Many minds, from different ages and backgrounds, were working in concentric circles of inquiry on the same fundamental problems. No wonder the tutors were so engaged. They were helping rewrite the rules of secondary-school education for a new cadre of students whose families had been barred from higher education.

"Of course we will make mistakes!" Mrs. Swanson told them. "How else can we learn what doesn't work? If an experimental method fails, try another. Keep our eyes on the goal. We are teaching, by example, that we constantly learn new ways of doing things. Learning is fun because you never know the answer ahead of time, and, the closer you get to solving one problem, the more new possibilities arise."

— ONTOGENY —
RECAPITULATES
PHYLOGENY

ONTOGENY: The developmental history of an individual organism.

PHYLOGENY: The evolutionary history of a species.

RECAPITULATION: A theory stating that, as an organism develops, it passes through a sequence of embryonic or juvenile stages that resemble the evolutionary forms of its successive ancestors. This is now regarded as a gross oversimplification.

—adapted from the *Miriam Webster International Dictionary*

Armed with definitions, Nina prepared her AVID troops for battle in the next day's biology exam. The stakes for their academic future—and AVID's survival—were high. Nina hoped that the tutoring principles and group-learning techniques would actually work. Yesterday, they had exhaustively gone over their Cornell notes, covering up the answers and quizzing each other until they could name dozens of the tissues, organs, and bones—as well as their functions—in a fetal pig. Then she had them cover up the answers and try to predict the actual questions that might appear on the test. Today, she wanted them to grapple with complex concepts of evolution and embryonic development, to gain a sense of nature's patterns.

"Ontogeny recapitulates phylogeny," she wrote on the chalkboard.

"Huh?" the students gasped.

"On-taw-genie re-ca-pit-u-lates fi-law-genie," the tutor explained phonetically.

"What language is that?" asked Kouang.

"Latin."

"I thought we're studying biology!" Bernice protested.

"Hush your mouth, we got an exam to study up for," said Tabitha.

"Let's break the phrase down into parts," said the tutor. "What does the word *ontogeny* mean?" The students in the biology study group shook their heads.

"The developmental history of an individual organism," a tall, freckled boy read aloud.

"Put it in your own words," she urged him.

"How a living being develops and such?"

"How an *individual* develops," she said, underlining the word *individual* in the AVID logo. "Advancement via *Individual* Determination. So, now we're talking about how an individual being develops from conception to adulthood. What does *develop* mean, biologically?"

Kouang raised his hand. "How body grow and change?"

The tutor smiled, "Now put it together."

"How individual grow and change from seed to full-grown?" he said excitedly.

"Right!" the tutor cried. "Now, what does *phylogeny* mean?"

"Evolutionary history of a species," the freckled student again read aloud from the glossary.

"Good," she said. "This time, I want you all to define *phylogeny* in your own words and write it in your notebooks."

They clawed the text, chewed pencils, and swallowed bits of erasers. Putting their heads together, the students came up with a definition that was close, but not perfect.

"Phylogeny is how a whole specious grows up," Bernice said.

"Species, not specious," corrected Nina, glancing at the clock. "Now, what does the verb *replicates* mean?"

"Repeat?" asked the freckled student.

"Close. It means 'reproduce,'" the tutor corrected. "Now, let's figure out the whole phrase." Hurrying, she divided the students into two groups, representing ontogeny and phylogeny. Bernice and Tabitha were in the ontogeny group; Clarence and Kouang in the phylogeny group. Sharing notes, they elbowed each other and giggled.

"Now, each group define what you stand for," the tutor said.

"How an individual organism develops," said the ontogeny group.

"How the species evolved," said the phylogenites.

Excited, the tutor placed Tabitha's hand in Kouang's. There was a moment of shock, then Bernice burst out laughing and it looked like Kouang was going to run away. But the tutor held their hands, saying, "Now, let's put it all together."

"An individual organism's development," Tabitha began, turning to the Vietnamese boy. "Reproduce evolution of species," Kouang said proudly.

The two groups looked at each other in astonishment, grasping the concept.

Looking up from the group she was tutoring, Mary Catherine had watched the biology tutor divide the students into groups and then bring them together, holding hands. She could not hear what they were saying, but that did not matter: She saw the recognition in their eyes, which brought joy to them all. A teachable moment makes lasting connections.

— THE ACCUSATION —

Another biology test was given early in December. The next morning, AVID students moaned about how tough it was, although a few dared to hope. Before school Monday morning, Mrs. Swanson was confronted by the biology teacher, Mr. Brundage. They stood awkwardly on the path outside the AVID room.

"I demand your immediate apology!" Mr. Brundage declared, clenching a stack of tests in his hands.

"What's the problem?" Mary Catherine asked.

"Your kids cheated on the biology exam."

"I don't believe it!" Mary Catherine cried in shock.

"The evidence is irrefutable." Mr. Brundage thrust out his hand like a card shark, displaying test papers topped by letter grades.

"Why, these are all As and Bs!" Mrs. Swanson quickly scanned the tests.

"Precisely. *Those kids* could never master these concepts on their own. They must have done some, excuse me, 'group learning,' while I was called out of the class."

"Did other students report AVID students cheating?"

Dismissively, Mr. Brundage changed the subject. "Look at their definitions! They're all virtually the same. Even the way they write down questions and topics. Obviously, your 'group-learning' model has only taught them that cheating is acceptable."

We have been colleagues and, I once believed, friends for a dozen years, Mary Catherine wanted to shout. *Knowing my commitment to the teaching profession, how can you accuse me of promoting dishonesty?* But she kept silent.

"Look at the essay question," Mr. Brundage raged, jabbing at one of the exams. "I asked them to compare physical development and evolution. In their answers, they use the same exact words, *ontogeny recapitulates phylogeny.* Now where are these Mexican kids, who can barely read sixth-grade textbooks, going to come up with such language?"

Mary Catherine had some explicit language of her own to answer Brundage's outrageous slur against Hispanics, but her students were filtering into the AVID classroom and she held her tongue. On principle, she never confronted a teacher in the presence of students, even if the teacher were wrong; it was a disservice to both the teacher and the students.

"Have you informed AVID students of your accusations?" Mary Catherine asked quietly.

"No, I wanted you to know first."

"Thank you for informing me of your concerns," she said. "I have no reason to doubt your sincerity. I believe there is only one way of getting to the bottom of this, and that is to bring the students in during our prep period to respond to your questions."

"They may have to retake the test immediately, under close monitoring," Mr. Brundage added. "No time to study, no second chance to cheat."

"Yes, good. That will clarify things," Mary Catherine retorted civilly. "If they don't know their stuff, we can proceed with the investigation."

"Indeed," Mr. Brundage sniffed archly. "If anyone should apologize, it should be you, Mary Catherine, for foisting this 'avid' charade on the faculty and on your poor, deprived students, who are only bound to fail and get hurt." With a wave of his glasses, Mr. Brundage turned on his heel, dismissing the AVID teacher as if she were an arrogant child.

Back in the AVID room, Mary Catherine's knees trembled so visibly that she took refuge behind her desk. In her 14 years of teaching, this was the worst attack she'd ever witnessed against her students. Her own reputation was at stake. She crossed forearms against her ribs and dug her manicured nails into the soft flesh of her arms—anything to prevent herself from breaking down in front of her AVID students.

At the moment when they had finally achieved excellence, they were accused of the ultimate crime—knowledge! The system could not admit that "poor, deprived" kids had scored as well as their middle-class comrades. The biology teacher considered it his duty to root out the AVID apostasy that threatened the dogma of "tracking." Mrs. Swanson was an infidel, leading students astray.

The inquisition was to be held that afternoon, in the conference room. Each student was to be brought in, alone, and questioned. If they ratted on their fellow students, they would be allowed to stay in advanced biology. If they persisted in the "lie" of their innocence, they would be humiliated.

Mary Catherine pictured Mr. Brundage as the Grand Inquisitor and wondered what fate awaited her students, who walked innocently into the AVID classroom, excited by learning and upbeat about their progress. She could not bear repeating the accusation: *Shame on you for doing well on your biology test. If you got an A or B, you must have cheated.* In her heart, she knew that if the white students had scored high, they would have been praised, not accused.

Yet she could not shield AVID students from this serious accusation. She wanted to present it to the group in as neutral a way as possible, so she wouldn't incite fear. She did not want to treat them like victims, powerless to defend themselves. Still, a doubt niggled her mind. What if they *were* guilty? Then they should accept responsibility and face the consequences.

"I need to meet with the biology study group," Mrs. Swanson said, leading Bernice, Joe, Clarence, Kouang, and the others to the back of the classroom. They gazed at her with trusting eyes.

"How did we do on the test?" they asked.

"As and Bs," she answered. "But we're going to test you again."

"Why?"

"Mr. Brundage accuses you all of cheating."

The students were thunderstruck.

News of the "cheating scandal" spread across campus like a brush fire whipped up by Santa Ana winds. In advanced classes, AVID students were the subjects of cruel jokes by their privileged peers.

"Here come the AVID Five!" a lookout cried, booing when Clarence, Joe, Máximo, Kouang, and Angelina entered. The class whistled and hooted. "Chea-ters! Chea-ters!"

Clarence walked past them to his seat.

"Do you know the punishment for cheating in America?" a heckler asked.

Kouang shook his head.

"We take off your clothes and lock you in the girls' locker-room."

Before Kouang could reply, the teacher entered the classroom, and the mocking students put on innocent faces. At the back of the room, Angelina hid her face, weeping.

In the faculty women's restroom, teachers talked behind Mary Catherine's back loud enough for her to hear in the stall.

"It's no longer a mystery what goes on in *her* classroom," said the history teacher who fancied tacos, vengefully clicking her tongue. "And that woman had the nerve to tell me I should be helping students prepare for a test."

"She's always boring us with new teaching ideas," the other teacher responded. "I guess Cornell notes is a new technique for cribbing."

Mary Catherine clenched her fists. Exiting, she held her head high, but her arms were trembling.

"This time," a leader of the old guard said, "she'll have her come-uppance!"

The night before the hearing, AVID biology students went home confused and frightened, not knowing what they had done wrong. The lack of clear discipline guidelines, multiplied by rumors that they might be suspended, magnified the danger each student felt. Their isolation was heightened because parents who lacked higher education did not necessarily understand the importance of school to their children's future.

Angelina waited until her mother returned from work at the sweatshop to tell her of the accusation.

"Mamá, yo tengo miedo." I'm scared.

Bowing with resignation, her mother never asked Angelina if she had cheated. Instead, her mother said, *"Pobrecita,* maybe you should stay home and take care of your little sisters."

"But *mamá,* I want to stay in AVID and go to college."

"Yo no comprendo esta cosa, 'college'!" *I don't understand this college thing.*

"Then I'll get a good job and take my sisters away, and we won't have to live like this!"

"Cállate!" Be quiet. Her mother froze, seeing the shadow of *el gringo* eavesdropping. Angelina hid in her room. When everyone else was asleep, the door was pushed open from behind. Stinking of beer, "Vince" sneaked into Angelina's bed. "Don't you worry about school, little thing," he whispered to the terrified teenager. "You just stay home and we'll have fun."

At Joe's house, the stereo was blaring, the baby was crying, the twins were kicking a soccer ball under the card table; his pregnant sister, who had just lit a cigarette, was screaming at the kids to be quiet, but this only increased the pandemonium.

Joe passed through the kitchen to his parents' tiny bedroom. There he found his father glued to the TV screen, playing PacMan. Ever since he'd been laid off from the tuna cannery, his dad had that crushed look, like an aluminum soda pop can stomped under a boot heel.

"Hi, Dad. I've got something important to tell you." Joe waved the biology test, trying to get his father's attention. "I got a B minus, but the teacher said I cheated."

"Huh?" PacMan's opening and closing jaws were reflected in his father's glasses.

"Never mind!" Joe backed away. There was no place to study in this house. He was way behind in algebra and also had to finish his English composition. He left the house and walked to the public library, passing drunks slouched against chain-link fences. Joe studied until the library closed; then he came home. There wasn't much dinner that night, and he left before breakfast in the morning. No wonder his eyes had that dull glazed look.

Máximo's mom snatched the biology test out of his hand. "Your teacher said you *cheated?*" she exclaimed in Spanish.

"I didn't do nothing wrong," Máximo whispered. "I promise."

"*¿Qué pasó?*" *What happened?*

"I memorized these Latin words, *ontogeny recapitulates phylogeny,* and Mr. Brundage said I cheated."

"What does *Señora* Swanson say?"

"We got to be *interrogado* tomorrow."

Mrs. Escobedo cleared a place for her son at the wrought-iron table in the kitchen. He took out his math and English homework. She brought him warm tortillas and a glass of milk. "Here, you study."

In a Vietnamese home, it was a great dishonor to be accused of cheating. To be suspended would cause his family to lose face.

Kouang could not bear putting his mother through this worry. Stoically, he kept it secret.

The trial of the students took place in a windowless room. Mr. Brundage sat in judgment. The student defendants faced him, from left to right: Clarence, unbroken; Tabitha, stunned; Bernice, glaring; Joe, hiding; Angelina, flushed; Kouang, staring at the floor; others terrified, clutching their binders. The students were the hues of the earth's clay in its richness, but fluorescent light drained color from their skin, leaving them shades of gray. The walls were prison green.

"We take cheating very seriously here," Mr. Brundage announced. "Not like the schools you came from," he said, raising his eyebrow. "I let you in advanced biology, not because you were qualified, but because Mrs. Swanson asked me to give you a chance."

Bernice rolled her eyes. Clarence bristled. The boys stared stonily ahead.

Undaunted, Mr. Brundage held up a contract: "On the first day of class, we went over the rules, specifically: Zero Tolerance for Cheating. You signed this contract. Right?"

Nervous gulps.

"Do you think this is funny?"

"No," said Bernice.

"I don't think so either. Because you stand accused of cheating. All of you. *Comprende?*"

Hispanic students bristled at being singled out. Angelina started to cry.

"Tears will get you nowhere," Mr. Brundage continued. "I am going to ask each one of you to explain how you suddenly scored in the 80s and 90s, when, frankly, you are not A or B material."

"Mrs. Swanson says if you work hard you can go to college," Clarence protested.

"Mrs. Swanson is an English teacher, not a scientist."

"But we scored high," Joe argued.

"That's why we're going to quiz you again." Mr. Brundage smiled cruelly, passing out last year's test and instructing them to start answering questions immediately. "Just to make sure."

Earlier, when Kouang was called out of class to meet Mr. Brundage in the conference room, Kouang considered the meeting a test of his character. Although he had trouble pronouncing many English words and still lacked vocabulary, he found biology an easy language to learn because the principles were in harmony with the pale green shoots growing out of the rice paddies, the piglets born in the spring and carried to market on a bicycle, the fish jumping in the Mekong River where he had played, watching bodies floating to the sea.

He wondered what punishments were given in America for stealing ideas. *America is such a strange country. Everybody is supposed to make it on his own, but students are punished for helping each other. In Vietnam, it is just the opposite. If you keep your own garden, you are an Enemy of the People; if you work hard, you have to give everything to the state.*

When Kouang opened the door, Mr. Brundage smiled sarcastically. "You're late, Mr. Kong," he said, pointing to a seat between his AVID classmates. "We'll continue with you next."

"My name is not Kong," Kouang said, taking a seat between Bernice and Clarence.

"Whatever. You scored at the top of the class," Mr. Brundage said, slapping Kouang's graded test on the desk. "Did you cheat?"

Kouang shook his head vehemently.

"Then how did you score 92?" asked Mr. Brundage. "Your last test was a 68."

"I study all night."

"And no one gave you the answers?" The teacher questioned, honing in.

"AVID tutor help me."

"Ah ha," Mr. Brundage said. "What inside information did the tutor give you?"

Kouang was confused by the word *inside.* He did not answer.

"Why are you staring at the floor?" Mr. Brundage jeered. "Do you feel guilty? Or do you people always lie to save face?"

Kouang's stomach sank, seasick, and he saw again the gunwhale rolling up on a huge wave; the broken mast stabbing the sky. Then there was shouting, and the pirate who called himself "captain" caught the old bearded grandfather rooting in the rice bag, his bony hand like a skeleton. "Throw him overboard!" the ravenous boat people cried. He heard the old man pleading. Then Kouang had closed his eyes. There was a splash. Silence. The boat rocked like a dead carcass on the deserted sea.

"Why don't you answer me?" Mr. Brundage cried, clenching his fists.

"I feel sick to stomach," Kouang said, imploring Mrs. Swanson with his eyes. She pushed her chair back, rising to her feet. "Mr. Brundage, may I have a word with you?"

The two teachers went out into the hall, closing the door behind them. "It's cultural, not personal, behavior," Mrs. Swanson whispered. "Asian kids rarely share. They come from a tradition of stoic silence." She paused. "By the way, his name is not Kong. It's pronounced 'kuh-wan.' Got it?"

Skeptical, Mr. Brundage turned his back on Mary Catherine and returned to face the impassive boy. "Kung, I am going to give you the test to take over." Mr. Brundage directed him to a seat at the back of the room.

Kouang gazed at the four-part test and sighed with relief. Pencil in hand, he filled in the blanks, skated through multiple-choice questions, and dove into the anatomy diagram, naming parts of the fetal pig. It was easier than the first time, because there were no distractions. Reaching the end, he felt as if an air hose had been attached to his chest. Kouang's self-confidence inflated his lungs and straightened his back, pulling his chin up. He virtually floated across the room, handing Mr. Brundage his test.

Mr. Brundage laid the punch-hole key over Kouang's paper and graded the questions. With each correct answer, his eyebrow sank a notch. Then came the essay at the bottom. This had been a trick question for extra credit. Kouang's handwriting blurred like a rice paddy in the mist.

"Kouang, you wrote 'ontology recapitulates phylogeny.' What does that mean?"

"It says story of one creature repeat history of evolution of species," Kouang answered, lifting his eyes. "But this old theory just gross generalize. Young people not have to repeat same old story of ancestors. Mrs. Swanson teach we can 'advance via individual determination.' That spell AVID."

The endorsement did not sit well with Mr. Brundage. He scrutinized the group, searching for the cheater in their midst. The Inquisition continued for another hour, keeping the students after school. Much of the time was used to repeat the same questions, followed by the wiping of tears. Relentlessly, the Grand Inquisitor grilled Clarence, Angelina, and the rest, saving Bernice for last.

"You have an attitude, young lady."

Bernice was about to talk back, but a dim memory of Mrs. Swanson's admonition not to confront teachers swam up from her unconscious and stilled her tongue.

"Trace the circulation system of the fetal pig," Mr. Brundage demanded.

"Your heart pumps blood from aorta to the lungs, where it picks up oxygen, and heads out to the organs and tissues," she answered. "Then the veins carry back the carbon dioxide to the lungs, where it's exhaled." Bernice traced the artery, dyed red, to the chambers of the heart leading to rubbery blue veins. "You know where Interstate 8 crosses the 5? That's the aorta of San Diego."

"Interesting analogy," Mr. Brundage allowed. "That will be all."

While Mr. Brundage scored the "retakes" to compare them to the original exams, the AVID students were ushered into an adjoining classroom and told to wait for the verdict. Tension was high. Much was at stake. The clock moved with agonizing slowness. They were stranded alone together.

Since this was not Mrs. Swanson's classroom, there were no tables to sit around, only battered desks arranged in rigid rows. Clarence and Máximo sat in the front, Angelina in the back, Bernice took a chair near the window, Kouang retreated to a spot beside a world map, Joe paced in circles, the rest of the accused scattered around the room.

"What's going to happen to us?" the freckled boy asked.

"I don't care," said Bernice.

They glanced nervously at one another, oblivious to the map behind Kouang's head that depicted the amazing distances AVID students and their forebears had crossed to reach this room.

Without thinking, they began scooting their chairs toward each other. Like iron filings, they were drawn by an invisible magnet. They talked quietly, not blaming, but reassuring one another. When Mrs. Swanson came to get them, they were sitting in a circle.

As they re-entered the conference room, Mr. Brundage wiped his glasses on his necktie and compared the scores. Kouang had scored 92 on the first exam, 93 on the second. Clarence was 82 on the first and 79 on the second. The range of difference between students was wide, but the differential between each student's two scores amounted to a few percentage points. The data was hard. Their knowledge was clear.

Still Mr. Brundage was not convinced. "Let me check your biology notes," he said to Joe.

One by one, Clarence, Kouang, Angelina, and the other AVID students opened their binders. Their biology notes, in the Cornell format, were detailed. The anatomical diagrams were complete, down to the names of the tendons. Then Mr. Brundage pointed to the hardest question on the test, the phrase that he had thought no one would understand. The phrase "ontogeny recapitulates phylogeny" was scrawled in the left columns of several notebooks. On the right side of the page, however, each student's definition was unique.

"How did you figure this out?" Mr. Brundage asked.

"I didn't get it the first time," Clarence said. "But our tutor made us read the text and write the definitions down in our own words."

"I see," Mr. Brundage said, grudgingly beginning to understand. "So the tutor helps?"

"Yeah, but they don't give us the answers," Clarence explained.

"We've got to figure it out ourselves," added the freckled student.

"But before the test, we exchange notes and quiz each other."

Mr. Brundage pondered, weighing the evidence. Before this moment, he had not believed that "underqualified" students could master these biological concepts. But objectively, the new scores, the verbal answers, and the detailed notes all reinforced the legitimacy of the original test results.

Mr. Brundage took off his glasses. The AVID students held their breath, waiting for the verdict.

"Based on past experience, I didn't think you kids could do it. That was my subjective opinion," Mr. Brundage said, clearing his throat. "But as a scientist, I have to rely on quantitative measures. The data have convinced me, beyond a doubt, that you are innocent of cheating."

A collective gasp escaped from the AVID students. "Yes!" cried Bernice.

"You have earned your As and Bs," Mr. Brundage said firmly, trying for the first time to distinguish their individual faces. Then he lost control of his voice. "I misjudged you," he said. "I'm sorry. I won't underestimate you again."

"What about other teachers?" asked Kouang, speaking for them all. "Will *they* respect us?"

"You are vindicated!" Mrs. Swanson cried in class the next morning, as students and tutors shared a quiet victory. Though their vindication did not make the school newspaper, it did temporarily silence some of Mary Catherine's critics in the teachers' lounge.

For a few days in December, AVID scholars were heroes on their buses, bearers of hope to their homes.

Mrs. Swanson saw this as a turning point. From that time on, AVID students showed greater confidence. They saw their hard work paying off, and they worked even harder, knowing that measurable results earned respect. They had entered the semester as strangers, been tested by the inquisition, and now emerged stronger from the heat, their fears forged into friendships.

As they left for winter break, they carried themselves a little higher. In four months, they had learned to take notes, to ask questions, to study in groups, to support each other. Their integrity had been questioned and they had proved themselves honest.

Still, the wintry fog of anxiety hung over them. When they came back in the new year, they would have to sit for semester exams. Could they compete with the best and brightest students? Would they pass, fail, or surpass Mrs. Swanson's expectations?

As Mary Catherine stood in the empty AVID room, she felt proud of her kids. AVID had survived its rocky birth, thank God for her tutors; and Jim had been her constant ally. Yet Mary Catherine regretted that she had alienated some of the faculty. And there was no proof that AVID would actually enable first-generation college applicants to gain acceptance to the American Dream.

Mary Catherine closed the door on AVID's first months, satisfied but unfulfilled. Would the next three years improve the lives of her students? Or would AVID follow hundreds of other acronyms to the graveyard of good ideas?

Outside the AVID classroom, the wind blew leaves off the liquid ambar trees. A cold front of recession swept down on the U.S. economy. Budget cuts for public schools loomed on the horizon.

Kids set up barriers and those become
their excuses. It's a defense mechanism.
They rationalize to themselves why they
fail in school and they accept it.
What we have to teach kids is that
they aren't victims.

—Mary Catherine Swanson

PART TWO
MIRACLES
1981–1986

— LETTER TO —
TEACHERS

When students returned from winter break, the flush of victory had drained from their faces, leaving a film of anxiety. Semester exams loomed. For some, the chances of passing advanced classes appeared no better than the odds of a snowfall in San Diego.

"Welcome home," Mrs. Swanson greeted them optimistically. "I just got back from a family gathering in my hometown of Kingsburg, in Central California. How were your holidays?"

Their responses were muted. Many of the AVID students had never seen a snowfall, never flown on an airplane, never been on a family vacation. How different from the privileged Clairemont students who went skiing in the Sierras.

"This is a brand-new year, 1981!" she exclaimed. "We have a newly elected president, Ronald Reagan." Cheers and groans. She smiled enigmatically, not taking sides. "We can make a fresh start. But first, we have unfinished business. What should we do to prevent more accusations against AVID students?"

"Tell teachers to stop putting us down!"

Mrs. Swanson listened to the complaints. She sympathized with their difficulties, but not with their whining tone.

"AVID students are not victims," she said. "What positive changes can we make?"

"They accuse us—accuse them back."

Mrs. Swanson crossed her arms. "If we confront teachers disrespectfully, we cannot expect them to show respect to us. What is a better way of communicating *what we are about* to other people on this campus?"

"Invite them to see AVID class for themselves."

"They won't come," moaned a skeptic.

"That depends on how we invite them!" Mrs. Swanson laughed. "How should we?"

"Write those prejudiced teachers a letter, Mrs. Swanson," urged Bernice. "Tell them we're trying hard. We are good kids."

"I could write a letter *for* you," Mrs. Swanson replied in a way that arrested the laughter. "But what would that imply about your confidence or ability to express yourselves?"

"Man, I'd like to tell my math teacher: 'Back off!'" muttered a frustrated student.

"You crazy? If we criticize them, they'll retaliate for sure!" an athlete retorted.

"What if we write the letter together?" Mrs. Swanson asked. "That way, we can express how we feel as a group. And nobody will be singled out."

She had not planned this as a lesson in composition, but that was how the interdisciplinary program worked. In this case, AVID students faced distrust from teachers who were suspicious of disadvantaged kids who showed up in advanced classes. Mrs. Swanson faced resentment and, perhaps, envy from colleagues who wondered what gave *her* the right to interfere in their classrooms. How could they solve this problem together?

"Let's brainstorm," she said. "What do we want to tell teachers about our class and our purpose?"

Silence.

"Why are we here?" This question, she knew, was the hardest for kids to answer, because it required teenagers to stand outside of themselves and look at what they were doing from an adult perspective. For children of violence, who doubt they will live to the age of 30; for children of poverty, whose families struggle every day to eke out enough money to buy food and pay rent; for children becoming adolescents, who have difficulty thinking past the weekend—for all of these kids, it was supremely important to learn how to inquire about the history, context, accuracy, and meaning of what they were studying, to contemplate different answers, to wonder if there were a deeper reason. For these children, it was vital to discover a purpose and to communicate it to each other, to parents, to teachers; to make their commitment real and public.

"In this letter, we need to answer some basic questions," Mrs. Swanson said. "What are our expectations? What are we willing to do to achieve our goals? What do we want from our teachers? How can we work together?"

She held her chalk high as the kids raised their hands to offer answers and the letter seemed to write itself.

To: Clairemont High School Faculty
Date: January, 1981

Dear Teachers,

We are enrolled in your college preparation classes without the prerequisites. Sometimes we are going to struggle in your classes. The reason why we are there is that we want to go to college. We are also enrolled in an elective class called AVID where we receive tutorial help with our work.

If we are not doing well in our classes, will you please tell our AVID teacher, Mrs. Swanson, so we can work more effectively? Also would you please stop by our AVID classroom, room 206, during fourth period any day to see the kind of work we do in our study groups from the binders that we keep?

Sincerely,

The AVID Students

All 32 students signed the letter. Mrs. Swanson placed a copy in the mailbox of every teacher and administrator at Clairemont High. Then she awaited the response with trepidation and hope: Who would reply? Would their evaluations show improvement?

The final exams were graded over the weekend. A week later, report cards were sent home. AVID students returned with worried faces. A chorus of Cs reverberated through the gloomy classroom, echoed by a dirge of Ds and a few mournful Fs. As students faced the music, nobody felt much like dancing.

"You took the hardest classes and competed against the top students at Clairemont," Mrs. Swanson said. "Your grades were not all they could be, or *will be*," she emphasized. "But they were *no lower* than when you took easy classes."

Were they disheartened? As they talked about their grades, she began to see they were inwardly pleased. For outsiders who had come to a new school and had taken the toughest schedules, it was a heady challenge to compete with Seminar students high on the bell curve.

"Hey, man. I took algebra and didn't flunk!"

Yes, she thought, *a first semester C is a high accomplishment.* But AVID students would not stop until they had turned the bell curve on its head, with the clangor ringing *Equality!*

— CAN A TEACHER — BECOME A LEADER?

AVID was no longer a secret on campus, yet it was not well known, either. The simple and direct letter from students provoked some teachers to respond with appreciation and the curiosity to learn more about AVID. Others vented frustration and anger, blaming Mrs. Swanson for changing the makeup of their classes. They refused to take responsibility for teaching kids whom they did not consider *their* students.

A few curious teachers began dropping by at lunch to check out the AVID classroom. They wanted to know why AVID students sat around cafeteria tables rather than at individual desks, where the tutors came from, and how the students took notes and studied together in groups. The bag-lunch conversations between Mrs. Swanson, AVID students, tutors, and visiting teachers focused on challenges, not complaints. They asked: *How could teachers become more effective? What were the difficulties in reaching non-traditional students? Were hard-charging teachers unwittingly setting up students for failure?* Mrs. Swanson certainly did not have the answers, but perhaps students could help teachers see what was working and what was not, and together they might help each other.

These energizing conversations, punctuated by searching questions and uproarious laughter, became popular among a small but growing number of teachers. They were glad to escape from the tiresome talk of retirement plans and bigoted code words in the teachers' lunch room.

One day, Mr. Brundage dropped by the AVID room. Mary Catherine tensed, fearing another accusation, but the biology teacher brought some *Scientific American* and *National Geographic* magazines to add to the AVID library. He wanted to learn how the program worked, and he talked with the tutors, admiring their youthful excitement. The students were wary at first but soon saw his sincerity. A place was made for him around the table, and AVID's earliest critic joined the search for solutions.

As the second semester got underway, Mary Catherine awoke at 3 A.M., breathing rapidly. She had dreamed of masked teachers pushing pointed sticks into the pit of her stomach. At such moments, her optimism failed her. She saw with stark clarity that the best intentions created the worst disappointments. AVID would not survive by goodwill and scintillating conversation alone. Unless students showed measurable progress, AVID would be sacrificed after one year, and the enemies of change would dance on its grave. Academic progress would require even greater motivation, hard work, and improved study habits on the part of students. Raising her head at dawn, Mrs. Swanson had little doubt they would persevere.

But students could not do it alone. Unless she and her colleagues found better ways of teaching this unique group of students, the teachers would keep on receiving their paychecks—and, later, retirement benefits—but the kids would crash and burn. Unless teachers challenged themselves to reach higher and deeper, students would lose this one gleaming chance that education offered—to raise themselves beyond their parents' limited horizons.

She had no power to compel teachers to change the ways they taught, no bully pulpit to motivate change, no funding to share in the hope that they would try innovative experiments. She was a teacher like thousands and thousands of her colleagues, a "knowledge worker" trained to convey *content* down the assembly line of an industrialized education system and to take orders from the administration. She had no authority. No position of power. Nor did she want power *over* other teachers. Instead, she wanted teachers to seize the opportunity *to make positive changes, not alone, but by pooling their experience, learning from each other.*

How could a teacher become a leader? She searched for a mirror in other professions. Doctors had morbidity and mortality conferences in order to go over cases and learn from their successes and failures. Teachers had a labor union to represent their economic interests. But public schools, at that time, did not foster meetings amongst teachers to discuss their students and come up with solutions. Nor was there an intellectual forum to share professional techniques, recount experiences, or pass on tricks of the trade.

If there were no structure for teachers and students to discuss ways to reform education from within the system, AVID would have to create a dialogue on effective teaching and learning. She saw no reason not to begin one here and now.

The next day, AVID students dared to be the first freshman class at Clairemont to host a dialogue between students and teachers. The possibility caused a sensation. AVID students were almost universally enthusiastic in their desire to meet with teachers in order to share their problems and search for solutions. They confidently composed and dispatched a second letter:

Dear Teachers,

On the second Monday in February, you are invited
to come to the AVID classroom, #206, from 2:30 to
3:30 P.M. for refreshments and a discussion of
effective teaching and learning. We sincerely
hope you will join us.

Sincerely,

The AVID Students

Who will show up? Mary Catherine wondered as she placed the letters in teachers' mailboxes. To her knowledge, there had never
been a dialogue at Clairemont High in which teachers and students
met on equal footing to discuss problematic educational practices
and to search for effective alternatives.

The unprecedented meeting demanded preparation on the part
of AVID students and tutors, permission from the principal, and
diplomacy by Mrs. Swanson. The pedagogical strategy was to
focus on common problems in teaching and learning that *were not
isolated to one teacher or class*, but, rather, were endemic at
Clairemont High. In order to effect change, *all* teachers were invited, regardless of whether they had AVID students in their classes.
The goal for the meeting was deliberately modest and achievable:
to focus solely on two isolated educational practices—not a litany
of gripes and grievances. Students and tutors would explain their
problems, teachers would respond, and together they would discuss ways to improve the transmission and acquisition of knowledge. Any changes would be strictly voluntary and subject to
review in a continuing process of refinement. If a new teaching
practice didn't show results in improved grades or standardized
test scores, "For heaven sakes, discard it and try something else!"
Mrs. Swanson urged.

Tutors played a crucial role as intermediaries between students
and teachers and would later be emissaries from AVID, serving as

teaching guides in willing teachers' classrooms. For months, Mrs. Swanson had asked the tutors to keep notes about what was making learning difficult for students. After much hashing out, they found two initial practices that were causing a lot of problems for students and that might easily be changed by teachers.

The first was the showing of films in science and history classes. Because red-blooded, late-night TV-watching, sleepy-eyed, high-school students—not just AVID kids—took advantage of boring film screenings to catch a snooze, teachers, assuming the role of *Sleep Police,* had adopted the practice of giving a quiz immediately after the film, to be completed in class. AVID students, who were exhausted from hours of studying and long bus rides, had trouble absorbing the complex concepts in the films, often because they did not yet have the verbal language skills to pick up the technical jargon. They needed to see the words in print, to hear the concepts repeated, and to put them into their own words through discussions with peers. They could absorb the concepts, but they needed *time* to do it. A pop quiz caused panic and incomprehension. They often flunked the quiz. This left the AVID students feeling like failures; teachers became frustrated and blamed the students, whom they were quick to stereotype as washouts. Instead of enhancing comprehension, the films became a stumbling block preventing students from learning what the films were about. Teachers lost respect for students—and, secretly, for themselves. Disappointment led to demoralization for both students and teachers.

Why not focus on content? she wondered.

The second practice drove Mrs. Swanson, as English Department chairwoman, crazy. Teachers in the humanities and social sciences gave writing assignments that were too broad and difficult for students to understand, much less to write about intelligently in a three-page essay. Students who had never heard a word of Elizabethan English two weeks before were assigned such broad topics as: "How does art mirror life in Shakespeare's *Romeo and Juliet?*" Survivors of the genocide in Cambodia, who had lived through a real civil war, were compelled to: "Discuss the relationship between slavery in the South and immigrant labor in the North in provoking the Civil War."

The essays were generally assigned on Monday and were due the following Friday. During the week, students were not required to write first drafts or to edit their work. This would have required teachers to do extra work. Instead, students listened to teachers lecturing by rote at top speed, frantically trying to cover all the material by the end of the semester.

How could a freshman possibly complete such an essay without several drafts, discussion, editing, and revision? The goal was not to recommend that teachers water down the material, but rather to concentrate it. Wouldn't it be better to demand analysis and original thought on a narrowly focused topic rather than a laundry list of generalized causes and effects, without evidence to back up the thesis?

Mrs. Swanson knew that the same principle of dilution versus concentration was relevant to the meeting itself. If she invited all students to attend, they would present teachers with a cacophony of complaints, punctuated by much wailing, in a game of Blame the Teacher!

"Our AVID class of 32 must choose several students to represent us," Mrs. Swanson said, the week before the meeting. "Those who want to participate can help the representatives speak for us by giving teachers concrete examples of difficulties you have experienced and helpful suggestions."

"I got one!" Bernice interjected. "Mrs. Brown, she's too busy staring out the window, thinking about her new baby. She's supposed to be helping us review for a test."

"No names or blaming, please," Mrs. Swanson answered. Bernice was sometimes impolite, but Mary Catherine admired her courage for standing up for what she conceived as justice when others remained silent. *Would Bernice learn the social skills to become an effective advocate for the underdog?* It was too early to risk Bernice's participation now, but this was one purpose of the dialogue: to teach students how to engage in constructive conversation, so that they might see that they are making a positive impact in their own lives and for others like them. The meeting was a crucible for combining school issues and representative democracy. *May the pestle not crush too many egos!*

Softening, Mrs. Swanson explained: "It is a privilege for us to have this meeting with teachers. If any teacher who takes the risk of participating feels that students are directly criticizing them, then we can bet we will never have another such meeting. No teacher must leave the meeting believing he or she has been personally singled out for attack. This is not about getting even. Not about ridicule or blame. It is about getting teachers to make changes that benefit AVID students. If we succeed and you gain the keys to a college education, you will have the skills to advocate for more fundamental change."

Bernice nodded, "I can get behind that."

"That's what's so good about this," Mrs. Swanson said, feeling a warm connection with Bernice after so many battles. "If we find an acceptable way of addressing a problem, the teacher will *want* to work with us—help us—rather than be offended."

"Isn't that brown-nosing?" asked Tabitha.

"No, when you look a teacher straight in the eye you convey self-respect," Mrs. Swanson answered. "The biggest power a teacher has over you is *grades*. If you want to do well in class, you have to work *with* teachers, not against them. Collaborating with teachers should not be confused with collaborating with the enemy. You are motivating teachers to work harder for your benefit. Collaborative learning gives you power to shape your destiny."

Students were nodding, first one, then two, then several together, as the idea took shape for them.

"Whom shall we choose to represent the class?" Mrs. Swanson asked.

There was no vote. No power struggle. No factions. No commotion. Within a few days, students were chosen by popular consent.

The last Friday before the meeting, AVID students worked with their representatives. Tutors led a back-and-forth dialogue of ideas that transformed complaints into questions, blame into suggestions. Other students prepared homemade ethnic dishes to serve as refreshments. After school, Mrs. Swanson quietly polled Jim Grove and a few other allies, asking them to come to the meeting and to talk it up with colleagues. AVID students formed the cafeteria tables to make a hollow square. Refreshments, redolent with spices: Vietnamese spring rolls wrapped in lettuce leaves; barbecued chicken wings; Mexican salsa, mild red and picante green chili peppers; homemade Italian foccacia bread with garlic and onions; and good ol' American potato chips and avocado dip were laid out on the counter at the back of the room. The chairs were arranged around the perimeter, waiting for their occupants. Teachers and students would meet on a level playing field. The final bell rang at 2:10, and students poured from classrooms. AVID representatives gathered their binders and books from their lockers. The meeting place glowed in the golden afternoon, a warm Santa Ana wind blew from the desert: summer's gift to February. All was ready.

Who would dare to come?

About 20 teachers wandered into Room 206 for the first conversation with AVID students. A majority of those present appeared genuinely curious about this controversial experiment, of which they had heard rumors, and about which they wished to make their own judgments. Some were eager to engage in a freewheeling dialogue with students about improving teaching and learning skills. A few suspicious teachers reluctantly showed up, merely because they were afraid students would talk about them behind their backs, and they were not about to let *that* happen.

The principal, looking relaxed, quietly took a seat with his back to the windows. He made a point of switching off his walkie-talkie so that he would not be interrupted by anything less than an emergency.

The chosen AVID students were there: several as representatives and a few to serve refreshments. The student representatives informally took their seats, looking a bit nervous, with their back to the bulletin board. AVID tutors took their places beside the students. Above them, college banners waved brightly and their heads were silhouetted against the Tutoring Assignment Schedule.

Several teachers were surprised to see their names listed beside the due dates of their own class assignments, with tutors' names assigned to each subject area. It felt reassuring to some to have their lessons reinforced by a team of tutors; others feared meddling from Mrs. Swanson and a bunch of untrained college kids.

Mr. Brundage took a corner seat, his appearance making a stir among the AVID students whom he had accused of cheating. His presence was a heartening sign of vindication (and of reconciliation, Mary Catherine thought to herself) for Kouang and other biology students. Mary Catherine was careful not to call attention to Mr. Brundage, not wanting to cause discomfort for her colleague, whom she respected for his courage in pursuing the truth.

A trio of grim-mouthed veteran teachers swept in late, elbowing past their younger colleagues. With pencils tucked behind their ears and eyes narrowed like sharpshooters, they glared at the AVID students through bifocal lenses.

Mary Catherine smoothed her blouse and straightened the hem of her navy blue skirt above her vulnerable knees. Anxiously she searched for allies and caught sight of Jim Grove's steady gaze, solid and supportive, with a glint of devilish excitement at the prospect of stirring the broth.

"How pleased we are that you have come to the AVID classroom," Mrs. Swanson began. "Your time is precious, so let's quickly get down to the purpose of this meeting. We have been working now in AVID for six months, and we've discovered that certain teaching and learning practices come up frequently in tutoring sessions." She glanced left and right at her freshmen. "Students have asked for an opportunity to discuss these problematic methods with faculty. It is their belief that, with not-too-difficult changes in methodologies, we can teach more effectively—and it will make it easier for students to learn."

The mouths of the grim grew grimmer, and one teacher cleared her throat at the mention of "not-too-difficult changes." Mrs. Swanson ignored her and pressed on: "The ground rule for students is never to single out any individual teacher for criticism. That is not our intent." She paused, waiting for this message to sink in. A few graying eyebrows were raised skeptically, and all the student representatives nodded their heads, as if to underscore her point—they were not out for blood.

"Now, since the students have a rule, then so must the rest of us," Mrs. Swanson pointed out. "The teachers' rule is not to single out particular students for blame." She waited a beat to underscore this point and several teachers nodded acceptance, but not all. Raising her hands to embrace all participants in an inclusive group, Mrs. Swanson ended on a high note: "Our joint task is to identify common difficulties and to come up with possible solutions."

Timidly, a Latino boy said: "They show a lot of films in class, 'specially on Fridays. They talk real fast and you can't catch the words. Then they give you a quiz. It's not fair." He turned to Mrs. Swanson for help.

Delicately, she explained to her colleagues: "Kids who are learning English as a second language have trouble grasping technical terms by ear. They need to see the terms and learn their definitions."

Several teachers were nodding. This had not occurred to them.

"So what solution do you suggest?" a science teacher asked, having just failed several AVID students on a film quiz.

"If we could share our notes and talk about the film, then have the quiz the next day, I think we would do better," the Hispanic student suggested.

"Sharing notes is cheating in my book," the teacher responded.

"I think you're missing the point," Mr. Grove interceded. "As teachers, what we are trying to accomplish is that students understand what is being taught in the film. Does it really matter how they get the information, as long as they master it?"

The conversation turned a corner, providing an opening for the students to explain how they took detailed notes and studied in groups. While one described the Cornell note-taking process, two others opened their AVID binders and demonstrated how they traded notes and asked each other questions. The teachers leaned forward, intrigued, and there was a subtle change of roles as the students became teachers and the teachers became learners.

"I was skeptical, frankly," Mr. Brundage admitted to his colleagues. "But I've seen the results and I have to tell you, this process really works. My AVID students have a deeper understanding of concepts, even if they started out behind."

A Vietnamese student raised her hand. "My tutor teach me by asking us good questions. Do you know what 'ontogeny recapitulate phylogeny' mean?"

"Please refresh us," answered an English teacher, to nervous laughter.

The student passed her notes to the teacher, asking her to put the biological concept into her own words. The teacher struggled and others got into the spirit.

"I wish all my students took Cornell notes," a history teacher interjected.

"We could teach them," Mrs. Swanson offered.

"How?"

"I would be happy to send an AVID tutor to your classroom," she said, gesturing to the tutors. "During the film, Judy, Nina, or James could take notes on an overhead projector, so the students could learn by doing it."

"Nonsense, they'll just copy the tutor's notes," a veteran chemistry teacher objected.

Judy shook her head. "We check their notes." As a highly respected graduate of Clairemont, Judy had credibility with teachers who had known her as a student with integrity.

"Some *will* copy," Mrs. Swanson responded. "But we reward kids who take original notes by giving them points toward their AVID grade."

"Oh dear, that means we'll have to read their notes," a weary English teacher sighed. "We have enough to do!" This touched a nerve with other teachers, who were overwhelmed with paperwork.

"Grading papers may be tedious," Mrs. Swanson admitted, to a round of applause. "Let me make you a second offer: For the first two weeks, AVID tutors will check students' notes and assign points. You can use these points in your grading systems, however you wish."

Nina smiled with satisfaction at the trust Mrs. Swanson showed her and the other college tutors.

The students waited expectantly, watching the teachers, who held the power, consider Mrs. Swanson's offer. Outside, the spindly liquid ambar trees, bereft of leaves, looked like curious observers, waiting for an answer.

"Okay, let's try it," a few teachers offered, while skeptics scowled.

"That's a start," Mrs. Swanson said, looking at the clock. "We have a second teaching practice that AVID students asked us to discuss. Then we get to taste the ethnic delicacies the students have prepared."

At the food table, Máximo Escobedo's eyes lit up as the savory aroma of corn tortillas floated among the teachers. Máximo had listened to the dialogue, catching familiar words like *Cornell notes*, but missing much of what was said. Nevertheless, his English was improving, and he was proud to present Mexican enchiladas, made from his mother's recipe.

Stomachs rumbled as the group considered the second issue.

"We get hung up by big essay topics that are too generalized, and we can't make sense of them," said a tall teenaged girl whose hair was braided in corn rows.

"Here's an example," said her colleague with coffee-colored eyes. "'What are the causes and effects of the Civil War?' How do you write a three-page essay on that?"

The teachers rustled uncomfortably. The topic had been deliberately made up, so that no teacher felt directly challenged.

"So you start writing the essay on the causes and effects of the Civil War and pretty soon you're all over the place, and nowhere," the student related breathlessly. "Really, we want to write a good paper and back up our opinions."

Mrs. Swanson intervened, turning to the teachers. "How does it look from your perspective?" she asked her colleagues.

"Glad you asked," a demanding history teacher flared up. "The papers I'm getting from AVID students are better than AVID students could possibly write *by themselves*. I think that tutors are writing the papers for them."

Nina and James bristled and Judy wanted to answer this charge, but Mrs. Swanson held up her hand. "How would you answer that?" she asked the students.

"It's not true," they said. "Nobody writes it for us."

"Then what *does* happen?"

"When we get an assignment, we put it on the board," the student explained, pointing to the tutoring schedule. "Then everybody from different class sections, you know, who's got that same paper, gets together to brainstorm."

"Brainstorm?" asked an American literature specialist, frowning.

"Yeah, we get together and talk off the top of our heads . . . or dig it out of our notes . . . or look in the textbook . . . brainstorming ideas!" the students cried, voices blending like a jazz band.

"Hold on, brainstorming is just the beginning," Judy interjected. "To write a good essay, we have to narrow the focus. Each student must come up with an original thesis. Then they have to defend that thesis to the group."

"Can you demonstrate this for us?" asked the history teacher.

Judy nodded, leading the students in an unrehearsed discussion.

"Okay," said the tall black girl with braided hair, "my thesis is: *The cause of World War II was that Hitler invaded Poland.*"

"But what caused Hitler?" piped up a shorter boy with freckles.

"Depression in Germany," answered the girl.

"What does *depression* mean?" James probed.

"People were sad because they lost World War I," she answered.

"Why else?" asked Nina.

"Too poor to buy bread," answered the Vietnamese student, who knew hunger.

"And why were they poor?"

"Inflation . . . their paper money became worthless, so they blamed the United Nations for everything."

"You mean the League of Nations," James said.

"Hold on, those are pieces of a puzzle," Mrs. Swanson interjected. "What was the underlying force driving Hitler?"

"Power," said a voice from the back.

"Go on."

"They thought they was Superman!"

"Were Superman," Judy gently corrected. "Now, look in your textbook for the analysis of the fascist ideology."

Mrs. Swanson explained the method. "The tutors don't give answers. That makes students dependent, as we discovered early on. Tutors respond to student ideas by asking deeper questions, forcing the students to probe for meaning. This collaborative learning is exciting, because it sparks inquiry. We call it 'writing, inquiry, collaboration.'"

The history teacher nodded, taking notes.

"But how does the actual writing of the paper occur?" asked the English teacher.

"After we defend the thesis, then we outline our papers," a sandy-haired student explained. "The thesis is always the first paragraph."

"You got to make it clear," explained a handsome boy with Aztec eyes, "because people are gonna try to break it down."

"We back up each point with evidence," the sandy-haired student jumped back in. "Then, near the end, you put this all in perspective."

"Like a big picture frame," smiled the Vietnamese.

Judy explained. "That first night, they go home and write a first draft. Then, next day, each one reads it aloud to the group and members respond."

The students acted it out: "Yeah, we'll say: 'This is clear' or 'This isn't' or 'I don't get it' or 'That's a good example.'"

"On the second night, they write a second draft," Judy explained. "Then, third day, students exchange papers. They become 'critical readers' of each other's work."

"It's to our benefit to share papers with the strongest students we can find and keep making improvement," the students added. "We get graded only on the final draft."

"You mean you're graded twice on the same paper?"

"Yes, once for the regular class and once for AVID. But in AVID you can always rewrite your paper because Mrs. Swanson says that's how real writers work."

"Tell us, please, how critical reading works," asked a language arts teacher.

The student explained, tossing her braids. "The first critical reader uses, say, a red pen, slashing up mistakes. They sign their name like Zorro in blood on the bottom." The teachers laughed, and she continued. "The second reader uses a blue pen . . . and so on."

"That could make one bloody unpopular with one's peers, couldn't it?" asked a student teacher. "What's the motivation to skewer your friends?"

"It's really helping them!" she answered. "Mrs. Swanson gives extra credit points to good critical readers. On the last night, we write our final draft, using all the critical comments to help us."

"So you see," Judy said, "the final draft has been conceived, outlined, developed, tested, and rewritten by the student. We tutors don't write the papers. The kids do. And they're remarkable."

The American literature teacher uncrossed her arms and raised her eyes, gold chains drooping from her spectacles. "Now that I understand the process you go through, I don't think it's cheating."

"All right!" the students cheered.

"But I don't believe that the majority of my students are capable of being good critical readers. On the contrary, I think students will multiply each other's errors."

Mrs. Swanson nodded. "In AVID we have begun to identify common errors: Run-on sentences are a huge problem. So I take some class time before we edit the papers and show how to look for run-on sentences. This gives the critical reader a tool." She looked up at her colleagues. "If other teachers start looking for common errors that are important for them—from math to science concepts to grammar—and those teachers teach the concepts to the class, there will be better critical readers, and this will reinforce the learning."

"Sounds great, but we don't have time!" a few teachers protested.

"I know your time is valuable," Mrs. Swanson said. "If you'll just tell us what one of your most common errors is, I will send in a tutor to teach that concept."

Their eyes lit up at the thought of tutors helping them with such unpleasant tasks, like grading papers and making photocopies— slave labor!

"The only rule," Mrs. Swanson said, reading their thoughts, "is that AVID tutors must work directly with kids."

"You've got a deal," announced four of the teachers.

The principal, who had been listening intently, seemed to waken, as if from a spell. A man of great heart but few words, he said: "I never thought I would see the day when students and teachers would sit down together and learn from each other." He congratulated the AVID kids and their tutors, thanking Mrs. Swanson and the teachers who had ventured to converse with students. "I think we have made a beginning. Who knows where it will lead. But I can tell you I will be back in two weeks with this contraption turned off," he held up the walkie-talkie, "and these antennae," he tugged his ears, "tuned in."

Adjourning the meeting, Mrs. Swanson expressed hope that such conversations could continue on a regular basis, helping participants become better teachers and learners. While not everybody was a believer, most agreed to return in two weeks, when they would report on progress and problems.

This group would form the nucleus of the first AVID Site Team, spreading innovative concepts and practices throughout the school. Over the next two decades, AVID Site Teams would form in hundreds of schools, involving thousands of teachers, students, and administrators in a broad-based educational reform movement. Two decades later, as she administered a network of site teams that circled the globe, Mrs. Swanson would look back at the early site team meetings as the apex of her teaching career.

But at this moment, all the participants were rushing toward the food tables. Máximo's eyebrows lifted to the top of his head as the same teachers who had ridiculed his accent in class devoured his mother's enchiladas with great relish. For some reason that he did not understand, Americans found it easier to savor the exotic tastes of foreign dishes than to accept immigrants as equals in their country. Mary Catherine stood back, watching her colleagues and students taste the savory Vietnamese spring rolls; smell the corn tortillas stuffed with frijoles; chew the barbecued ribs, dripping spicy sauce on their chins. They had done good work. Together, they partook of the delicious fruits of the earth. A feast of learning.

THE THREE Rs: RIGOR, RESPONSIVENESS, AND REASSURANCE

The Clairemont Site Team met faithfully every two weeks until the end of the 1980–1981 school year. Support grew. A consistent group of about 20 teachers came regularly, representing about one in four faculty members at Clairemont High.

The AVID class developed a routine that was rigorous, responsive, and reassuring: a humanistic extension of the traditional three *R*s. Grades gradually improved from the D and F range to the lower reaches of the Cs. By the end of the second semester, AVID students had not yet caught up with their peers from more privileged backgrounds, but they made enough progress to see that, with hard work, individual responsibility, and support from AVID classmates, they could meet the expectations set by tutors and Mrs. Swanson.

Tutors made their way into math, science, and history classrooms, teaching note taking and helping teachers try out new techniques. One method was for the tutor to write a question on the board for kids to answer quickly in writing, while the teacher took the attendance roll.

"Tell everything you learned about binomial equations," the tutor would ask. Students had five minutes to dash off as many examples of binomial equations as they could. This helped students review what they had learned and warmed them up for the next lesson. It gave teachers a chance to take roll without having to deal with as many discipline problems—the kids' heads were down, pens streaking across lined paper. Finally, brainstorming gave teachers, tutors, and Mrs. Swanson an idea of what students were learning easily and what they were having trouble absorbing.

This instant snapshot showed, with painful accuracy, how little knowledge students had acquired in comparison to how much material teachers *believed* they had successfully conveyed. The tutors soon realized that many teachers had little or no idea of the level of their students' comprehension of specific subject matter. Instead, teachers were hypnotically focused on their own deadlines to make sure they covered the material required by the curriculum. Students fell further and further behind until they were left in the chalkdust as the teacher reached the finish line.

Knowing what students had learned—and what they hadn't—helped Mrs. Swanson design creative techniques for reviewing, reinforcing, and reinvigorating learning. If a new technique helped—great. The idea was passed on to other teachers through notes dropped in their mailboxes. If experiments failed—like the time math tutors tried to help kids with English grammar—they were quickly discarded, with a throaty release of laughter.

All was not humorous, though. With some teachers, tutors discovered a pattern of neglect, incompetence, and, worst of all, verbal abuse. Before outsiders were allowed to observe classes, students who had complained of being ridiculed or humiliated had been held suspect by the administration unless they could show proof. But if no other adults had been present during the incident, it was the student's word against the teacher's. In any "You said—I said" confrontation between teacher and student, the teacher reigned supreme.

One day, Angelina was facing the wall and staring at a paper with a big F at the top. Her tutor, Judy, noticed that there were no editing marks or comments on the paper, only the flunking grade.

"*¿Qué pasó?*" asked Judy.

Angelina hid her face, refusing to tell. She'd laboriously written the paper in English, using a dictionary, but "Vince" had barged in on her.

"Go to bed," he had ordered.

"I have to finish my homework."

He laughed, pushing the papers off the table and stepping on them with his muddy boots. He didn't leave her alone until 3 A.M. and she didn't have time to copy the whole paper over. In her hurry, she had misspelled the title and even used a few Spanish words. When Angelina turned the paper in, the teacher, Mrs. Bellows, became furious.

"This is American history! Not Mexican history!" Mrs. Bellows shouted in front of the class, hurling the paper in Angelina's face. "This mess is unacceptable work for an advanced class. Go down to the office and have the counselor reschedule you for a lower level."

"*Que bruja!*" *What a witch!* Judy hissed to the frightened student. "I'm going to tell Mrs. Swanson."

"*Por favor, no.*" *Please don't.*

"Why?"

Angelina's lip trembled. After her horrible treatment from "Vince," she didn't trust Americans. But Angelina could not say this, so she nodded, giving Judy permission to talk with Mrs. Swanson, as long as she didn't have to speak with her. Angelina didn't want anyone to discover the reason for her sloppy work.

"My God!" cried Mrs. Swanson, on hearing the story. She was furious at the mistreatment of this uncommunicative student but made a policy that she would never reprimand another teacher. Instead, she took Angelina's paper and spoke with Mrs. Bellows privately.

"I agree with you that this paper is a mess," Mary Catherine said. "I'm not making excuses for Angelina. I don't know what's going on with her, although she *is* learning English quickly."

"Not quickly enough," Mrs. Bellows argued, crossing her arms. "Her spelling and grammar are horrible! I've got 36 kids in a class designed for 28, and I've got to cover the textbook. I can't afford to have AVID students dragging down the class."

"We're all overcrowded," Mrs. Swanson sympathized. "But the point of AVID is to help these kids catch up. AVID students have to rewrite their papers in the AVID class. Angelina will rework this as many times as it takes to make it acceptable."

"Just this one time," Mrs. Bellows relented. "But she'd better improve fast."

Mary Catherine brought the news to Judy, who passed it on to Angelina, who actually smiled. Still, Angelina turned away when Mrs. Swanson approached.

"I've got to break through this wall," Mary Catherine later told Judy. "But how?"

This is not to say that students were never at fault. Tutors observed the instances when students were smarting off, acting out, or disrupting classrooms. When those same students then came wailing to AVID with a complaint against a teacher, Mrs. Swanson was able to sit them down and explain, in no uncertain terms, that they must stop the behavior or they would lose the privilege of being an AVID student. She always disciplined students respectfully in private, refraining from humiliating them in front of their peers.

AVID tutors infiltrating other classrooms added a subversive element to AVID's out-front campaign to raise teaching and learning standards. College kids were closer in age to students than they were to teachers, and they could sympathize with student complaints.

Teachers were accustomed to teaching without being observed by anybody. The classroom was sacrosanct, the teacher's private domain, and nobody had the right—except in extreme cases—to interfere in the interaction between the lordly teacher and the serfs. Some teachers had been reciting the exact same lectures for 10 or 15 years. Disciplinary practices that had worked when many Clairemont teachers had begun their careers in the 1950s were clearly not able to cope with the complex social and psychological issues of the 1980s.

The inspiration for improving teaching techniques was contagious. Mrs. Swanson placed a "suggestion box" in a convenient place. Soon, teachers were dropping notes about what worked and what didn't. Instructors who had innovated new ways to convey knowledge passed on their lesson plans for others to adapt to their needs. The collegial environment generated an atmosphere of experimentation, evaluation, and incremental improvement. The climate was alternately electrifying, trying, conflictive, resolution-oriented, and inspiring. Teachers looked forward to freewheeling discussions about teaching styles and strategies. At midday, a group frequently gathered around the AVID room to share lunch and ideas.

Nevertheless, it became clear that opposition was still strong from some teachers, who questioned Mrs. Swanson's unconventional methods and who saw AVID as a threat to their way of teaching.

By the second semester of AVID's first year, Mrs. Swanson realized that, for a variety of reasons—lack of motivation, rebelliousness, problems at home—the AVID class was not working for all her students. Attrition was inevitable, with 2 students out of the original 32 refusing to sign up for the AVID elective in their sophomore year.

By the end of their first year, the rest of the students in the AVID class did remarkably well, in her eyes. Major improvements in their study habits and attitudes came first, followed by tiny improvements in grades. The grades on their first-semester report cards were below average in comparison to the other kids, usually from more privileged backgrounds, in the same advanced classes. But in comparison to their fellow bus riders, who were stuck in regular or remedial classes without any tutoring or moral support, the AVID students moved ahead rapidly. By second semester, small incremental improvements added up to improved grades in academic classes. There were a lot more Cs and Bs, and even a few As. Their conduct grades also improved, revealing deeper involvement and more positive attitudes toward learning.

Clarence was terribly shy at the beginning of the year, but had slowly begun to raise his hand and participate in class discussions. He had always worked hard in school, but now he worked more effectively, using notes to focus in studying for tests. His writing also began to improve, as he used his own words to describe concepts. Mrs. Swanson valued Clarence's presence in class. Even-tempered and friendly, he was a quiet leader who led by example, on and off the playing field. She saw in him great potential, if only he could overcome his family's lack of resources and the absence of a father to guide and protect him. His 1981 report card had more Cs than Bs, but no Ds.

Angelina spent most of the year facing the wall. For months, Mrs. Swanson had been unable to make contact with the girl who was ashamed of her crooked teeth. Her blemished skin reflected the impact of emotional and hormonal turmoil. Sometimes Mrs. Swanson noticed that Angelina was talking with a Seminar student named Alice, who was her English peer tutor. Angelina was constantly reading, but the books were not the ones she was supposed to read for classes. Instead, Mrs. Swanson discovered that Angelina was reading *Don Quixote* in Spanish, one of the most difficult novels to understand in any language. In the spring, Angelina sat by the windows, which were open, and one day Mrs. Swanson saw Alice, who was outside, pass a book through the window to Angelina. It was an unabridged edition of *Moby Dick* in English! Mrs. Swanson was startled: Here was a girl who had spent the entire preceding year, eighth grade, stultified in a remedial English class, learning such challenging concepts as how to read a clock in

English. Now, with the help of Alice, Angelina was challenging herself to read Melville's classic. *How can I reach Angelina?* Mrs. Swanson asked herself. The teacher thought she could establish contact by talking about great books that both she and Angelina loved, then guiding Angelina to open up on a more personal level about herself—turning a literary relationship into a bond of trust.

Máximo, on the other hand, ended the year with an A in math. From his education in Mexico, he was actually ahead of the American students, who didn't have to work nearly as hard, it seemed, as students in his old *colegio*. In English class, Máximo got a C, an amazing accomplishment for someone who had arrived at school knowing five words in English: *Who, what, why, where,* and *when*. Quiet, conscientious, and very kind, Máximo asked deeply intellectual questions. His eyes, Mrs. Swanson believed, were windows to a profoundly artistic soul. Máximo loved art, but in order to take AVID class, he had to sacrifice art class. Mrs. Swanson arranged for Clairemont's art teacher to work, one on one, with Máximo after school—a private course of independent study.

In the spring, Mrs. Swanson had begun recruiting new students for the second AVID class next fall. Among them was Jaime Escobedo, the next brother in line in the Escobedo family. In the interview, she found Jaime to be sensitive and introspective. Although he had been in America for a year, he had trouble communicating in English. Jaime's mother (with Máximo translating) told Mrs. Swanson a harrowing story about Jaime's debut in the San Diego City Schools. Soon after they immigrated, Jaime enrolled in middle school. His eighth-grade science teacher called Mrs. Escobedo in for a conference and told her that Jaime was "retarded." His mother was shocked, because Jaime had excelled in science in Mexico. The school counselor explained that because Jaime did not raise his hand to ask or answer questions in class, the teacher presumed that he was mentally deficient. Defiant, Jaime memorized all of the elements of the periodic table, a feat that proved his teacher wrong. He excelled in science and mathematics. Now Jaime was coming to Clairemont High, and Mrs. Swanson was eager to have him in her AVID class. Mrs. Escobedo thanked her, hinting to Mrs. Swanson that there were three more Escobedo brothers coming after Jaime. When their time came, could they all take AVID class?

Kouang finished the year with strong Bs and a C in English. Revealing the story of his escape from Vietnam had broken down the boundaries of prejudice and fear and had created bridges of compassion and understanding. He made friends easily, socializing with kids outside the Vietnamese circle, who helped him to acculturate rapidly. On any given afternoon, he could be seen playing ball on the grassy area with American kids. They talked constantly, and soon he was learning idiomatic expressions. As Mrs. Swanson watched the changes taking place in Kouang, she realized that he was a young man of extraordinary intelligence, perhaps one of the smartest students she had ever had in any class. All he needed was to learn English and he would be on his way.

Bernice was still defiant, finishing the year with Ds in her classes, but always with bright shiny fingernails. Mary Catherine sadly recalled a field trip to UCSD she had arranged, when Bernice had gone out of control, running around the campus. Mary Catherine had taken great pains to assure the nervous university administration that her inner-city students would not cause disruptions. Much to her chagrin, she received an urgent call from UCSD campus security, "We've got a young lady here who propositioned a soft-drink delivery man." When Mary Catherine angrily confronted her with this accusation, Bernice would not look her teacher in the eye. She sat sullenly, paring her nails. "You done, teach?" she muttered sarcastically, walking away. Bernice quit AVID after her first year, but her friend Tabitha remained in the course. Mrs. Swanson discovered, to her regret, that the program was not for all students.

Summer provided a brief interlude before the fall semester, when Mrs. Swanson would teach two AVID sections of freshmen and sophomores. The program was designed as a long-term project. Each class of AVID students would stay together, with Mrs. Swanson as their teacher, for four years. This contrasted with the normal way of doing things, when students were randomly assigned new teachers each year, with no continuity. AVID students would, she hoped, be sharing trials and triumphs, making and losing friends, coming to know one another almost as a family (with all the blemishes and beauty marks exposed), hurting and helping each other as they struggled individually to achieve their common goal—a college education.

The test of this long-term investment in 30 lives each year would be measured by concrete results. How many AVID students would go to four-year universities? How many would still be enrolled in college after two years?

— BUILDING A BRIDGE —

The pressure was on to increase the diversity and diminish the attrition rate of minority students at the University of California. To accomplish this, UCSD needed to attract candidates from the same pool of students who came to Clairemont under the court-ordered busing program. Mrs. Swanson believed the ivory tower in La Jolla had an interest in helping high-school students from minority backgrounds prepare for college. Yet there were yawing gaps—in teaching and curricula—between secondary schools and public universities. Although the two systems were both supported by the taxpayers, they operated as if they were on different planets. Minority students were lost in space.

Mrs. Swanson wanted to build a space shuttle, bridging the gap. As the policy of affirmative action opened up college admissions policies, university faculties had become increasingly critical of high schools for failing to prepare students adequately. For their part, high-school teachers were in a quandary. What skills did colleges want high-school graduates to master?

In 1982, all segments of California public universities approved a voluminous report laying out the basic competencies that university-bound students were expected to acquire in secondary school. The massive compendium was called *Competencies Expected of Entering Freshmen*, and individual volumes were prepared for each discipline: competencies in English, mathematics, and other subjects. Like many academic reports that arrived from on high, this one was largely ignored by secondary schools, but not by Mrs. Swanson. She found the report on English competencies gathering dust in the school office and read it with great interest. As chairwoman of the Department of English at Clairemont, she took her job seriously. If these were competencies in writing, grammar, and literature that the university demanded, she would be certain that her Clairemont students attained them.

For AVID students, the competencies for history, science, mathematics, languages, and English were especially welcome. Knowing the importance of basic competencies in her own life, Mrs. Swanson had wanted such a guide to make sure that AVID students were on the right track to college. She had been searching for a blueprint for college preparation, and now she discovered one. What could she do, as a secondary-school teacher, to bridge the gap?

Tremendously excited, she received her principal's permission to fly to Berkeley to meet the chairwoman of the report committee. The administrator who had written the guidelines appeared shocked, almost offended, by the visit of a high-school teacher to her office. Mrs. Swanson enthusiastically embraced the competency standards and asked breathlessly what the next step was to implement them.

"What next step?" the administrator asked querulously.

"I believe it would be a good idea for secondary-school teachers and college professors to work out how to make this happen," Mrs. Swanson replied earnestly. "How are these standards going to be incorporated into secondary-school curricula, unless the two systems work together?"

Astonished silence. The administrator shook her head: The report was it, *finis*. In its arrogance, the university system had not thought it necessary to meet with leading secondary-school educators from around the state. No dialogue between high-school teachers and freshman college professors was planned. No task force had been created to implement the report.

To her dismay, Mrs. Swanson was the only high-school teacher who had come to Berkeley hoping to get involved. But she knew that hundreds of California teachers who worked hard to send their best students to top-echelon California universities truly wanted their high-school graduates to be well prepared for arduous college curricula. It was especially cruel to admit minority students through affirmative-action programs, only to have them fail because they lacked basic competencies that they could have gained in high school.

"Let's start a statewide dialogue," Mrs. Swanson suggested. "We could develop a high-school curriculum to match the university's goals."

"I'm sorry, but I have another appointment waiting." The administrator ushered Mrs. Swanson out the door with a dismissive look.

Undaunted, Mrs. Swanson helped organize a series of meetings in San Diego, which continued throughout the 1982–1983 school year. She got a go-ahead from the San Diego City Schools, which provided $5,000 to fund the effort. Teachers from public schools and college professors from local universities participated. It was, perhaps, the first time that local secondary and post-secondary faculty had sat down together and seriously considered the problems each group faced in educating a new generation of students.

One of the most important findings of the report was that many college freshmen simply could not write a cogent essay, lab report, or term paper. Mrs. Swanson teamed up with a UCSD professor to draft a writing curriculum. UCSD doctoral students were vitally involved, along with AVID tutors, who provided support and student perspectives.

During the summer of 1983, the team wrote a comprehensive new writing curriculum, largely based on the AVID program's "Writing, Inquiry, and Collaboration" methods. The struggles of Kouang and other AVID students to communicate their stories served as a touchstone of what worked and what didn't. In this way, the children of illiterate refugees made important contributions to the development of teaching methods and exercises that would help their peers in the future. Group learning methods that had enabled AVID students to pass the biology test became a paradigm for the collaborative efforts of teachers, professors, graduate students, and tutors to develop winning teaching techniques. *Ontogeny recapitulates phylogeny* echoed in these efforts: The development of the AVID learning model was replicated in the evolution of a new teaching paradigm.

Would the original AVID classroom evolve into a new species of classrooms?

After much discussion, the structure of the program was divided into 16 forms of written communication—essays, lab reports, history research papers, and the like—that students needed to master in order to succeed in college. These formats were called Writing Domains and, by the end of the summer, the group had developed a 16-unit course that could be adapted to teach high-school or college students.

The idealistic goal was for teachers and professors to learn from each other by teaching as a team. During the first semester, the teams would teach classes at Clairemont High. Later, in the second semester, they would teach freshmen at the University of California.

A UCSD professor's doctoral students who taught writing to college freshmen were offered as candidates to teach at Clairemont High.

Mrs. Swanson chose older doctoral students who had taught in high schools earlier in their careers, believing that they would have the classroom experience to cope with adolescents. In retrospect, she realized that this might have been a mistake.

Appearances mean a lot to teenagers, who are easily embarrassed and are quick to ridicule adults who look "weird," especially teachers. Most teachers at Clairemont adhered to a dress code: ties for the men, dresses for the women; Mrs. Swanson made a point of dressing *up* for her students. But the UCSD writing teachers, many of whom had gone to college during the Vietnam War, dressed like

1960s hippies, with jeans full of holes, iconoclastic messages on T-shirts, and ragged sneakers. One might have thought that this would make them look hip to students, but the Reagan Era had given birth to a new style—later labeled Generation X. When these new, cynical Generation Xers looked at the aging denizens of the '60s, rather than regard them as hip, they immediately lost respect for them as teachers.

Conversely, the UCSD writing teachers, who had attended high school during the disciplinarian era of the late '50s and early '60s, were shocked by the lack of respect shown them by 1980s students. The doctoral candidates might have dressed *down*, but they wanted to be looked *up* to by students, especially ghetto kids who appeared ominous or threatening.

The experiment in team teaching was, sadly, doomed from the start. One female writing teacher couldn't cope with the cacophony of foreign tongues that greeted her each morning. Unable to quiet the class down one afternoon, she freaked out.

"Listen," she screamed, with one foot on a chair, pointing at the class. "When I'm on, I'm on!"

"On what? Drugs?"

The class erupted.

Mrs. Swanson began to wonder if the reason some of these writing teachers were going for doctorates in education was because they had wiped out as high-school classroom teachers.

In contrast, the experiment in Writing Domains was highly successful. Not that all the exercises worked, because they didn't. But the laboratory of interaction helped the faculty and the students to refine the 16-unit course, to discard some exercises, and to invent new ones. The Writing Domains, at first so amorphous and confusing to the students' ears, gradually provided a dozen maps to guide students through wildly different kinds of intellectual terrain, from summits of rational discourse to profound depths of self-reflection. The students carried a backpack of writing tools so that, whatever cliff or chasm they ran into, they would have a model and a method to guide them—and the rest was finding their voice.

The problems in several Clairemont classrooms (not in AVID) would, by the second semester, cause the team-teaching initiative's demise. To Mrs. Swanson's disappointment, if not surprise, the University of California refused to allow secondary-school teachers to instruct college students.

Convincing two major public-education institutions to work together was an impossible goal, of course. Teachers and professors might build bridges within the local community, but the systems for which they worked were not integrated. The university looked down on the public school, the University of California looked down on the California State system, the high school looked down on the elementary school, and so on. Everyone looked down at the students, especially those labeled with euphemistic names: minority, free-lunch, low-income, disadvantaged, under-represented. . . .

Ironically, the integration of students from minority communities into the American Dream of a college education could not be accomplished while educational systems remained structurally segregated: kindergarten through twelfth grade versus university level. Intuitively, Mrs. Swanson understood that all students needed some form of guidance in order to bridge the gap, but she committed AVID to focus its limited resources on those students whose parents had not gone to college, kids who needed her most.

For all the work and painful disappointment, the valiant effort to develop a "writing for learning" curriculum was not in vain. Far from it. Some of the basic elements from Mrs. Swanson's curriculum would be incorporated into the freshman writing program at the University of California that is being used to this day. As a spin-off, a UCSD writing professor and others would develop writing as a means to assess student knowledge and comprehension of subject matter.

Incredibly, California students had up to that point been tested on their writing skills by answering "objective" questions on multiple-choice, fill-in-the-blank, and true-or-false tests. How is writing style evaluated by a true-or false-test? The state needed a way to evaluate writing skills based on students' actual writing samples and to make these evaluations based on an objective reading. This, of course, was a difficult task.

Yet Mrs. Swanson had found ways to use writing samples to evaluate AVID students' knowledge and understanding, as well as reasoning, analysis, and communication skills. These formed the basis for UCSD to develop the first statewide assessment program, called *Direct Assessment in Writing*. Sadly, the challenging texts used as writing prompts were attacked by fringe groups, politicians bowed to political pressures, and the California writing-assessment program was eventually abandoned.

Strangely, the courageous effort to develop a curriculum that bridged the gap between institutions got Mrs. Swanson in trouble with her own school district. The district's Committee on Curriculum was incensed: *Why was this high-school teacher meeting with college professors? What gave this rogue teacher the idea that she and her students could develop a better curriculum?* The message came down from higher-ups threatened by a lowly teacher's zeal: *Stop messing around with our curriculum, or we will squash your little AVID program.*

Mrs. Swanson despaired of ever creating institutional change when she did not have a base of power within her own institution. She opted to continue creating a solid program that would incorporate these principles, yet remain within the control of a teacher in the classroom. She would have to struggle long years to find another way to build a seamless learning curriculum between high school and college.

No Good Deed Shall Ever Go Unpunished would be a fitting essay topic for analyzing the perverse forces that conspired to undermine initiatives to reform educational institutions from the bottom up. In AVID, Mrs. Swanson vowed not to be defeated again.

On the English-language front, Mrs. Swanson had a surprising breakthrough in her own classroom with Angelina. Back in her freshman year, Angelina had resisted every attempt to establish a personal relationship with anyone: When Mrs. Swanson approached her table, Angelina turned away, cringing from physical closeness, almost like a burn victim. But by sophomore year, Mrs. Swanson established contact with Angelina by talking about books by Jane Austen, the Brontë sisters, Herman Melville, and Miguel de Cervantes. Only then did Angelina turn from the wall with expressive eyes and speak with a remarkable vocabulary she had acquired from reading classics. As long as they talked about books, Angelina was open, but when personal subjects came up, she closed down.

It took a year for Mrs. Swanson to gain Angelina's trust. The girl always looked sad, with dark circles under her eyes, and Mrs. Swanson thought this was because she stayed up late at night reading novels. After school one day, Angelina was not able to talk about books. She broke down, her body curling up in a fetal ball, and told Mrs. Swanson her terrible secret. Mary Catherine was shocked, reaching out to hold the sobbing student. She believed Angelina, but had never heard of such a thing happening to one of her students, and she was caught unprepared. Angelina shrank from touch. Terrified of what she had revealed, she pleaded with Mrs. Swanson not to tell her mother what the tattooed trucker was doing to her. She begged, "Please don't report to *policia*, because they will take me away. Then who will protect my sisters?"

Naively, Mrs. Swanson followed Angelina's wishes and never betrayed her secret to the authorities. This was before California mandated that teachers and counselors report allegations of sexual abuse to the Department of Child Protective Services. Today, all teachers are given workshops in child abuse prevention and detection and are expected to obey all applicable laws and protocols. In retrospect, Mary Catherine realizes she might have handled this differently. Yet these dilemmas continue to face teachers in a land where abuse threatens one in three children, and where, tragically, some children are also abused by the institutions designed to protect them.

In Angelina's case, the emotional breakdown established a powerful bond between student and teacher, a bond that enabled Angelina, with great sacrifice, to protect her sisters at home and to come out of isolation in school. Her English improved dramatically, and this gave her confidence to engage in classroom debates, in which she expressed strong opinions. She grew taller and more self-assured. She could not yet be called pretty, because she could not afford braces to straighten her teeth nor dermatological treatments to clear her skin, but she became an accomplished student.

— CLARENCE THE — DRAGON SLAYER

In the archetypal coming-of-age myth, the young hero must leave his home and enter a dark cave where a fearful dragon awaits. The monster has been terrorizing the countryside, incinerating castles, thrashing knights, and carrying off maidens. The monstrous shadow of fear lies upon the land, feeding the dark fires of distrust and hatred in the hearts of neighbors. In every generation, from medieval to modern times, frightened voices whisper: *Who will slay the dragon?*

In the 1980s, the shadow of white supremacy fell across the landscape of America. Through a network that stretched from the Southeast to the Pacific Northwest, the leader of a white-supremacist group spread racial bigotry to a national audience. He would later be exposed as a hate-monger and implicated in the fomentation of hate crimes against minorities.

But in 1980 he was viewed as a novelty. The leader was rumored to have once been the "Grand Dragon" of the Ku Klux Klan, but no one seemed to know if he had ever been affiliated with that organization. Still, the image persisted. He did not wear the outlandish theatrical costume—pointed hat, masked cloak, sash and satin robes (if indeed he had one)—as his public personae. Instead, he sported a business suit and tie. His message of black-baiting and virulent anti-Semitism was slicked up for a suburban audience. His fiery breath teased hair-raising threats into a trendy, blow-dried image.

As part of his speakers' series, Mr. Grove invited the white supremacist to address his Seminar class. Mr. Grove saw this as an opportunity for his students to confront a controversial issue face-to-face, in a neutral forum that promoted rational discussion. Yet, there were no African Americans or Hispanics in Jim's Seminar class, and this presented a problem—the critical lack of balance.

When Jim mentioned this to Mary Catherine, she jumped at the opportunity to bring AVID students to the forum. This was a risky undertaking that could blow up in her face. When asked, two decades later, to explain her rationale for exposing minority students to a white supremacist, Mrs. Swanson reflected: "I never believe in sheltering people from knowledge. See what's out there. Understand other points of view to understand your own. Being unprepared and ignorant makes you vulnerable. Things blind-side you, and you don't know how to handle them."

She did, however, believe in preparing her students for new and uncomfortable situations. If AVID students were accompanying Seminar students to the opera *Romeo and Juliet,* she had them read the Shakespearian play and discuss the characters first.

So it was that she prepared her students for the encounter with a bigot: *Racism is out there, face it. Always be polite, but stand up for your beliefs.*

Clarence Fields accepted the invitation to the forum with an anxious heart. Although he had earned respect in the AVID class and on the football field, he did not feel comfortable with Seminar students. He was intimidated by their high IQs, in the genius range, and by their sharp tongues, which were quick to ridicule students they deemed "average" or "dense." It was especially difficult for

Clarence to speak up before Seminar students, even if he believed he were right.

Bigotry at Clairemont High was more subtle and complex than merely the issue of spoiled white kids putting down blacks. Racial resentments reflected deeper social and economic divisions between groups and among neighbors. There were those who assimilated into a pluralistic society and there were those who remained isolated in what social critic Michael Harrington called *The Other America*. Like a child running from a bogeyman into a funhouse, old hatreds chased childish fears into a mirrored labyrinth where racism and reverse-racism bounced off the walls, shattering identities and fragmenting friendships.

Clarence was caught between the distorted reflections of racism and reverse-racism mirroring the *Disunited* States of America. Each day, he ran a gauntlet between the predominantly white students in his advanced classes and his black buddies from the old neighborhood. As he listened to Mrs. Swanson preparing him to encounter the mythical Grand Dragon, Clarence was more worried about facing his own dragons on the playing field. Clairemont was not favored to win the upcoming City Championship football game against rival Lincoln High. He would have to confront his neighborhood friends as foes in front of thousands of fans at the Chargers Stadium.

On forum day, the guest speaker, dressed in a conservative suit, cut an engaging figure in front of the joint Seminar–AVID class. For all outward appearances, he was a middle-aged man with dark hair and a medium build. He displayed no overt rancor and was outwardly cool and reasonable.

"He's very convincing," Mrs. Swanson recalls, with hindsight. "If you're not ready for his arguments, you can be naively pulled in by his rhetoric."

Clarence recalls now: "That man talked about the role of white people in the building of America. He thought African Americans had nothing to do with the building of the nation. We were really just taking up space here in society. He felt African Americans should have their own states back in Africa."

Clarence thought about the contributions of his family to the country he loved. His grandmother, M'Dear, had been born on a plantation and had picked cotton during the Great Depression. She migrated to San Diego, where she raised a family, supporting her children by working as a domestic for a doctor's family. Had she not contributed to the well-being of this community? His mother had worked hard all her life, cleaning homes and then working long hours at the sandwich shop at the Navy base on North Island. She always had a warm meal ready for him and his sisters. Yet this smooth-talking speaker said the Fields family had contributed nothing. It did not make sense.

Clarence raised his hand. "I have listened to your views about my ancestors. Now, I think it is fair to ask you to tell us: Where did your ancestors come from?" he asked, staring down the Grand Dragon.

"Well, that's really not the point here," the flustered speaker replied, showing a flash of dragon's teeth. "It is not where *my* ancestors are from. It is where *your* ancestors are from."

The Seminar students laughed, surprised that an AVID student had verbally confronted the white supremacist. Mrs. Swanson felt a wave of pride that Clarence had gained the confidence not only to confront a racist, but to do so in front of the Seminar students.

An African American track coach who was attending the talk could barely contain his rage. But Clarence remained calm and collected, just as he had practiced in facing the opposing team across the line of scrimmage.

The patriarch of white supremacy talked about his own children. He didn't let them read any textbooks provided by the public-education system. Those books, he said, were filled with lies. They distorted "true" American history. They taught about the contributions of African Americans, when, in fact, blacks had had nothing to do with the building of this nation.

Clarence's palms were sweating and Seminar students scoured his face for a flicker of fear. "Pardon me, are you saying that because African Americans had nothing to do with the building of this nation, that whites built the weapons of violence that are tearing this country apart? Do you mean that white people are responsible for the problems of this country?"

The Grand Dragon drew in his breath. "You're monopolizing the conversation," he said. He turned away from the AVID students, seeking support from the white kids. "We're going to let other people ask questions."

The Seminar students closed ranks with the AVID students. "Answer the question!" cried a chorus of voices, united behind Clarence.

"I am not going to answer that question!" raged the deflated supremacist. "Or we can end it right now!"

Clarence Fields, whose family had risen from slavery, a junior at Clairemont High, had outsmarted the Grand Dragon. He had defended his family, his peers, and gained the respect of the intellectual elite.

Mrs. Swanson's heart filled her throat. Teachers live for such moments. Her vital task in AVID was to instill pride and self-confidence so that her students knew they could tackle things in life and conquer them. Clarence had not resorted to name calling or threats; he had used words backed up by reason to make his point.

On the way out of the room, the track coach came up behind Clarence. "Man, you did it! I wish I could have kept my cool."

Clarence, the dragon slayer, walked down the hall to the locker room and suited up for football practice. Alone with his own dragons of self-doubt, he wondered how he would face his neighborhood friends, now fierce rivals, who played for Lincoln High.

— CHAMPIONSHIP GAME —

San Diego's high-school football championship was a grudge match pitting brother against brother in a fight for supremacy in America's Divided City. Clairemont had beaten Lincoln earlier in the football season. Now, before thousands of fans in Jack Murphy Stadium, home of the Chargers pro football team, it was pay-back time for the Lincoln Hornets. Their strategy was to use guilt and intimidation to frighten the Clairemont Chieftains into submission.

You betrayed your brothers. We will crush you.

Underlying the conflict between schools was an ugly backlash. Lincoln's team members were nearly all people of color. Clairemont was newly integrated, with several of its best players coming from Southeast San Diego.

After outsmarting the white supremacist in the classroom, Clarence had to do battle with the barely disguised bogeyman of black supremacy on the playing field.

He remembered warming up before the season game, when the Hornets got off the bus at Clairemont High and swaggered onto the Chieftains' playing field. Clarence and his teammates stood in a circle, stretching. It was a bright sunny day, but each Lincoln player was wearing a green rain cape. One by one, the Lincoln players swirled off their capes and glared at the capeless Chieftains, outfitted in royal blue and orange.

"Boy, those guys are big," whispered the Chieftains' five-foot, ten-inch captain.

"They look mean!" quivered the Chieftains' right end.

"Don't worry, we played with these guys in Pop Warner," Clarence replied. But he could not help but notice the massive size and aggressiveness of his neighborhood friends. Nor could he miss the resentment in their eyes.

They had been buddies from the halcyon days of sandlot baseball, before gangs and drugs had infiltrated the neighborhood. There were about a dozen friends, tight as brothers, who grew up together, sharing the bruises of boyhood, tussling like puppies in the dust. Clarence never realized that they would be labeled "underprivileged," for they were rich in love and laughter and had suffered no overt discrimination that he could remember.

Then fate divided the dozen in two. Roughly half stayed at Lincoln, the other half were attracted by the promise of a better education. Clairemont welcomed the handsome black athletes, four of whom—Clarence, J. J., Marquise, and Reggie—were enrolled in AVID. Their popularity grew when they helped the Chieftains move to first place. It was the first time since Clairemont High's opening in 1959 that the Chieftains reached the football championship. Clarence and his friends became heroes on campus. Yet, on their home turf, they were considered traitors.

The days leading up to the game put almost unbearable pressure on the athletes. All the odds were on Lincoln to smash Clairemont, even though the Chieftains had beaten the Hornets in the regular season.

The Friday before the game, Mrs. Swanson asked the football players to sit with her around a table, while tutors worked with the other AVID students.

"I know there is some concern about threats from a few of your opponents at Lincoln," she led off.

Silence.

"Let's talk about it," Mrs. Swanson urged in a soothing voice. "What are your concerns and fears?"

If a coach had ever asked them to share their feelings, they would have died of embarrassment. It didn't seem so strange with Mrs. Swanson. Reacting to intimidation from Lincoln, J. J., the quarterback, acted tough.

"Hey, if they start it, we will finish it!" he boasted.

"I don't think it's a big deal," scoffed Reggie, a running back.

"Yeah, right! You don't have to tackle them," moaned Marquise, a lineman.

"I just hope we don't let our school down," sighed Clarence, the fullback.

"I don't care who wins tomorrow," Mrs. Swanson said, looking clockwise around the table, meeting each student in the eye. "I care dearly about how you handle yourselves, on and off the playing field. I want you to feel proud that you have come this far, where no Chieftains have come before. You will be playing in Charger Stadium, before your families and friends from Clairemont. And you will also be playing before your opponents and their classmates and families, who may be your neighbors or friends. In victory or defeat, I want you to acquit yourselves with dignity. I'm rooting for you."

By the time Mary Catherine took her seat at the 50-yard line, Lincoln fans had turned the stadium into a Hornets' nest. They had scaled the end-zone fence and posted green-and-white Lincoln banners. The blue-and-orange Chieftain banners were relegated to the sidelines.

The Chieftains ran out onto the field, and the AVID classmates stood and cheered. Clarence looked up in the stands and saw his mother and sisters. Right behind them, Mrs. Swanson was waving a banner.

The Hornets won the coin toss. Just before the kickoff, the announcer's voice boomed from the P. A. system. "The New York Athletic Club has just announced the 1981 Heisman Trophy winner is Marcus Allen, a graduate of Lincoln High!" The announcement hit the hornets' nest like a stick. Screaming Lincoln fans shook the stands with their stamping feet.

On the field, Clarence wanted to shout with pride, for the Heisman Trophy winner had brought fame to his neighborhood. There was also a personal connection. Clarence had grown up with Marcus Allen's younger brother, who was playing for Lincoln today. It seemed like the gods were on the Hornets' side.

Clarence raised his helmet in a half-hearted salute, and a piercing pain shot through his shoulder. He'd been injured in the last game, and today they'd taped him so tightly that his shoulder pads jutted under his chin. Lining up for the kickoff, he had no time to think. The ball sailed high and the teams collided. He was lost in a flood of colors that washed back and forth between goalposts, splashing numbers on the scoreboard.

Clarence carried the football, charging through the line to make a few yards. Then Lincoln captured the ball, and Clarence was a defensive linebacker, falling back to block a pass. At the scrimmage line, it was clear who was on his team. But as exhaustion set in, the chalk lines blurred in his mind. He was playing for Clairemont and against Lincoln, with his teammates and against his friends.

Insults flew across the scrimmage line. *Keep your dignity,* Clarence told himself.

The teams were well matched: Lincoln was bigger; Clairemont, craftier. It was a close game. Closer than anyone had predicted. By the fourth quarter, Lincoln was ahead by one touchdown.

Mrs. Swanson watched with a teacher's pride and a mother's anxiety. She squealed unabashedly—she had been a cheerleader at Kingsburg High—while she kept up a running conversation with Mrs. Fields and the other parents. When the Chieftains scored, tying up the game, the AVID section cheered and clapped and pounded feet. The Hornets charged back, pushing to the Chieftains' five-yard line. Then Lincoln fumbled and Clarence recovered the ball, running to the 30-yard line. In the final minute, J. J. threw a touchdown pass. Victory!

Cheering teammates hoisted J. J. on their shoulders. Chieftains fans swarmed onto the field, attempting to tear down the Hornets' banner. A fight nearly broke out between blacks and whites. Clarence stayed out of it. Although he savored victory, he could not revel in his brothers' defeat. Up in the stands, he saw his mother and sisters and M'Dear and Mrs. Swanson and his AVID class-mates. The sight of them gathered together brought tears to his eyes. Overcoming the incredible pain in his shoulder, he waved at them. Now all he wanted was a shower and to go home and cele-brate quietly in his neighborhood.

His loyalties were undivided.

— A NATION AT RISK —

In April 1983, the United Somnambulists of America was awakened from the nightmarish decline of its public-education system—and stirred by a call to arms. The Carnegie Commission on Education released a damning report called "A Nation at Risk" that upset the education establishment's applecart, shocked teachers to the core, and set a new agenda for school reform into the next decade.

"Our nation is at risk," the report read. "Our once unchallenged preeminence in commerce, industry, science, and technological innovation is being overtaken by competitors throughout the world," it declared. "If an unfriendly foreign power had attempted to impose on America the mediocre educational performance that exists today, we might well have viewed it as an act of war. . . ."

Bringing this message home was the fact that the chairwoman of the Carnegie Commission, Yvonne Larsen, had been a member of the San Diego City Schools Board of Education. Mrs. Swanson began reading the report during lunch hour. She could barely put it down so that she could teach in the afternoon. Following her last class, she barricaded herself in her conference nook and read the entire report.

With concern quickening to excitement, she pondered her response.

She no longer felt alone. The report seemed to be speaking for her when it said: "We have even squandered the gains in student achievement made in the wake of the *Sputnik* challenge. Moreover, we have dismantled essential support systems which helped make those gains possible."

She underlined "support systems" in red ink, punctuated with an exclamation point. How shortsighted it had been to bus minority kids across town to schools where they were viewed as alien invaders, and then to abandon them to hostile teachers and remedial courses, without guidance or support. No wonder they were failing in many schools. In reality, the schools were failing them.

As the daughter of a small-town newspaper editor who crusaded for democratic institutions, she had been raised to believe that public education was the foundation of a free society. Without free and universal access to rigorous public education, America would lose not only its economic power but, more importantly, would cut the threads holding together the fabric of a pluralistic society. With students from diverse cultures studying together toward a common goal, the AVID classroom became a one-room schoolhouse of American democracy.

"A Nation at Risk" underscored the importance of teaching not only subject matter, but the values of decency and equality that Mrs. Swanson and her tutors had inculcated in students through relationships that grew stronger as they shared ups and downs— and by personal example. These intangibles could not be tested by academic measures, but were tested, day after day, in the crucible of the classroom.

As the wife of a banker, Mary Catherine shared her husband's faith in free enterprise as the energy source for America's productivity. She did not want to redistribute wealth through socialism, although she did support effective social programs like Head Start. Instead, she wanted to pass on the tools of mental productivity, prized by the professional elite, to ordinary people. By studying their way from humble homes into elite universities, they could one day share the wealth of nations. She saw the AVID classroom as a greenhouse. Outside her door, the seasons revolved like the sun brushing the branches of the liquid ambar trees; each young mind was a leaf, and, like Dylan Thomas's poem "The Force That Through the Green Fuse Drives the Flower"—AVID ignited a *green fuse.*

The Carnegie Commission said it less poetically, but with straightforward force.

> Our concern . . . goes well beyond matters such as industry and commerce. It also includes the intellectual, moral, and spiritual strengths of our people which knit together the very fabric of our society. The people of the United States need to know that individuals in our society who do not possess the levels of skill, literacy, and training essential to this new era will be effectively disenfranchised, not simply from the material rewards that accompany competent performance, but also from the chance to participate fully in our national life.

With broad brush strokes, the Carnegie Commission zeroed in on specific educational problems documented in testimony. As an English teacher who had devoted most of her career to the teaching of analysis and essay writing, Mary Catherine was deeply disappointed when she read a condemnation of the nation's students:

> Many 17-year-olds do not possess the "higher order" intellectual skills we should expect of them. Nearly 40 percent cannot draw inferences from written material; only one-fifth can write a persuasive essay; and only one-third can solve a mathematics problem requiring several steps.

"The AVID method of 'Writing, Inquiry, and Collaboration' directly addresses this problem," Mrs. Swanson wanted to reply. Imagining herself testifying before the commissioners, she explained the writing-to-learn program:

"Writing is a core skill that is used in every step of the learning process, from note taking to study questions to analysis to essay writing. The constant, comprehensive, and very demanding use of writing in AVID forces students to absorb what they read and hear and distill it into their own words. Writing engraves knowledge into the crevices of the brain," she explained. "Writing structures thought into phrases, sentences, paragraphs. And when students have to read each other's run-on sentences, garbled phrases, and interminable paragraphs, peers become tough editors, demanding simplicity, clarity, and structure."

This was fun! The report was forcing her to think on a higher level, to analyze the reasons for the impromptu exercises that had sprung up in creative brainstorming sessions by the AVID Site Team.

"The *I* is for inquiry," she continued in her mental testimony, feeling not the least bit intimidated by the august—and, luckily, imaginary—body of educators listening from a raised dais. "AVID tutors are taught not to answer students' questions directly, but to turn the questions around. If a student asks how to balance a binomial equation, the tutor might ask, 'Why is this exercise given? What is the purpose for learning this algebraic formula?'"

Carried away, she continued: "If the student asks, 'What do I need to know for the test?' the tutor answers: 'If you were the teacher, what questions would you ask to test whether the students have really mastered the material?' Suddenly the students are trying to outsmart the teacher, and their perverse glee in thinking up the most twisted and obtuse questions enables them to 'ace' the actually banal test."

Was this stuff getting over to the brain trust? She imagined Clarence falling asleep. But in Mary Catherine's imagination, Yvonne Larsen, the Carnegie Commission chairwoman was rooting her on.

"*C* is for collaboration," Mary Catherine cheered back, kicking her bare legs and shaking pompoms. (How embarrassing to be caught in her Kingsburg High cheerleading outfit!) But her enthusiasm for the AVID team was a hundred times greater than her rather awkward displays of football spirit at age 16.

"When bright but poorly prepared students are isolated in advanced classes, especially if they don't come from an academically supportive environment, they can't possibly compete with kids who, by virtue of their birth and family background, know the rules of the game and get private coaching at home," she explained breathlessly. "In AVID, we work together as a team. It may sound corny, but being part of an academic team gets kids motivated to play in a game that was denied their forebears. Imagine how intimidating it is to be the first in your family ever to take a college board test. Then think of the powerful motivation of seeing your AVID brothers and sisters sitting beside you in the testing room, silently cheering each other on."

The commissioners were standing up, their wooden chairs creaking (or was it their knees?) as the committee chairwoman held a single finger aloft to signal that the witness, dressed improbably in a cheerleader's outfit, had one second of testimony left before they turned off her microphone.

"Commissioners, if you want to get 17-year-olds to 'possess the higher order intellectual skills we should expect of them,' to 'draw inferences from written material,' to 'write a persuasive essay,' or to 'solve a mathematics problem requiring several steps,'" she heard herself shouting, "then come to my classroom and see it all happening at once."

"My dear lady, we have run out of time," the ghostly commissioner protested with a skeptical frown before vanishing into the footnotes of the report.

"Writing, inquiry, and collaboration work!" she exclaimed to the world. The microphone went dead.

Mary Catherine awoke with a start. She was not addressing an august body but only her reflection in the dirty windows of her classroom after dark.

— ENGLISH TO — THE MAX

As AVID's third year drew to a close, Mrs. Swanson went from table to table, talking with students she believed were qualified to take Advanced Placement English in their senior year. This college-level course, taught by Mr. Grove, was known as one of the hardest classes at Clairemont High, one of the top AP English classes in San Diego. She knew that Mr. Grove had no intention of lowering the high standards that had enabled him to send past graduates to the finest universities in the nation, where many got college credit in English. The class would be made up almost entirely of Seminar students. She believed it would be too demanding for some AVID students.

"Clarence, I would like you to take AP English with Mr. Grove," she said to the shy hero who had shown his mettle and his eloquence in the dragon's den.

A smile spread across his lips. He had never expected to be asked to take AP.

"Are you sure I can do it?"

"If the Grand Dragon couldn't intimidate you, why should Mr. Grove?" she assured him.

"Because Mr. Grove is smarter and tougher."

"Clarence, I think it will be a tremendous challenge, and it will give you the confidence to communicate wherever you go in life," she said, touching his sleeve. "You can do it."

"All right, I'll try."

At a table nearby, Máximo overheard Mrs. Swanson's conversation with Clarence. Máximo waited for her to approach his table, but she skipped over him, going to Angelina's table and whispering to her. A shadow fell over Máximo's deep brown eyes, and his lashes glistened like wet brushes dripping with turpentine. He swallowed, feeling in his throat the humiliation he had experienced that first day in public speaking class.

How he had worked to learn English, only to be passed over by Mrs. Swanson! The injustice hurt deeply because it came from the one teacher he most wanted to recognize him. *If Clarence can do it, I can too!* he vowed to himself.

Máximo screwed up his courage and approached her desk. "Mrs. Swanson, why don't you invite me to take AP English?" he asked. "Do you think I can't hack it?"

"Oh, Máximo!" she cried, flushing with guilt for her shameful insensitivity. "I never meant to hurt you. I just didn't even consider . . ."

"Why, because I'm Mexican?"

She met his eyes, feeling his hurt.

"No, Máximo. It was because I thought the language barrier would be an impediment. I presumed, wrongly, that you would not be interested, and I deeply regret it."

He was stunned speechless by her apology.

She took the initiative. "Máximo, I'm not going to fool you. If you take AP English, you will be one of only a few AVID students. The rest are Seminar kids, and you know how cutting they can be. Do you want to take this challenge? "

"If Clarence can do it, I can too," he repeated.

She wrote "AP English" on his schedule and signed it, saying, "Máximo, I believe in you."

So it was that the immigrant from Tijuana, who had mumbled *"Mi* name is Máximo. . . . I got *siete* brothers," as a freshman, took college-level English as a senior.

The first thing Mr. Grove demanded of his students in AP English was that they memorize the prologue to Chaucer's *Canterbury Tales* in Olde English. Then each student was ordered to come before the class and recite it perfectly. This was no small feat for Clarence or Máximo to accomplish, but they did it, with Mrs. Swanson's help. For two long semesters, the AVID students struggled with the readings and the essays in Mr. Grove's class and managed to finish the course, all with the support of the AVID tutors.

Mr. Grove was moved by their individual determination and impressed by their advancement relative to where they had begun. But he was also concerned about how far and fast AVID students could advance over the course of a year in comparison with his Seminar students. Jim shared Mary Catherine's commitment to stimulate and support all students to achieve to their utmost, but, in the final analysis, he believed that individual determination could advance students only so far, and that beyond nurture's reach soared the gift of intelligence.

— FIRST GRADUATION — CLASS

The acid test for AVID came in the spring of 1984. The college applications had been filled out, the essays written, the letters of recommendation sent.

Who would get into college?

Mrs. Swanson was as anxious as a high-school senior to see the results of four years of hard work, struggle to change the system, and growth. She had taken an immense risk with the lives of her students. Had it been fair to put them in advanced classes? Would they fail to compete successfully against gifted and talented students? Would the experiment work?

The stakes were high, not only for AVID students, but for all disadvantaged students to attend college. If America could not provide educational opportunity to students in the middle, then this would have awesome consequences for the future of the republic.

The letters altering the AVID students' fates had been sealed. Envelopes bearing news had been mailed. The mailboxes were watched like hawks. Each student had to face this ordeal individually, and the letters quivered in their hands.

Angelina hid in her bathroom and tore open the envelope from San Diego State University. As she read the letter welcoming her to the freshman class, her hands shook and tears streamed down her cheeks. She was going to major in English and become a teacher of literature like Mrs. Swanson! She could not wait to thank Alice for giving her so many books and Mrs. Swanson for believing in her. But she kept the letter secret from her family. She wanted her mother to be proud of her, but she did not want her sisters to feel abandoned. She would live at home and commute to college until she found a job and an apartment. Before that bastard tried to climb in her bed, she would slip away and take her sisters with her.

That same afternoon, Máximo received the envelope embossed with the SDSU logo. It was bulging with information packets and he knew instantly he had been accepted. But he did not want to savor this moment alone. When his family gathered for dinner at the wrought-iron table that his father had forged and welded in Tijuana, the sturdy table where eight brothers ate and studied and fought together, he waited until his mother took off her apron and sat down. Then he pulled out the envelope and read it aloud in English, translating for his parents. Luz and Victoriano showed their pride in their eyes, not only for Máximo, but for all their sons. His older brothers were working their way through community colleges, struggling because they did not know the system. Máximo was the first Escobedo ever to be accepted to a four-year university. Yet behind him was coming Jaime, who was getting As in science and who dreamed of applying to UCSD the next year. Máximo's mother pointed to the blank wall in the living room that was waiting for their graduation portraits.

Kouang's mailbox was stuffed with letters from UC campuses: Berkeley, Los Angeles, Riverside, Irvine, and San Diego. He waited for his mother to put down her thimble and come out from behind the curtain where she sewed sleeves and embroidered wedding dresses, and he collected his little sisters and his grandmother. They kneeled beneath the Buddhist altar, where the sepia-toned picture of his father stared down, surrounded by photos of their ancestors. Kouang placed the acceptance letters on the altar and lit joss sticks and made offerings, giving thanks. The journey that had begun on a sinking boat had led him to San Diego, where Mrs. Swanson had helped him get on his feet. In the last two years, he had earned straight As in the toughest classes at Clairemont and had taken college-credit classes in calculus and political science. On his college boards, he scored a perfect 800 in math and a respectable 550 in English. He was fascinated by the NASA space program and wanted to study engineering and astrophysics at UCSD. Beside the altar hung a poster of "Earthrise," a photograph by astronauts who had landed on the moon. Kouang was shooting for the stars.

In Clarence's home, his sisters were always watching television and their favorite show was the Academy Awards presentation. But now it was their big brother's turn to open the envelopes. *And the winner of five college acceptances is . . . Clarence Fields!*

For his leading roles as student and athlete, Clarence was awarded thousands of dollars in scholarships to UC Berkeley, West Point, Colorado State, San Diego State, and the University of Utah.

The long bus rides, the pain-in-the-butt AVID notebook checks, the bruised shoulder and hurt feelings, the moral confrontation with the white supremacist—all paid off. Clarence wished the Grand Dragon could see him now.

I believe it really doesn't matter where one's people come from, but it truly does *matter where the children are going. I am proud of my African and Native American ancestors. Whether the Fields family nursed babies, picked cotton, or cleaned toilets, they never lost their dignity. I have taken the hardest classes and competed with the smartest students, without giving up. This is because Mrs. Swanson believes in me, and when someone in our class falls, we help each other up. I feel sorry for your children, Mr. Grand Dragon, who aren't allowed to read history books and are being schooled in hatred. What is their future? I have great expectations!*

Clarence did not seek approval from those who hate, but rather from those who love. *What would his mother and grandmother say?*

Upon seeing the acceptance letters, hearing the calls from recruiters, receiving the congratulations of the pastor and neighbors, his mother burst into tears of joy. The great grandson of slaves would be the first in his family to attend a four-year university. Before the Lord, she gave thanks. *My prayers have been answered.*

Despite her grand pride in the cherished letters, M'Dear greeted the news with a jaundiced eye. She did not trust the promises from bigwigs who wanted him to sign on the dotted line and sell himself into slavery at the white man's plantation. If they took Clarence away, who would look after him when he was hungry or blue? She wanted Clarence to go to college close to home.

His girlfriend also pleaded: "Please don't leave me, Clarence. Go to San Diego State."

After this meteor shower of glory waned, Clarence's face gathered shadows, his bright eyes clouded over. *Where do I belong? Should I leave? Who will guarantee me a place on the team?*

For the first time in Clarence's life, he alone had to make a choice that would likely determine his future. Everyone had an opinion about what he should do. He felt isolated.

As a teacher, Mrs. Swanson took deep satisfaction in the success of Clarence. Indeed, almost all of her AVID students had done famously. Out of 30 students in the senior class, 28 were accepted at four-year universities. AVID's four-year college-bound rate was 93 percent. The national average was 31 percent.

AVID passed the college entrance test with flying colors.

As Clarence's mentor, the only question in Mrs. Swanson's mind was: *Which university ought Clarence choose?* She had definite thoughts about it. Was there any secret that she had taken English courses at Berkeley while getting her bachelor's degree from San Francisco State University? The academic opportunities at Berkeley were greater than at any public university in America, surpassing Harvard in many graduate departments.

Berkeley was tough on freshmen, flunking people out to winnow the weak and the unwanted. But Mrs. Swanson knew professors there who would be delighted to be Clarence's mentor. Berkeley was her first choice. Utah, with its Mormon traditions, was her last choice. Despite changes in the Church of Latter Day Saints, any lingering prejudice against blacks would hurt Clarence deeply. After all, a teacher knew best where a student would shine, or be shunned.

Or so she believed.

When Clarence looked carefully over his offers, he felt dispirited in the knowledge that he did not qualify for a football scholarship to Berkeley. Instead, he was offered an *academic* scholarship to the flagship campus of the University of California, a greater honor, in Mrs. Swanson's mind, because it represented academic excellence. But he would have to "walk on" the field at the fall football tryouts. There was no guarantee that he would get on the team, much less get off the bench.

For Clarence, the middle linebacker, Berkeley meant risking that he might never play football again. For Berkeley, under the gun to improve its racial percentages, Clarence was a truly desirable scholar, for he had proven through AVID that he could do the scholastic work. At Mrs. Swanson's suggestion, an admissions officer flew down to Southeast San Diego especially to meet with Clarence.

The deadline to accept or reject colleges was two days away. Clarence came to Mrs. Swanson's classroom after school to make his choice.

"Clarence, I am so proud that you were accepted to so many schools. My goodness, Berkeley!"

His lips curled slightly downward. "Mrs. Swanson, at Berkeley I will have to *walk on!*"

She nodded, understanding that "walk-ons" had less-than-great chances of making the team.

"Clarence, this is a question of values. What is most important to you?"

He lifted his chin, his lips straightening. His throat struggled to clear itself.

"Most important?" he smiled, daring her with his eyes.

"Yes, tell me."

With the earnestness of an 18-year-old who has thought things out through many a sleepless night, he spoke from the heart: "Mrs. Swanson, you got to remember my priorities are eating, football, sleeping, and education."

My God, in that order? she gasped, stifling a laugh.

Clarence was dead serious. He had sacrificed meals, rest, and fun in order to get an education. But his heart was in football. He loved it more than he loved his girlfriend. More than money or power or anything. Football was life itself to him.

Mrs. Swanson was rent by his words. She could barely hold back tears. *Don't think of yourself,* she cautioned: *What is best for Clarence?*

"Where would you like to go?" she asked gently.

"Utah offered me a football scholarship. They guaranteed I could play as a freshman!"

"Utah?" Her hair gleamed, perfectly in place, golden in the gloom of her office.

He nodded yes quietly, with granite strength. Light from the Great Salt Lake was reflected in his eyes.

Mrs. Swanson saw it and knew he had made his final decision. She respected his courage to take this unlikely path to his dream. But she did not want him to go in ignorance.

"You're going into Mormon country," she said, acquiescing. "I know they want you, but I fear that some Mormons still look down on blacks. You need to know that you are the best. You have already proved that in so many ways, both with the Seminar students and to your friends at Lincoln. If anybody ever tells you that you are less than the best, don't you believe them. Remember, I have a telephone in this classroom, you can call me anytime."

"Thanks, Mrs. Swanson!" And Clarence Fields, soon to be a freshman at the University of Utah, light-footed it to the bus.

— CLARENCE *AGONISTES* —

In the final weeks before graduation, Clarence the running back stumbled.

In a recurring nightmare, he was climbing the steps of the stadium. But just before he made it to the top and reached for the prize, the stairs flew like pigeons before his blind footing. He fell down the steps and could not stop himself from tumbling lower and lower.

Why am I leaving home? Who will cook for me? Will my friends forget me? How soon can I come back?

At odd moments, tears welled up. He couldn't figure out why. When he saw his mother's strong back, bending over the stove; or heard M'Dear's voice sing out in church; or watched his sisters playfully fighting, he was overcome with throat-choking emotion. He hid his eyes in shame.

"Congratulations, Clarence!" A coach would slap him on the back. "You're the Man!"

Wincing, he wanted to crawl away.

Why couldn't he be normal, like the other guys? Why did he have to be so ambitious? He no longer worried about not being good enough, but feared being shunned because he thought he was too good.

"Utah! Are you crazy?" taunted his old neighborhood buddies. "Those Mormons gonna whitewash your black ass!"

Clarence saw envy in their eyes. Suddenly, the dragon slayer's tongue felt ashen in his mouth. He wanted to run away. But where would he go? After all he had worked for, he felt lonelier than ever before, and weaker as summer approached.

One day in AVID, he confided his dark thoughts to a friend named Willa. Nothing specific. Just a few words. He was thinking forebodingly, as heroes have done before battle since ancient times.

Willa had never heard Clarence talk that way before. It frightened her; she wondered if Clarence planned suicide.

"Mrs. Swanson, I think you better talk to Clarence," she pleaded.

"Why? Is something wrong?"

The girl shifted from leg to leg. "He's been down lately."

"That's normal. There is a lot of pressure on you kids. Going to college is not easy, especially for the first generation."

"But Mrs. Swanson, Clarence isn't usually scared of anything. He talked like, well, you know."

"No, I don't know." Mrs. Swanson was taken by surprise. She had her hands full, with 30 teenagers freaking about going to college. But Clarence had been ominously silent.

"Where is Clarence?"

"He's gone," said Willa.

"I'll be sure to talk with him tomorrow."

"That might be too late. I'm scared he's gonna do something stupid."

Mrs. Swanson put everything down. She dialed Clarence's home phone number. His mother answered. Tempering her voice so not to spread panic, Mrs. Swanson inquired: "Do you know where Clarence is?"

"I think he went to get a haircut."

"Is it okay if I come to your home?"

Mrs. Swanson hopped in her car. If Clarence harmed himself, she never would forgive herself. How had she missed the warning signs? She drove south and east, along the freeway dividing San Diego's communities, an unspoken border between rich and poor. She exited into a neighborhood of used-tire repair shops and barbecue joints, shadowy in the dusk—a place where she was suddenly conscious of her blonde hair. Searching for the right street, she slowly passed Lincoln High, hidden behind wire mesh fences. She would not have driven here alone at night but, knowing that she was going to Clarence's house, she was not afraid—for herself.

Clarence looked in the barber's mirror, his image reflected in infinite regression, and saw the ghost of a dragon slayer. His hair looked nappy and sad.

"Shave it way down," he told the barber.

"Are you sure?"

"It don't make any difference."

Mrs. Swanson passed the barbershop, not knowing he was inside. She reached a rundown residential street, locked the car, and approached a house that had seen better days. The shade was pulled up in the front window and eyes watched the street from behind it. Composing herself, she climbed the broken steps and stood on the cleanly swept porch.

The screen door scraped open, and Mrs. Swanson was greeted by a large woman with Clarence's eyes. She had met Mrs. Fields at parents' meetings at Clairemont and, of course, at the championship football game, and had had conversations with her. But that was in AVID territory. This was Mrs. Fields's home.

Mrs. Swanson fumbled for an excuse for her visit. Frankly, she did not know what she was going to say. It was an awkward moment.

But Mrs. Fields held open the door, welcoming her son's teacher with an apologetic smile, as if to say: *Pardon the mess.*

"Pardon me for interrupting dinner," Mrs. Swanson extended her hand. "I really appreciate your taking the time to see me."

They sat in the parlor. Mrs. Fields and her mother faced the pretty white teacher. Their housedresses contrasted with her suit and high heels. The aroma of collard greens and bacon wafted from the kitchen, mixing with the musty smells of washing and smog.

"It has been a great privilege to have Clarence as my student," Mrs. Swanson beamed. "He deserves every honor he has received. I have great expectations for him."

A smile like the sun burning through June gloom warmed the anxious mother's face. "I am so proud of my boy!"

"You have a right to be proud."

The grandmother shifted uneasily on her seat. "Is there something wrong?"

Mrs. Swanson was about to speak when the door creaked open. Clarence entered, his closely cropped hair showing the roundness of his head, accentuating the whites of his eyes.

The moment she saw Clarence, Mrs. Swanson feared he would take flight.

When he saw his teacher in the sitting room, his mouth fell open. He was conscious of the furniture and the walls, the TV, and his sisters' toys. His mother sat on the edge of her seat. M'Dear darted a look of warning.

"Clarence, can I speak with you?" Mrs. Swanson asked.

He nodded, looking from Mother to M'Dear. *Was he in trouble? Had the scholarship to Utah fallen through?*

When they were alone, Mrs. Swanson asked him how he was feeling.

"It's a hard time," he admitted.

She listened as he poured out his troubles. He had a great football career at Clairemont, but he did not know if it would happen again in college. His other concern was about going away to college, leaving the community. His voice sounded depressed. "There are a lot of changes. I'm getting ready to leave, and my girlfriend is not too happy with me. I'm the only one from around here who is going to Utah."

"You have an acceptance to a four-year college in hand," Mrs. Swanson said. "You may never have that again in your lifetime. You can always go to work or attend a community college. You can't *always* go to a four-year university."

Clarence shifted in the seat, looking at his mentor. As she talked, his body lost its tension. His shoulders loosened up.

"Seize the opportunity while it's here!" Mrs. Swanson encouraged him. "Even though it is scary, we have to do it. I will always be here to support you." She got up to go.

Now Mrs. Fields joined them. She could not speak directly to her son of her feelings, so deep they would pull her asunder, for she would miss him terribly. So she turned to Mrs. Swanson and spoke to Clarence through his teacher.

"I want for Clarence not to have to work as hard as I have had to do," she said, hiding her calloused hands. "I never got a chance to go to school. I want my son to have an education, so he don't have to struggle through no tough times."

Clarence turned toward her. He wanted to thank his mama for sacrificing for him, and there was only way to do so. Someday, he would come back from college and get a good job and buy them a house.

Mrs. Fields shook Mrs. Swanson's hand warmly, and M'Dear even gave a nod. The three women stood with Clarence. His two sisters were looking through the screen door, swinging back and forth between the light and the shadow.

"I'm glad you came to talk with us," said Mrs. Fields.

"So am I!" Mrs. Swanson laughed, relieved.

As Clarence watched her drive away, he drew closer to his family. It was a strange visit, but good: He would *never* forget her coming to his home. Yet, years later, he would have trouble remembering *why* she had come.

The day before graduation, Mrs. Swanson was up at 5 A.M., watching the network news. She saw a profile about a student who had fled Vietnam and was graduating with honors from a Florida school. *That's nothing compared to Kouang,* she thought. She called the local television affiliate and told a producer that there was an even better story about a Vietnamese student in San Diego.

Later, a television reporter taped an interview with Kouang in which he recounted his story in clear, colloquial English. It was broadcast that evening and the next morning, to her surprise, Kouang's picture was prominently displayed in the *San Diego Union*.

On graduation day, the AVID students proudly sat in the auditorium. As their names were called, "Angelina . . . Clarence . . . Kouang . . . Máximo . . ." Mrs. Swanson watched them rise. In their caps and gowns, they were almost indistinguishable, except for their eyes and hands, but she recognized them by the way they walked, tall and proud. She remembered the scared 14-year-olds she had recruited and raised, along with her own son, Tommy, as her children. AVID had not so much changed them as it had helped them become themselves on a higher level.

Their parents watched from grandstands: the seven Escobedo brothers, ascending like stairsteps; Kouang's diminutive mother in a silk Vietnamese dress; Clarence's proud mom and M'Dear beaming; Angelina's mother and two sisters, awed by the spectacle. These were the faces of a new America, one that would not be seen in the heartland for another decade, and they showed pride and not a little gratitude. As their sons and daughters proceeded to the stage and received diplomas, their parents cheered and their friends cheered for each other. They grasped the slender diplomas, knowing that this was not an end, but a beginning.

— BLOWING THEIR — SOCKS OFF

Vindication for Mary Catherine's methods came not in flowery praise from plenipotentiaries of the Carnegie Commission, but from data collected annually by the San Diego Unified School District. Early on, she had relied on hard statistics, not fuzzy feelings, to evaluate her experiment and to guide the evolution of effective teaching and learning techniques. Her methods of collecting data were limited at first by a lack of funding and expertise, but her commitment to statistical measures was firm. The reliance on data proved to be one of AVID's strong points, which would distinguish it from programs with high hopes but no scores. Data spoke with quiet authority amid the cacophonous cries of competing educational initiatives shouting for attention in an acronym-crazed society.

While it was tempting for some program directors to cull selective data to back up their optimistic claims, Mrs. Swanson made it quite clear to the AVID Site Team that she would rather see AVID fail than dishonestly appear to succeed.

"Accurate data is good data" was her motto. This imposed a stern discipline on the AVID program, a discipline that, over the next decades, would enable university-based researchers to document the program's successes and failures over a 20-year period.

In 1984, the district released data comparing achievement scores in area high schools. Scores were not broken down to the classroom level, but the school averages gave the first indication of how the bused students were doing.

Clairemont High School surpassed the district average by 46.6 percent in language arts and 35 percent in mathematics.

Although the AVID class was statistically insignificant, only 120 students out of a student body of 1,200, the program did help bring up the Clairemont average. At the District Headquarters, analysts scratched their heads at the anomaly. But the AVID Site Team was not surprised by the results because teachers, students, tutors, and the administration had participated in a schoolwide effort to incorporate effective teaching and learning skills. As a stone splashing into a pond creates ever-widening circles of motion, AVID's influence spread in waves that touched many students and classrooms.

This phenomenon would, one day, be called affectionately "AVIDizing" a school. The AVID Site Team influenced the ways other teachers conducted classes and how students took notes and studied collaboratively, raising expectations for what so-called "average" students could achieve. As students from different racial and linguistic backgrounds crossed boundaries, studying together and depending on each other, the original purpose of integration was being served, not in name, but in friendships and in working relationships. Clairemont avoided some of the tense racial and ethnic conflicts that afflicted other schools, and this was, to some degree, a byproduct of AVID's social influence on the entire campus. Without AVID's positive influence, both academic and social, the dire predictions of the old guard back in 1980—that busing would doom Clairemont—might have come true.

However, the success of AVID almost caused its downfall.

The school district was engaged in an undeclared war of acronyms. In this noble, but flawed, contest to improve minority students' academic performance, the district's Achievement Goals Program, AGP, was highly favored. AVID was an obscure guerrilla band on the periphery.

The district had invested millions of dollars in its pet project, hoping that AGP would raise the test scores of minority students in inner-city schools. The impetus for the program had been the court-ordered desegregation plan. To spur progress, the judge ordered that schools with high concentrations of minority students score *above* the fiftieth percentile on standardized achievement tests. At first glance, this would appear to be statistically impossible: How could a majority of minorities score higher than its own average? But, it was argued, the fiftieth percentile was measured by a much larger pool of test-takers from many school districts, so it was technically possible for a majority of San Diego's inner-city students to score above the fiftieth percentile.

Possible, but unlikely.

To achieve this unrealistic goal demanded by the court, the AGP curriculum was specifically designed to prepare students in inner-city schools for the standardized test. Suburban schools like Clairemont, which attracted busloads of minority students, were not required to teach the AGP curricula. So a Clairemont student like Clarence Fields was free to participate in AVID, while Clarence's peers from the old neighborhood at Lincoln High were enrolled in AGP. In 1984, the number of AGP students was exponentially larger than the number of students in Mrs. Swanson's AVID class.

The roles of teachers in the two programs were diametrically opposed. An AGP teacher was given strict guidelines, rigid lesson plans, and a tight schedule. The motive was high-minded, but the method was rote learning. The unspoken presumption was that teachers in low-performing schools didn't know how to teach. So their individual teaching styles were ground down into cogs in a test-preparation machine: One size fit all learning styles. This undermined the fragile personal relationships between teachers and students, a sacrifice that the district leadership was willing to make to comply with the order of the court.

To be fair, the challenge of undoing generations of separate and unequal education was an immense task, and American society didn't know how to go about righting the wrongs of racism and prejudice. It was a time of turmoil and conflict, with the threat of cities burning. If gains weren't made quickly, the backlash might take the country backward.

Things look different from the top and the bottom of any organization, and schools are a prime example of how top-down efforts often thwart and crush the creative efforts of individual teachers. While the administration put its eggs in the AGP basket, teachers in the trenches struggled to find ways to touch and improve the lives of the under-prepared students in their classes who were now expected to meet higher standards. Thousands of teachers devoted millions of hours and untold energy to find ways to cope with the greater needs of students—and to obey the demands of the administration. Their efforts were often successful for individual students and classes, but they lacked a coherent and practical method that produced repeatable results.

The AVID approach was philosophically opposed to mass-produced rote learning. Mind-dulling remedial worksheets gave way to intensive writing, inquiry, and collaboration in accelerated classes. While Clarence had been thrust into classes above his past experience—but not beyond his ability—his Lincoln High friends were condemned to boring monotony.

AVID challenged students to achieve *above* the fiftieth percentile. Mrs. Swanson inspired them to take risks and, if they fell, to pick themselves up and try again. Writing, Inquiry, and Collaboration was a metaphorical fulcrum to leverage hard work into achievement. The AGP curriculum was drafted at headquarters. AVID relied on ingenuity: If one approach didn't work, try another. AVID did not "teach to the test"; it tested students' character, encouraging determination and endurance, and provided plenty of support.

The danger of classroom-based initiatives is that they often depend on charismatic teachers whose personal styles are impossible to replicate on a large scale. Another pitfall is that many caring teachers value intangibles that feel good over hard test results. Still others question the very measures of achievement. Radicals protest standardized tests as a sellout to the power structure: Why should blacks and Latinos be judged by white people's standards?

AVID was a unique combination of support and rigor, fostering strong relationships *and* measuring achievement. Mrs. Swanson did not question whether minority kids should adopt the values of the dominant culture, but provided tools so that they could have the opportunities of their wealthier peers. She incorporated contributions from other teachers and refined methods developed in universities. She had that rare ability to think on two levels, the creative and the systematic, and her program combined the best of both worlds: freedom and discipline; relationship and structure.

But did it work?

Mary Catherine never set out to compete with the Achievement Goals Program, the purpose of which was to raise test scores for minority students. AVID had a broader intention—to help minority and low-income students prepare for college. As a byproduct, she discovered that AVID raised test scores higher than AGP did. AGP scores improved, although in many cases they fell short of the fiftieth percentile goal. AVID not only raised test scores, but 93 percent of AVID students went to college, an enrollment rate that was 75 percent higher than the national average.

"We blew their socks off," Mary Catherine recalls with a glint in her eyes.

Creating a program is like bearing a child: With the birth pangs comes the miracle of a new life, followed by painful struggles for support, funding, and survival.

The first four years had been as joyful and rewarding for Mrs. Swanson as for a new mother raising a baby. Every crisis was a new stage of life as AVID moved outward, like a developing child, through concentric rings of growth. The first ring was the intimate relationship between two teachers, a few tutors, and dozens of students. Within the warm embrace of the AVID room, it felt like family.

The second ring of growth comes when a toddler reaches beyond the mother to explore the immediate world. As AVID students fanned out into their other classes, the program touched teachers of English, math, and science who were amazed at the progress of their AVID students. They worked together collegially to help their students succeed.

The third ring of healthy growth is provided by a supportive community. Within a large, racially divided school, AVID created a community of learning where everyone belonged.

A father, or father figure, is vital for the balanced development of a child. Mr. Grove was involved from AVID's conception and always was there to support Mrs. Swanson.

After the first AVID class graduated, Mary Catherine had great expectations. But she did not take into account the destructive forces within American society in the 1980s that saw the dismantling of public institutions, the break up of families. In the shadows of the Reagan recession, factories closed and working families struggled, two or three paychecks from homelessness. When a desperate father skips out on his family and the mother carries on alone, against incredible odds, to support her young ones, children are put at risk.

Most of the kids in the AVID program had lived in single-parent families at least one time during their lives. In San Diego, "America's Finest City," one in four children was growing up in poverty.

AVID's reputation spread and Mrs. Swanson received inquiries from teachers at other schools. How did this program achieve such results? But there was silence from the district's central administration.

Mrs. Swanson dreamed of AVID spreading to other schools, a reform movement that began in the classrooms, not boardrooms, and was led by teachers. She believed, perhaps naively, that a low-cost program that so obviously benefited kids would be welcomed by the district and maybe even would be encouraged to expand to other schools.

Instead, the negative reaction from Big Brother (and Sister) at headquarters seemed to issue from George Orwell's surrealistic portrayal of totalitarianism, *1984*, which was making a comeback that year. In place of an Orwellian future for her students, Mrs. Swanson envisioned a hopeful world, where minds would be nurtured, not crushed; where freedom of speech and thought would be cherished by a new generation.

As fortune would have it, each time AVID would gain victory, a new obstacle was thrown in its path. As a classroom teacher, Mrs. Swanson would exult in her students' triumphs. But, as an educator dedicated to innovative change, the next two years would be painful and demeaning—the most hurtful she had ever experienced in her career. At times, she would feel like the exhausted single parent, cast out, barely able to carry on in such a hostile environment. Like a lioness, she was a fearsome protector of her students.

Forces beyond her control were conspiring to turn AVID's pointed success into a blunt weapon against its founder. Pride comes before a fall.

— GIFTED —

The district administration had trouble absorbing AVID's success. What could explain the fact that Mrs. Swanson's students performed better in advanced classes than did their peers in AGP classes? Why did nearly all AVID students attend college, while only a fraction of non-AVID kids from similar backgrounds gain the keys to higher education?

It couldn't be the AVID curriculum, tutors, and study groups. No, it must be the students Mrs. Swanson had recruited. They must be gifted!

These views were championed by Dr. Virgil Sexton in district meetings. He happened to be the honcho in charge of the district's Seminar Program for gifted students. Dr. Sexton was Mr. Grove's boss, and when Jim came back from meetings at headquarters, he told Mary Catherine about Virgil's views.

The assumption was that minority students couldn't have earned good grades and gone to college by virtue of hard work, determination, and individual responsibility. Sexton presumed that they must have been certified as "gifted"—according to intelligence tests used by the district—but, in fact, they had not been so identified.

This assumption riled Mrs. Swanson. Not because she didn't think her students were smarter than some teachers presumed. It bothered her because the Establishment assumed that white students who were bright, but not geniuses, could study their butts off and become valedictorians. But non-whites? No way, José.

In 1985, Dr. Sexton called Mrs. Swanson to say he was declaring the AVID students "gifted."

"I hear that you are discounting AVID's role in my students' success," she said.

"There's no other way of explaining the results," he answered. "They are *unidentified* gifted."

"I invite you to send a school psychologist to test AVID students here," she replied.

Dr. Sexton complied with her request. All AVID students took the district's gifted test. When the results came back, Mrs. Swanson read them in her office. The typical AVID score was 101; a score of 100 was generally considered average. The highest AVID score was 115; some students scored as low as 90. The district required a score of 145 to be certified "gifted."

Clearly, they were in the average range. Yet they were performing in the top range.

Mrs. Swanson felt the students had been vindicated.

At this time, the Seminar Program was under fire. The court decreed that all San Diego public schools integrate minorities. The Seminar Program, not only in Mr. Grove's classroom, but throughout the district, was nearly 100 percent white. Asians were beginning to filter into Seminar classes. But there were virtually no African Americans or Hispanics. State funding was going to be cut if San Diego didn't incorporate minorities into the gifted program—pronto.

AVID was a rich mix of ethnic groups. Why not draft AVID students into the Seminar Program? That would bring up the percentages and fulfill the state's requirements—*and* bring Mrs. Swanson under the control of the district. Kill two birds with one stone.

One day early in summer vacation, Dr. Sexton called her at home.

"Mrs. Swanson, you're coming to work for me!" he crowed. "Got a pen? I want you to produce in writing the following items: A brochure explaining AVID, a curriculum, a recruitment procedure . . ."

"Hold on," Mrs. Swanson said, astounded. "Are you telling me I will no longer be teaching at Clairemont? That I've got to move to the Ed Center?"

Dr. Sexton sidestepped the question. He was winging it, she realized. He thought she'd be flattered to join the Seminar team. He couldn't understand her negative reaction.

She knew two things. She wanted to stay in the classroom and work with kids. And AVID must not be taken over by the Seminar Program, where the students would not receive the AVID support structure.

"I'm sorry, Dr. Sexton," she said politely, "but I am not willing to sacrifice my kids."

Dr. Sexton was taken aback. She heard him sputtering to himself, then his voice came through, loud and clear. "Mary Catherine, you will not be able to get along in your life on good looks alone. At some point you're going to have to produce something."

She was livid. Immediately after hanging up the phone, she called her principal, Chuck Raleigh. She relayed the conversation. "Chuck, what do you think my course of action should be? Not about the job. About the obnoxious insult."

"Call Sexton's boss and report it," Chuck answered, adding with fervor, "that remark was totally inappropriate."

Dr. Sexton's boss, Deputy Superintendent Angstrom, reported directly to the superintendent of the district. She related the conversation again, her heart pounding with hurt and rage. Angstrom listened. He made no comment. No resolution. Nothing.

She hung up the phone again, terrified. *Have I made a horrible faux pas?*

Later, she realized that Dr. Angstrom could not answer until he had talked to Dr. Sexton. The chain of command ruled the Ed Center.

She was left with an uneasy feeling. School was out and she felt utterly alone.

The following week, she got another call from Dr. Sexton.

"I understand you are not going to work for me," he said snidely. "Let me tell you one thing. I will see to it that your career is ruined in the San Diego City Schools."

She called Chuck Raleigh again, repeating Sexton's threat. "I don't know what needs to be done," she said in desperation. "I needed to report to you what has happened. So a person in authority will know—so that if this escalates, it's not just my word against somebody else's."

This time, Chuck Raleigh did not offer a solution. She hung up, more frightened than before. She didn't know what Sexton could do to her. She *did* know that if he tried to ruin her career, she would not take it lying down. She would fight.

Deputy Superintendent Angstrom never contacted her. She never learned what Dr. Sexton had told him, or even if the deputy superintendent had inquired about the insult. The brooding silence from the district headquarters was ominous. Gossip traveled quickly along the corridors of the Ed Center. The superintendent's office was right next to Angstrom's. It was virtually impossible that he hadn't heard something about the incident—from his deputy's perspective. She had no friends in high places.

But Jim Grove was her friend. The gentlest man in the world, and the most cultured, he listened to her plaint. The insult blanched his rosy complexion chalk white.

"Mary Catherine, if I find out I have a terminal disease," he said with spiteful laughter, "I'm going to do you and mankind a great favor. I'm going to invite Dr. Sexton for a trip to Coronado Island and drive off the bridge!"

Later, when Mrs. Swanson told her friend Martha Tower about Sexton's threat, Martha exclaimed, "Why, Mary Catherine, you can't let that happen!"

"But I informed the principal," Mary Catherine said. "I called Dr. Angstrom. They didn't do anything."

Martha was the head of the Language Arts Department for the district. Her office was next to Dr. Sexton's. "You have to report this to another assistant superintendent," she said. "I'll go with you and we'll make sure this is taken care of."

Martha set up the meeting with Assistant Superintendent Elliot Arnson in Dr. Arnson's office at the Ed Center. The room was furnished with a desk, from which a rectangular table jutted. Mrs. Swanson sat on one side of the table, facing the door. Martha and the assistant superintendent were on the other side of the table. In the blonde wooden door, there was a little six-inch-square window that looked out onto the hallway.

As Mrs. Swanson began to tell her story, she looked up. Virgil Sexton was staring at her through the window, trying to intimidate her. She must have looked stunned, because Martha suddenly asked, "What's wrong?"

"Virgil is staring in the window," Mrs. Swanson explained.

They turned around. He was gone.

"To my knowledge, nothing was ever done," Mary Catherine reflects, years later. "But nothing bad happened to me. Although there might have been a lot of behind-the-scenes stuff."

Soon after, Martha Tower left San Diego City Schools and went to work for the County Office of Education, a move that would one day have tremendous implications for Mary Catherine's career—and for AVID.

— MRS. CHIPP COMES —
TO CLAIREMONT

In the middle of a hot summer day, Mary Catherine was waist deep in roses, clipping shears in hand. The phone rang. Her teenage son, Tommy, picked it up.

"Mom, it's for you!" he cried, adolescent voice cracking. Tommy cupped his hand over the receiver and whispered, "It sounds like Ronald Reagan."

"Why in the world would the president call me?" she laughed, wiping the dirt from her dungarees. "Hello?"

"Sorry to interrupt you on vacation," the voice had Reagan's timbre and relaxed warmth. She only knew one person who sounded like Reagan, and that was her friend, Chuck Raleigh, Clairemont's principal.

"Chuck?" she asked.

"The district has named my replacement," he said. "Come on down to school. I want you to meet my successor."

Something in the way he said the word *successor* made her squeeze the shears. Accidentally, she nipped a rosebud. It fell, guillotined, to the ground.

"I'm warning you, Mary Catherine, don't get all embarrassed," Chuck said. "But I intend to brag about you and your AVID kids to the new honcho."

The next morning, freshly bathed and glowing, Mrs. Swanson dressed fastidiously for the meeting, anxious to make a good impression. Excited to meet the new principal, tell her new boss stories of AVID students' hard-earned achievements and share her plans for the future, she rushed to school. Atop a mesa, Clairemont High gleamed in the sun. In four years, it had surmounted the loss of half its students and faculty, absorbed 500 inner-city students, and transformed itself into a new institution: diverse, innovative, and committed to excellence. As America absorbed new ethnic groups, it was a model of what a high school could achieve with limited resources and much heart. Yet there was still much to accomplish.

"Mary Catherine!" Chuck patted her warmly on the back, ushering her into his old office. Heavyset, with a salt-and-pepper crewcut and high, Cherokee Indian cheekbones, his turquoise eyes danced, admiring his star teacher. Animated, jovial, and personable, Chuck knew his strengths and weaknesses and had no ego problems. He had started out as a coach, and he knew how to lead teams. He was a *laissez faire* administrator who believed that if you trusted teachers as professionals and inspired them to reach a goal, they would use their individual talents to the utmost. This approach motivated teachers like Mr. Grove and Mrs. Swanson to work tirelessly on behalf of their students because they took responsibility for making their classrooms citadels of learning. Chuck had created a climate of freedom within a hierarchy that rewarded conformity.

And now he was leaving. Who could replace him?

"Meet Clairemont's new principal, Mrs. Blanche Chipp."

Mrs. Chipp was broad of shoulder, sober of demeanor, and approximately five feet, six inches tall, with closely cropped hair.

She was sharply dressed in a dark gray suit with charcoal stripes, a silk handkerchief, and pointed black pumps.

Mary Catherine extended her hand in greeting. Mrs. Chipp flinched slightly, holding back. She had the careful eye of a woman who looked twice before taking a step forward into new territory.

Who could blame her if she were uptight about her position? Mrs. Swanson wondered. Mrs. Chipp was the first African American who had been promoted to a position of power at Clairemont High. She appeared young for the post, yet determined to look mature and in control. The new principal's discomfort was obvious, but Mary Catherine could not understand why Blanche looked at her suspiciously. Mrs. Swanson felt ridiculous holding out her hand while Mrs. Chipp held hers back. Yet Mary Catherine did not want to insult her new boss. On the contrary. She was eager to get to know Blanche, see her vision for the future, to become allies in the struggle to usher more students of color into college. She saw the black administrator as an ally in her struggle for justice. Of course, Mrs. Swanson needed to brief Mrs. Chipp as soon as possible on AVID's financial crisis for the coming year. Without a new grant, AVID would have no more money to pay tutors.

The frosty silence grew into a glacial stalemate.

Chuck tried to break the ice. "Blanche, I want you to know what a privilege it has been to work with Mary Catherine. I'm sorry if I'm embarrassing you, Mary Catherine, but I mean it." He described her roles as English chairwoman, founder of AVID, host of meetings between teachers and college professors, and instigator of schoolwide reforms.

Mrs. Chipp stared down, seemingly fascinated by the shimmering patina on the toes of her shoes. As the list of Mary Catherine's credits lengthened, Mrs. Chipp seemed to grow bored. Slowly, as if tugged by a drawstring, the corners of her lips tightened. She did not acknowledge a word of praise for her new subordinate.

"Well, I guess I'll leave you two alone to plan for a great year!" Mr. Raleigh smiled warmly.

Mrs. Swanson hugged him. "Hope you get a good new assignment, Chuck."

The door closed, leaving the new principal and teacher alone, a tableaux. Mrs. Swanson felt Mrs. Chipp's unease, a heavy weight bearing down on her shoulders. *The weight of prejudice? The weight of responsibility?*

Mrs. Chipp drew her head upward. "Hmmm," she said. "Are you aware that you have something in your left nostril?"

"Excuse me?" Mary Catherine's hand flew up to her nose in disbelief and shame.

"That will be all," Mrs. Chipp smiled, excusing her from the principal's office.

This was only the beginning of a disrespectful relationship that would worsen over time, alienating Mrs. Swanson from the school she loved.

— CAFÉ GELATO —

It was a slow evening at Café Gelato in early December 1985. Lisa was behind the counter, trying to study for an English lit final and simultaneously swab down the espresso machine. She was exhausted, as usual. To put herself through college at UCSD, she held two jobs: tutoring AVID kids by day, scooping Italian ices by night.

Lisa had been hired in AVID's third year, and Mrs. Swanson had given her major responsibilities for a 22-year-old college student. She not only tutored AVID kids, she observed faculty members' teaching styles, brainstormed new tutoring techniques with Mrs. Swanson, and actually guest-taught in the classroom. The experience had been so exciting that it had thrown the rest of her life into confusion. She was torn between two career dreams: pursuing the bright lights of Broadway theater and influencing young lives as a teacher. Mrs. Swanson had become Lisa's mentor and dear friend. Lisa would do virtually anything to help Mrs. Swanson.

AVID needed help. The foundation grant was long gone. The program was nearly broke. The new principal was openly hostile. The district refused to pay for tutors. Mrs. Swanson was constantly searching for money to keep the program going, and the strain was grinding her down. Lisa worried about Mrs. Swanson's health.

Lisa spent as much time writing grant proposals for AVID as term papers for UCSD. The answer from foundations was always: "We regret we cannot grant your request. AVID is an outstanding program. But it is appropriate for the local school district to provide funding for tutors."

Lisa cleaned the espresso machine, sighing as she wrung out the rancid rag. She felt eyes watching her back and turned round. A man in a trenchcoat smiled sympathetically and ordered a double espresso. He tipped her and sat down at a nearby table.

San Diego's trendy espresso bar was deserted. Lisa came out from behind the counter to wipe off the tables. The trenchcoat intrigued her.

The customer scoured the local newspaper, jotting down items in a reporter's notebook. He peered over the Metro section. His eyes were piercing but guarded; newsman's eyes.

"What a rag," he said.

She looked at the damp cloth in her hand, feeling wrung out.

"No offense—I meant the local paper," he said.

She laughed. "I never get time to read what's going on in the world."

"Nothing's happening," he said. "Slow news day."

His handsome, haggard face looked vaguely familiar. Where had she seen him before? He saw her looking at him and flashed a smile, as if mugging for a camera.

"Are you a newspaper reporter?" she asked.

"TV, the *11 O'Clock News*."

"Really, how exciting!"

"Not really," he said, inviting her to sit down. They made small talk. She looked at her watch. He stood up to go.

"So what do you do when you're not steaming milk?" he asked.

"Oh, I'm a student at UCSD," she said glumly. Her eyes brightened. "I'm also an AVID tutor at Clairemont High."

"Why are you so *avid* about teaching?" he asked. "Schools are going to hell. It's a national scandal."

"A-V-I-D is a program," she said, spelling out the acronym. "Haven't you heard about it?"

He brushed off his trenchcoat, skeptical. "Johnny can't read."

"But this one works!" She rattled off the statistics. "Ninety-three percent of AVID students go to college."

"Really? I'm impressed."

She frowned at the sour-smelling rag in her hand. Maybe if she could get the reporter interested, he could get out the word that AVID needed funding. "That's why it's so sad that AVID is running out of money," she said, calling on her theatrical skills. "If something doesn't happen soon, they'll have to fire me and the other tutors."

"If AVID's so good, why won't the district fund it?" he asked.

"Between you and me, I think it's jealousy," she said, looking him in the eye. "AVID beat out some million-dollar program and now they're trying to kill it."

He opened his notebook. "Who?"

"I don't really know, maybe some bureaucrats?" Lisa said. "Do you think you could help?"

"Just the facts, ma'am." He smiled, showing a glint of incisors. "I need sources."

Lisa jumped up. "I almost forgot! Mrs. Swanson, that's AVID's founder. She's going to be interviewed tomorrow night by the superintendent on educational TV."

"Will she talk to me first?" he asked. "I'll need her home phone."

Lisa hesitated. Something in his tone made a warning light go on in her head.

"It's late," she stalled.

"But the show's tomorrow," he said convincingly.

She looked at his pen poised above the notebook. Mrs. Swanson was always talking about taking initiative, not giving up. *Maybe I can make a difference!* Lisa thought innocently, giving him the number.

"Thanks for the tip," he said, stuffing the notebook into his trenchcoat.

"I'll tell her you're calling," she shouted after him. The door closed. The café was empty. "Yes!" she cried, tossing the rag into the air.

The reporter's late-night call awakened Mary Catherine. She squinted at the glowing clock dial in her darkened bedroom. Tom moaned. It was nearly 11 P.M. They both had to get up at 5 A.M. Who could be calling at this hour?

"I hope it's not too late," the reporter apologized.

"Too late for what?" she asked groggily.

"To get the lowdown on AVID's funding crisis."

"Crisis?"

"Yes, a source has told us that you are meeting with the superintendent of schools to resolve a budget conflict."

"Source?" she asked. Then she remembered: Lisa had called, bubbling with excitement. She'd met a TV reporter. He wanted to give AVID publicity. Mary Catherine had been busy preparing for tomorrow's interview with the superintendent and hadn't paid much attention. She'd heard the goodwill in her tutor's voice and thanked her. Before hanging up, she'd said: "Oh, and Lisa, please don't forget to look after the AVID students tomorrow evening. They are excited to see the broadcast, but most don't have cable TV at home. They'll be watching the interview on the cable set in the Clairemont office. If they call in to the show, make sure they are truthful and to the point." Lisa had promised she would take care of everything.

Now, the TV reporter was on the line, making demands and citing "sources," as if he were a Watergate reporter. Mary Catherine remembered the polite way her father asked questions: The more penetrating the question, the more respectful he became. Ed Jacobs never called people out of bed unless it was an earthquake or flood. Now TV reporters were jabbing microphones in shooting-victims' families' faces and asking, "How do you feel?"

She did not want to talk to this reporter. It was late and she was weary, but there was also something sinister about his tone. She feared intuitively that publicity could endanger AVID.

"Listen, I appreciate your interest in AVID and am happy to send you some materials," she said. "But I have nothing to say about a supposed 'budget crisis.'"

"Then you deny AVID is, quote, 'broke?'"

"No comment," she stonewalled.

"You're not firing tutors?"

"No, I'm not."

"Look, I'm just trying to do a story."

"I'm sorry, but it's awfully late."

"I'll see you at school tomorrow," he said. "With my camera crew."

The phone line clicked. Her hand was trembling.

"What happened?" asked Tom.

"Oh, some silly reporter," she said, not wanting to alarm him. She needed to grab a few hours of sleep. Tossing and turning, she remembered Lisa's excited voice. She did not blame her loyal tutor. She resented the reporter for taking advantage of her enthusiasm. In her gut, Mrs. Swanson feared that controversy could provide AVID's enemies with ammunition to kill the program.

In retrospect, Mrs. Swanson wondered, *If I had answered the reporter's questions more openly, would I have defused the potential conflict with the superintendent?*

Awaiting dawn, she felt a calming presence from her childhood. Ed Jacobs was a stalwart supporter of the First Amendment. Mary Catherine was her father's daughter: outspoken, fierce in debate, respectful of differences. She had confidence that she could defuse the crisis. Tomorrow, she'd inform the superintendent's office about the reporter. She must act with integrity, even if it blew up in her face.

The next morning, she swallowed her pride and called an administrator who was not a supporter of the AVID program. "Please inform the superintendent that someone is trying to foment a conflict and that I don't want any part of it," Mrs. Swanson said.

Since Mrs. Chipp was not in her office, Mrs. Swanson reported to the assistant principal, Mr. Swarz, that a TV reporter may be trying to come onto campus.

"Let 'em try," he growled, rubbing his hands together.

AVID HITS THE
11 O'CLOCK NEWS

The TV reporter, brilliantly clad in a blue blazer and crimson tie, arrived at Clairemont High at the stroke of two. He was wired for sound. Video crew in tow, he crossed the circle drive and passed a line of school buses.

"Are we rolling?" he asked the camera operator. Affirmative, answered the red light glowing on the video monitor. Chin jutting, the reporter strode toward the school office.

"Stop right there," Mr. Swarz barked, barring the door. "Do you have ID?"

The reporter smiled, flashing his press card. "May I speak with Mrs. Swanson?"

"She is in her classroom, teaching." Mr. Swarz snarled.

"Great, we'll interview her with the students!"

"No, sir. You will turn around and proceed off school property."

"This is a public place." The reporter turned to the camera, addressing an invisible audience: "Freedom of the press . . . call the American Civil Liberties Union."

"Not on my watch!" Mr. Swarz approached the lens, hand thrust forward.

"Watch out!" The camera operator stepped backward off the curb and kept filming from the street.

At that moment, the bell rang. Hordes of students poured from the building. *Wow, TV!* They swarmed around the reporter, mugging for the camera.

"What's happenin'?" the reporter asked, attempting to be "with it."

The boys started flexing their muscles, flashing gang symbols. The girls cooed: "Hi, Tammy! Hi, Mom! Way cool!"

"We're here to interview San Diego youth. . . ." he told them.

The noise was deafening. "Whaaat?"

"We need to find somebody from AVID class," the reporter shouted into the sea of expectant faces.

The ensuing traffic jam was making communication impossible. Horns honked. Bus drivers revved engines. Miraculously, the sea of students parted to allow locals to head toward cars, commuters toward waiting buses. Yellow doors swung open. The reporter leapt aboard a school bus and waded down the aisle, jabbing his microphone in young people's faces. Finally, he found a Vietnamese girl who agreed to talk.

"Here we have an AVID student," he said, turning to the embarrassed student. "What is your opinion of the controversial funding battle with the superintendent?"

"What controversy?" she answered, dumbfounded.

"Do you think your teacher, Mrs. Swanson, should fire your tutors?"

"Why? They helping us study!" She panicked.

"Off the bus!" ordered the driver.

The intrepid reporter pressed on. "We have information that the AVID program may be forced to close, preventing you from going to college." He turned the microphone on the frightened student. "How do you feel?"

Mr. Swarz clambered aboard the bus to hustle the reporter off. The hand-held camera captured it all: the red-faced vice principal, the self-righteous media personality, the mob of students, the noise, the tumult.

"That's a wrap!" shouted the reporter, back on the sidewalk, anxious to get video footage back to his producer. "We've got enough for the *11 O'Clock News*."

Within minutes after he and his crew sped off to their glitzy commercial TV broadcast studio, the "student riot" disappeared into thin air. When Mrs. Swanson emerged from the building several hours later, en route to the cable TV interview, she saw the quiet greensward and smiled to herself, "Much ado about nothing."

At the modest television studio operated by the County Office of Education, all was ready. Dr. Thomas W. Payzant, superintendent of San Diego City Schools hosted a weekly talk show, discussing local school issues with a variety of guests. Dr. Payzant was a soft-spoken man of strong convictions and keen intelligence. Although he had few years of experience as a classroom teacher, he was a dynamic administrator, alternately charming and tough. When he had come to San Diego several years earlier as the new superintendent, he was a breath of fresh air and quickly won the support of the local newspapers. San Diego was a conservative town with growing urban problems, and the superintendent was viewed as the man who could balance the two. He was seen as a firm administrator who both saw the big picture and immersed himself in detail, a brilliant combination of vision and supervision. Payzant inherited the AGP program from his predecessor and, rather than buy an off-the-shelf curriculum, he implemented the one that had been developed by the district staff. AGP was specifically designed to be quite proscriptive, with little flexibility for deviation from classroom to classroom. Teachers were told what was to be taught and how in a particular class. This was formally called "direct instruction," but was privately said to be "teacher-proof."

With a court-ordered agenda to improve student test scores above the fiftieth percentile, Payzant believed that teachers were critical to raising student performance, but he did not always see things from the perspective of a classroom teacher. By the same token, it seemed to some teachers that the superintendent was averse to changes he could not control.

Mrs. Swanson was never out of control with her students. But from a supervisor's perspective, this headstrong teacher was not easy to control.

In terms of personality, if not power, the two educators were evenly matched: Both were forces to be reckoned with, and each would emerge as a national figure in public education.

Yet in the bright studio lights, they respectfully avoided school politics and focused on an issue of overriding importance: preparing under-represented children for college.

A transcript of that discussion, if the videotape still exists, would almost certainly make dry reading. Not that their ideas were not refreshing. But the format of two talking heads debating remedial versus accelerated learning curricula in education-speak certainly did not attract an audience from, say, *Wheel of Fortune*.

Still, in Mrs. Swanson's memory, the interview was less important for what was said than for what was *not* said. What was not openly discussed on television was the delicate question of why the district was not funding AVID tutors. Mrs. Swanson did not know at what level of the bureaucracy opposition to her program was coming from—the superintendent or district administrators—but she was too polite to raise such questions publicly. The superintendent did not lead the discussion toward the subject of funding, but rather focused on issues of effective curricula and motivation for minority and low-income students. Their conversation was polite, informative, and benign.

Near the end of the show, the telephone lines were opened for viewers to call in. One of the callers was an AVID student. No doubt, it was a heart-felt testimonial. Dr. Payzant expressed delight in the student's success. Under the warmly lulling lights, controversy evaporated like smoke from dry ice.

Back at Clairemont High, under Lisa's watchful eye, a dozen AVID students gazed at a flickering blue screen, transfixed by the wavy images of their teacher and her top boss. The talk about curricula went over their heads. But it sure was exciting to see Mrs. Swanson on TV, bragging about their achievements to that funny guy in the suit!

Outside, a camera operator surreptitiously climbed onto a ledge and poked a video lens through a louvered window into the school office. While the TV reporter held his legs, he filmed the silhouettes of teenagers gazing raptly at grainy blobs on a television screen: A video-on-video exposé.

Lisa saw the one-eyed monster peering in the window. She panicked. "Get down!" she whispered to the kids, pointing at the camera.

Kids hit the floor and rolled away from the window.

Lisa fought back panic, nightmarish images of being spied on by a shadowy voyeur in a trenchcoat. *It's my fault . . . never should have spoken to that reporter.* Guilt gave way to rage. *You scum bag!* She wanted to strangle the reporter, tie his belt around his neck and lynch him from the flagpole. Someone must have tipped him off that AVID students were watching the show at school. A major conspiracy!

Unaware of the implications of this invasion of privacy, the students stifled giggles, writhing on the floor to evade the glassy cyclops panning the room. They crouched against the wall and defiantly watched the show. Some even took notes. Others prepared thoughtful questions. Excited to participate, they eventually forgot the camera that kept filming. One student screwed up her courage and phoned in to the show, innocently praising AVID for giving her a chance to go to college.

When the music and credits came on the screen, Lisa switched off the TV. They huddled in darkness. Finally, the camera crew withdrew. *All clear.* Students hurried to a waiting van, giggling and laughing under the stars. Lisa rushed home to catch the *11 O'Clock News.*

After leaving the TV studio, Mrs. Swanson relaxed on the long drive north to her home and family. The interview had gone exceptionally well. The superintendent couldn't have been more cordial. They shared faith in public schools, in equal access to higher education. They may have disagreed about how best to improve education for minority and low-income students, but at that time of debate among educators, who could claim a unilateral hold on truth? All people of goodwill were needed to put their minds together to heal a Nation at Risk. She felt confident that the superintendent and she could work things out for the benefit of the kids. Exiting the freeway, she opened the window, smelling the sage and roses of Olivenhain. The closer she came to her family, the more peaceful she felt. Her house was quiet. A star hung in the sky. She stared up at it, wondering.

The present is terribly uncertain. But a teacher can alter the future. Students are America's future. That's why AVID is so important. It gives the children of divorce, the offspring of teenage mothers, the war refugees who come to school speaking no English—it gives teenagers who might otherwise fall through the cracks—a chance to make it. Not by sneaking through the back door of the admissions office, but by being prepared for the rigors of college.

Surely the media could see the value of such an endeavor.

"A blue-ribbon panel flunks America's schools!" chirped news anchor Waverly Snow, as "A Nation at Risk" flashed on the screen, upbeat music tinkling in the background. "But there *is* hope in San Diego. A special report by our reporter Dirk Bender."

"Thanks Waverly," Bender replied from the left side of the Plexiglas anchor desk. Ruggedly handsome against a sky-blue background projected behind him, the reporter looked straight through the camera, into Lisa's living room and Mary Catherine's bedroom.

"This is the story of a teacher from Clairemont High who devised a formula to boost poor kids from ghetto slums to the ivory tower," Bender explained evenly. On screen, the image of teenage gang members cut away to clean-cut collegiates gathered around the flagpole of San Diego State University. Bender's voice dropped: "It's also the story of a superintendent who makes tough budget choices and must depend on the honesty of his staff." Photograph of the superintendent looking serious and idealistic.

Lisa hugged a teddy bear on her living room couch, fingers crossed. Mary Catherine sat up in bed beside her husband.

"AVID stands for Advancement via Intellectual Discipline," Bender said crisply.

"No! Individual Determination," Mary Catherine whispered. It was a common mistake, but she was impressed by Bender's upbeat tone.

"AVID has sent hundreds of hopeless kids from tough neighborhoods to four-year universities—a 95 percent success rate!" he enthused.

"Dozens, not hundreds," she shrugged at his exaggerated figures. At least he had done some background research. His portrait of AVID was consistent with a major profile of the program that had appeared in the local edition of the *Los Angeles Times,* an article that had also caused a small stir in the County Office of Education. He gave a cogent, if superficial, description of a "homeroom atmosphere," where tutors worked one-on-one with students. "Some of us wish we could have had college tutors," he winked at the camera.

Lisa cringed.

"But strange things happen in Byzantine bureaucracies," Bender averred with an ironic twist. "A source reveals that AVID faces the budget ax. Today, AVID students protested on campus." The screen exploded with gritty images of riotous students. A red-faced administrator stood cross-armed, blocking a gate.

"It looks like a riot at Berkeley!" Lisa cried, taking off her shoes.

"The woman behind it all is Mary Catherine Swanson," Bender said ominously. The screen projected an outdated yearbook photo of Mrs. Swanson looking young and naïve. "In a potential infringement of First Amendment rights, a school official drove cameras from the school grounds. We are investigating a cover-up."

"He thinks he's Carl Bernstein investigating AVIDGATE!" Mary Catherine howled, not knowing whether to laugh or cry.

"After stonewalling our news team," Bender continued bitterly, "Mrs. Swanson was all smiles when she appeared on the superintendent's cable TV talk show." A video clip showed her and the superintendent conversing pleasantly. "But what the superintendent *didn't* know," Bender paused melodramatically, "was that Mrs. Swanson had set him up. While the superintendent answered a call from a student, he did not see what was going on—simultaneously—at Clairemont High. Look at this scene." Dim silhouettes of AVID students crouched before the TV screen. It looked as if a coven of student radicals had taken over the principal's office. When the camera panned, they hid their faces. Now Bender's voice froze Mary Catherine's blood. "On school property, using the principal's cable television and private telephone, Mrs. Swanson had arranged a trap. Coached by their teacher, student callers put the superintendent on the spot."

The intrepid reporter turned to Waverly, the news anchor, who appeared overcome by shock and disbelief.

"Isn't that the most incredible story?" Bender deadpanned.

"Absolutely!" Waverly admitted, on cue.

"Bastard!" Lisa screamed at the tiny TV screen in her student flat. She hurled a shoe at Dirk's leering face. The vacuum tube imploded. Sparks flew. The sound bleeped off. In the eerie darkness, Lisa put her head in her hands. *I've destroyed her career. How can I ever ask her to forgive me?*

In bed, Mary Catherine was shaking with rage. How could the media provoke a virtual riot and call it a student protest? She did not question a reporter's right to investigate a story. But to insinuate that she had done something underhanded—when she had done everything in her power *not* to put the superintendent on the spot.

She did not blame Lisa. The idealistic college student had only wanted to help AVID obtain funding, so tutors could keep helping kids.

No, Mary Catherine blamed the reporter. He had taken advantage of a naïve girl's faith in the media as a white knight crusading for "truth, justice, and the American way." *Did Bender harbor grudges against a program that helped minority kids?* Most reporters she knew had *sympathy* for the downtrodden.

No, it was apparently done for sheer exploitation. Did the *11 O'Clock News* really need to stir up conflict to garner rating points? Emotionally, she wanted to curl up and hide. But the warrior inside her refused to be a victim. She had to be strong, not for her own sake, but for her students. *A teacher must teach by example, not by preaching.* And so she tossed and turned: sleepless, hurt, nauseous, angry, fearful. Hours later, in the pre-dawn cold, she rose from bed and dressed for a new day of teaching.

The hyped "student riot" at Clairemont High was rebroadcast on the early morning news. In case anybody hadn't seen it, the farce was repeated at noon.

Mrs. Swanson went straight to her school mailbox, half expecting a pink slip. When she slipped outside for a breath of fresh air, a colleague pointed up at the seagulls circling above the guano-stained pavement.

"Well, looks like this time the Big Bird crapped on you!"

She whooped until she cried.

All day long, she expected a call. She wanted the chance to tell the superintendent the truth. Not to apologize—for she was not guilty. She merely wanted to explain her side of the story. Was there no institutional memory of her contributions? After teaching for nearly two decades, with never a complaint against her; after developing programs that brought credit to the district; after devoting everything she had to the AVID students, she deserved the chance to be heard.

"From my limited perspective at that time," Mary Catherine now recalls, with the benefit of hindsight, "I had given heart and soul to the district—and they didn't care."

Lisa came to AVID class, her eyes puffy, cheeks pale.

"Oh, Mrs. Swanson, I'm sorry, I'm sorry, I'm sorry!" she cried. "It was all my doing, but the consequences are going to fall on you. I can never forgive myself."

Mrs. Swanson put her hands on the anguished tutor's shoulders and gazed firmly into her eyes: "Lisa, you had good motives," she said gently. "The only time that it is difficult to forgive people is when there is malicious intent." She raised Lisa's chin. "There *will* be consequences, but I surely hold no animosity toward you."

Lisa looked up. She would never forget the strength and determination in her mentor's eyes. *The most enduring lessons are taught by example.*

Mary Catherine taught her AVID class, reassuring her students that neither they nor she had done anything wrong. She used the debacle to teach a lesson about "point of view" reporting, to be skeptical of polarized conflicts they saw on television.

"Are they going to cut AVID?" Angelina asked.

"Not as long as I'm here," Mrs. Swanson said.

At lunch she made a point of eating in the faculty room. A few colleagues came up to her with condolences and wry cheers. Her enemies had a field day, whispering behind her back. When Mr. Swarz passed, some wit shouted, "The Russians are coming!"

All day Mrs. Swanson waited for a note, a call, some acknowledgment from the superintendent's office. It never came. The silence was devastating.

— LETTER OF ⸗—
RESIGNATION

The fight over AVID's future reached a turning point in 1986. A power struggle between the entrenched school system and a pioneering teacher had jeopardized Mrs. Swanson's career—and AVID's survival.

Since 1980, AVID had sent over 170 disadvantaged students to universities, and another 30 were heading to college in the fall. But, over these six years, Mrs. Swanson had suffered a series of emotional blows: Jim had retired from Clairemont High in 1985, grant money for tutors ran out, the central administration opposed the program, and the principal showed contempt for what Mrs. Swanson had accomplished. She felt abandoned, the single mother of a fatherless program.

In conflicts between teachers and administrators, many factors are at work—personality, power, and principles—and at Clairemont all three levels were at play. After Mrs. Chipp drew attention to Mary Catherine's nose, she picked at her teaching methods, departmental priorities, evaluation reports—even her speaking style. These small criticisms added up, annoying Mary Catherine to distraction. More perplexing to her was her new boss's attitude toward the program. With a wave of her hand, Mrs. Chipp dismissed AVID as a trivial elective, yet she took credit for its accomplishments. The principal seemed to make a point of humiliating Mary Catherine before other teachers.

One day, Mrs. Swanson was summoned to Mrs. Chipp's office. A number of black and Hispanic faculty members had also been invited, among them Edna Bellows, the history teacher who'd humiliated Angelina.

"Clairemont is being honored for increasing the number of minority students who go to college," the principal said, smiling at the teachers. "Clairemont is leading the way in black and Hispanic admissions."

"That's wonderful!" Mary Catherine cried. "I'm so glad Clairemont is getting credit for our work."

Frowning at Mary Catherine's remark, Mrs. Chipp turned her charming smile on Mrs. Bellows. "Edna, you've done a fabulous job with your history students. I want you to lead our delegation of teachers to the celebration at Sea World." Turning to the other teachers, she flashed free passes to the park's penguin exhibit. "We are very proud that you fine teachers will be representing us at the minority enrollment awards ceremony. Afterwards, enjoy the penguins. Good work!"

Mrs. Chipp passed out the passes to all the teachers, but ran out when she reached Mary Catherine. Walking back to the AVID classroom, Mary Catherine felt a shooting pain in her stomach. She didn't give a hoot about going to Sea World, but she wondered what Chipp's reasoning was behind selecting those particular teachers, several of whom did not even teach college-preparation classes.

"Why do you think she didn't invite me?" Mary Catherine asked Jim, meeting her retired friend for coffee away from campus. "AVID's responsible for preparing most minority kids for college."

"Easy," Jim warned, pointing at her hair.

"Because I'm a blonde?"

"You don't fit the mold," he said.

"In other words, I can't represent Clairemont because I'm not a minority?"

Jim shrugged. "People are more interested in symbols than in content."

Mrs. Chipp was promoted at a time when affirmative action was the social engine that accelerated racial equality in America. Whatever her personal merits, the rapidity of her promotion to principal made her suspect in the eyes of some teachers. Yet it was not easy to be in her place, facing a predominantly white staff that was firmly entrenched. Mary Catherine was caught between the old guard, who resented her for putting minority students in advanced classes, and the new principal. She didn't know if Mrs. Chipp just didn't like her or if the principal was being instructed by higher-ups in the district headquarters to make her life miserable.

"Why are they coming down so hard on me?" Mary Catherine asked Jim. "I don't know if it's Blanche Chipp or the district or the superintendent."

"You're a subversive," he said, raising an eyebrow.

"My goals are anything but radical! The Declaration of Independence holds that all men are created equal. I believe in hard work, determination, and never giving up on a child. What's more American than that?"

"The Declaration was a revolutionary manifesto, and it's still shaking people up," Jim said. "You are dangerous because you are changing the system from within, and you're getting results."

"If it's subversive to fight for kids to achieve the American Dream, I'm proud to be a subversive," Mary Catherine said.

"Then you must be willing to take the consequences," he said.

Mary Catherine was neither saint nor martyr. Nor was the superintendent an authoritarian who crushed new ideas. Quite the contrary, when the AGP program stopped making progress and was criticized roundly as "lockstep learning," he slowly dismantled it. Later in his term, Dr. Payzant invited citizens to propose reform measures to make schools more democratic and community-oriented, and he was generally regarded as a forward-thinking and highly intelligent educator.

Even leaders can be petty, however. But Mary Catherine knew it was out of character for the superintendent to retaliate against a teacher whose low-budget program bested the district's million-dollar initiative.

Today, Dr. Payzant, who is superintendent of Boston Public Schools, praises AVID's curriculum, reliance on data, and use of tutors as harbingers of both the standards movement and national tutoring programs. But, looking back on the 1980s, he acknowledges that there were tensions between Mrs. Swanson and some district administrators who derogatorily labeled AVID as a "boutique" program—not to be taken seriously. He attributes this simmering conflict to resentment by people in a large organization of a teacher who received media attention promoting her program. Also, he reflects, the AVID program was "entrepreneurial—in the best sense of the word," but this raised eyebrows in an era before choice and risk-taking were valued in public education.

Dr. Payzant asserts that millions of dollars in budget cuts during the mid-1980s recession prevented the district from funding any new initiatives, including small programs like AVID, but Mrs. Swanson believes the district could have easily found the two thousand dollars per year necessary to keep the program going.

This larger context of educational trends underlies the climate in which the storm was brewing. But, for those caught in the vortex, it felt as if AVID was being scuttled and its treasures were being allowed to sink to the ocean floor of mediocrity.

Others sum things up less dramatically. "Some resented Mary Catherine's personality, and resentment against her was transferred into resentment against the program," says a former administrator who viewed the conflict from within the district headquarters.

In California, all ideas are reduced to bumper stickers: *Power to the teachers!* In the comic-book version of what happened at Clairemont High, the uppity white teacher had threatened an insecure black administrator. Mrs. Chipp depended on the establishment for her position, and Mrs. Swanson was fighting the establishment for her students' welfare. Both fought for the advancement of minorities, but the forces of change had placed them in opposition to each other.

Mary Catherine didn't know if she was exaggerating her fears or if she—and AVID—were really in jeopardy. All she knew was that the point of pressure was being applied by the principal.

Yet Mrs. Chipp had more issues than AVID to contend with that year. Her daughter Jacqueline, a junior at Howard University, and Jacqueline's fiancé had been walking across Dupont Circle in Washington, D.C., when she suddenly felt dizzy and blacked out. At the emergency room, the intern glanced at her youth and race, presumed that the cause of Jacqueline's black-out was a drug overdose, and looked no further for a cause. But Jacqueline didn't use drugs. Later in the semester, she had trouble focusing on exams and suffered severe headaches and was treated for migraine. Then, three months later, she had a seizure. A scan revealed a benign brain tumor that, because it had been left untreated, caused epilepsy. Her grades plunged, her driver's license was revoked, her fiancé broke up with her, and she was forced to move back to San Diego to live with her mother. Blanche Chipp was struggling with a tough job and caring for her daughter, a strain that would push anyone to the limits of endurance.

It was in this climate that Mrs. Chipp called Mrs. Swanson into her office for a special assignment. For once, the principal greeted her with a smile.

"Clairemont's accreditation is under review by the Western Association of Schools and Colleges," Mrs. Chipp said formally, lifting a pile of papers from her desk. "If we lose our accreditation, your students won't be able to get college credit for their courses."

"That would be terrible," Mary Catherine said, wondering what her boss was getting at.

"Indeed it would!" Blanche scowled. "That's why I want you to draft a comprehensive report on the school's performance over the past six years." She plopped the papers into the teacher's hands. "The report is due next month."

Mary Catherine was speechless. The WASC report was the principal's responsibility, not hers. It should have been drafted months ago. It required input from all academic and athletic departments, health and food services, students, parents, and the community. Mrs. Chipp had delegated the report to procrastinating staffers, and now the principal's job was on the line and Mary Catherine was supposed to save Blanche's rear end.

"I have no administrative experience to compile this report," Mary Catherine said. "I am a teacher. My students need me."

"You know how to write a report, don't you?" Mrs. Chipp shot back. "You *will* write this report. I am giving you a desk in the library."

"What about my classes?"

"You have expensive tutors," Blanche answered. "Your classroom is next-door to the library and you can monitor from there."

What if I refuse? Mary Catherine thought. If Clairemont lost its accreditation, none of the students would get credit for college-preparation classes. The whole purpose of AVID was for students to take college-preparation courses. If she refused, the answer was clear: *My students will suffer.*

"I will write the report," Mary Catherine said.

"My, my, aren't we acting like a D-I-V-A," Blanche sneered, spelling AVID backwards.

Mary Catherine was wearing high heels with blunt toes, and she struggled to restrain herself from kicking Blanche in the shins. The walk back to AVID class was the most bitter of Mary Catherine's teaching career. She felt used and disrespected, but she would not act like a victim. She would do this for all the students who were working for college credit, and she would not show AVID students her hurt and angry feelings. She would rely on her tutors and on the AVID students themselves, and she would be there for them before and after school.

The next day, she seated herself at the desk in the library, buckled down and started working. In the next weeks, she interviewed teachers, gathered statistics, and began writing. Inside, she seethed. She was appalled at having her values turned upside down, putting administrative duties over students.

After two weeks, her fingers were sore from batting the typewriter keys. She went to the principal with a modest request. "I would like an assistant to type up the report," she said. "I'm a teacher, not a typist."

Mrs. Chipp looked down at the floor, shaking her head. "After only two weeks, you are making demands of me!" she cried.

This, finally, broke Mary Catherine. She had worked so hard for so many years, never blaming others, always shouldering responsibility. She no longer had the strength to fight back. Stumbling back to the library, she felt utterly alone. Jim Grove was not there to support her. The district administrators, with the exception of the curriculum chief, were against her. After six years, AVID had not gained a secure source of financial support. She had pleaded for money from the board of education, but bureaucratic maneuvering had blocked her efforts. She had written grant proposals until she was blue in the face, but none had come in. She was spending over a thousand dollars a year of her own money to pay for tutors. The constant search for money and the lack of support from the district had drained her emotionally; today's indignity was the final blow.

Approaching her beloved classroom, the milestones of her career passed by. She had taught for 20 years, chaired the English Department, sent hundreds of students to college. When busing had scared other teachers away, she had stayed at Clairemont and welcomed the new students. Together, they had created a new program. It wasn't an alternative to affirmative action. It was positive preparation. And the results had been spectacular.

But now she was a glorified typist for a principal who neither respected nor supported her, nor valued her relationship with students. For besting the district, she was considered a threat to the system and should be crushed. Without outside support and funding, enthusiasm was not enough to sustain AVID. It would follow other doomed programs to the graveyard of discarded acronyms. For the first time, this visionary teacher could no longer see the future. All she knew was that her own survival as a self-respecting teacher was imperative if she was to be of any use to future students.

Mrs. Swanson sat down at the typewriter in the library and, as tears streamed down her cheeks, wrote her letter of resignation.

— KISMET —

The weighty, well-documented report to the accreditation commission was Mrs. Swanson's final gift to Clairemont High. She delivered it on deadline and it won Clairemont the highest accreditation rating possible.

With a heavy heart, she slipped the undelivered letter of resignation in a drawer and returned to teaching. The welcoming faces of the AVID students, so hopeful and appreciative, made her decision even more wrenching, for she could not tell them. How could she save AVID without abandoning them?

Two days later, she visited her old colleague Martha Tower. Martha had worked with Mary Catherine on many projects in the City Schools before moving to the County Department of Education, where Martha kept track of AVID's progress.

The city and county departments of education had separate administration centers and roles. San Diego City Schools, America's seventh-largest school district, was administered from an aging Ed Center in University Heights. The County Department of Education was responsible for the 43 districts in San Diego County.

Mrs. Swanson's efforts had been blocked by the city, for reasons that she could not understand. At the county, she thought, perhaps there might be support for her program.

"Martha, you'll never guess why I'm here," Mrs. Swanson said. "I've got to leave Clairemont. For years you've been telling me to go but I couldn't bear to abandon my students. Now I have no choice. To save AVID, I've got to replicate it. Can you help me?"

Martha listened sympathetically. "I'm sorry," she said. "I don't know of any openings."

When Mrs. Swanson left that day, she knew that if she didn't find another job, her family could make do. She wasn't in the same position as many teachers, who were two or three paychecks away from losing their mortgage. Yet she could not rip up the letter of resignation, even if it meant never again working in the San Diego schools. She could not return to Clairemont High in the fall.

When she faced her class, she could not look her students in the eye. Yet she could not look herself in the mirror if she backed down. She saw no way out. When her students left the AVID room after school, there was no Jim Grove to help her plot a strategy. She felt utterly alone in Room 206. How could she teach hope if she didn't feel any? West of Clairemont High, the sun sank into a brown layer of smog, a tarnished disk dissolving in gloom.

It was the lowest point of her career.

Next-door to Martha Tower's office worked an educator named Jack Tierney. A towering figure of a man with skin like red clay, Jack had a passion for helping the underdog. He was a former priest who brought a sense of mission to public education. He'd run a high school for juvenile offenders and had taken a Ph.D. in leadership, learning from brilliant minds like Rollo May and Max Lerner. No bureaucrat, Jack believed the County Office of Education should take a pioneering role as a laboratory for experimentation. "We are the research and development arm of public education," he would advocate. "Teachers in the trenches don't have time to write grants and develop curriculum." Jack was searching for small local programs that worked, and he was on a constant lookout for funding to support them. Jack had never met

Mrs. Swanson, much less spoken with her. Nor had he overheard the conversation between Martha and Mary Catherine.

Jack was a voracious reader. Every morning, he devoured the papers. Jack had read the profile about AVID in the *Los Angeles Times*. The article by Scott Harris was entitled "Minority Students Avid Fans of College Readiness Program."

The story began with a heartwarming profile of four immigrant girls who were studying geometry in a local college-preparation program. There were testimonials from students who had raised their grades from Cs to As and predictable words of praise from city school officials cornered by the reporter looking for a good quote. *Was it all lip service?* Jack wondered skeptically. The program had a feel-good name, AVID, like so many others that had impressed reporters and sank into oblivion.

What caught his eye was that the teacher kept records. The numbers were impressive: 170 students had completed the program—*all had gone on to college*. The budget? A $7,000 grant from Bank of America, which had run out, he noted.

The program reminded Jack of a successful initiative called Boost that he had worked on. The Navy had been searching for minority candidates for officer training. They scoured the ranks for enlisted men who showed leadership potential but who lacked basic skills. They put them through an intensive seven-month course at the Naval Training Center. It was competitive, but instead of a sink-or-swim approach, Boost provided tutoring and moral support.

Jack liked the idea that AVID was rigorous academically *and* intellectually supportive. It seemed highly effective and motivational, and it ran on a shoestring budget. He filed the article amid the piles on his desk and turned to other pressing duties.

A little while later, Jack had occasion to visit the State Office of Education in Sacramento. There, he listened to the grim statistics that revealed the failure of public schools to prepare under-represented students for California's preeminent universities. For once, the legislature was putting its wallet where its mouth was. Assemblywoman Sally Tanner sponsored legislation, Assembly Bill 2321, which was targeted to improve minority performance on college entrance exams. The State Office of Education put out a request for districts to apply for Tanner Grants to fund pilot programs.

It rang a bell. Jack flew back to San Diego. The next day, he barged into Martha Tower's office.

"Is this thing for real?" he asked, slapping down the *Times* article on her desk.

"You're damn right! It's the real thing," she said without hesitation. Jack sat down and quizzed Martha about the program and its young teacher.

So it was that two days after Mrs. Swanson left Martha Tower's office feeling utterly disconsolate, she got a call at school. A man with a booming voice introduced himself as Jack Tierney.

"I liked the article and checked you out with Martha Tower," he thundered. "If you're half as good as she says you are, and these minority college admissions figures hold up, you may be onto something big. I can't guarantee the County Office of Ed will support you, but maybe we can help you get some state funding to replicate this thing."

Mrs. Swanson was speechless.

— MIRACLES —

Quietly eating a homemade tuna fish sandwich at her desk, Mrs. Swanson got a call from Martha Tower at the County Office of Education.

"Dr. Rosander wants to bring a group of administrators and board members to observe the AVID program," Martha said.

"Dr. Rosander?" Mrs. Swanson cried, mid-bite, her mouth filled with pink albacore.

"Yes, Jerry Rosander, county superintendent of education," Martha laughed. Rosander was the top education official in San Diego County, overseeing state education programs for all the local school districts, including the City Schools. In California, local superintendents ran the schools on a day-to-day basis, while the county superintendent, who was appointed by a countywide board, administered state programs and provided services for the smaller school districts in the county.

"My God!" Mrs. Swanson swallowed. "One second." She dropped the bread crust into the wastebasket and hurried to get her appointment calendar, thinking: *I'll need at least a week to get things ready.* She composed herself. "When would Dr. Rosander like to come?"

"Two o'clock this afternoon."

"What an honor. Of course," Mrs. Swanson finally managed to reply, with the disquiet of a prisoner awaiting execution at dawn. Her mind raced. The visit was undoubtedly in response to Jack Tierney's call about the state grant. She couldn't miss this opportunity. After two years of struggling with grant applications and pleas for funding to keep AVID afloat, she had two hours to prepare for the visit of the top county educator. She modulated her voice to a semblance of dignity. "We are always delighted to receive visitors."

Mrs. Swanson bolted the rest of her lunch. It was noon, and school let out at 2:10. *How can I possibly round up the kids? They'll have to stay after school and miss the bus. No time to coach them.*

Struggling to contain her excitement and hide her anxiety, Mrs. Swanson announced the visit to her two afternoon AVID classes. She asked for volunteers to speak honestly about their personal experiences.

"Anything less than the truth will immediately be picked up by the county superintendent," she pleaded. "Just be yourselves."

She also asked a few faculty members with AVID students in their classes to attend. Hurriedly, she rearranged the cafeteria tables into a hollow square, dragging screeching chairs around the periphery. Somehow she managed to find a few bottles of soda pop and chips.

When the distinguished educators came through the door, Dr. Rosander introduced himself to Mrs. Swanson. In his mid-fifties, with a round face, sandy hair, and blue eyes, he was a man who appeared comfortable and pleasant in manner, but he had a non-committal air about him. He was there to inspect the program that the county was considering sponsoring for a grant application to the State of California.

Mrs. Swanson sized up "the Supe" as a hard nut to crack. She smiled sweetly, but with the steely determination of a nutcracker.

She touched the sleeve of his coat and led him to a corner. Up her own sleeve, she was in possession of an important bit of information. By coincidence, Mrs. Swanson had been reading her father's newspaper, the *Kingsburg Recorder,* which she received weekly by mail, when she came upon a news story about Dr. Rosander's appointment to the county superintendent position in San Diego. With surprise, she read that Rosander had grown up in her hometown and had attended the same high school. But he was of an older generation, and Mrs. Swanson was sure that she had never met him before.

She offered him a soft drink. "You and I have something in common, about which I'm certain you're unaware," Mrs. Swanson said, flashing her high-school cheerleader smile. "We're both from Kingsburg."

"Is that so?" he replied, poker-faced.

"My name is Mary Catherine Swanson," she interjected, hoping to make a connection. To no avail. "But my maiden name is Jacobs. My father is the publisher of the *Kingsburg Recorder,* where I read about your appointment as county superintendent when you moved to San Diego."

"Nice to meet you," he said with an apparent lack of enthusiasm, and he sat down.

Chairs scraped as the dignitaries, students, and teachers took their seats around the hollow rectangle. Dr. Rosander sat at the head, with Mary Catherine on the far side of the table. Half a dozen students slouched or sat bolt upright, depending on their personalities, around the periphery.

Dr. Rosander began the meeting. "We are here to learn about AVID. I would like to go around the table and hear each person say something about the program."

The students shifted nervously in their seats. They had no idea why the group of educators was visiting, only that it was important to Mrs. Swanson. She did not discuss the program's monetary difficulties with her students, not wanting to alarm them with the fact that she had virtually run out of money to pay tutors. She especially did not want the underclassmen to know that AVID was hanging by a thread and she might not be there for them next year.

With amazing aplomb, for they had not had a moment to pre-pare, the students offered simple but eloquent testimonies about AVID's effect on their personal lives. Their serious tone was bro-ken occasionally by nervous laughter, as when one student admit-ted that she hated taking Cornell notes and another confessed that he was proud to be a nerd.

Finally, it came time for a petite girl to speak. Her name was Li and she had a shy expression in her eyes, like a gray cloud over the Mekong River of her birth. Her long black hair was immaculately combed straight down her back. Her voice was so quiet that the educators had to lean forward to hear her story.

"Mrs. Swanson came to me and told me I should be in AVID because I am getting good grades, but bad grades in English because I come from Vietnam two years ago and I don't know English very well." She stared down at her delicate hands clutched together on her lap and avoided the eyes staring from around the table. "Mrs. Swanson also told me if I come in AVID I have to take advanced English. I was so scared! I didn't do good in English. But Mrs. Swanson say she will help me, and so I come and I work very hard." Her head began to rise with these proud words, and a smile broke forth like the sun returning after the monsoon.

She looked the county superintendent straight in the eye. "I can do it," she said with determination. "I'm getting As and Bs. I will go to college and study English."

Mary Catherine felt awe at the quiet blossoming of this child. The deputy superintendent, a brass-tacks man, wiped dampness from his right cheek.

Two honors-level math and science teachers spoke about the effects they had seen in their classes. At first, they had opposed allowing students who had not fulfilled preparatory requirements into their classes, fearing they would fail. Yet they noticed that some kids were assiduously taking notes. AVID students started out behind their peers but, over the course of the year, they moved up.

"I was skeptical and resisted AVID at first," one teacher admitted.

Mary Catherine held her tongue. Painfully, she remembered the "cheating scandal."

The teachers spoke about the collegial atmosphere that developed when teachers worked together to help AVID students.

When all had spoken, Dr. Rosander gazed around the table and said, "Now I would like to tell you a story about a boy named Jerry Rosander. By looking at me, with my blonde hair and blue eyes, you may not think I was a disadvantaged student—but I was."

Describing his own boyhood to the AVID students, Dr. Rosander spoke in the third person. "Jerry was the descendant of Swedish immigrants, one of nine children. When his family arrived in America, they spoke no English. They settled in a rural California community and worked hard for little money. When Jerry was in eighth grade, his father died. Jerry had to get a job to help support his family."

Pausing, Dr. Rosander glanced at Mrs. Swanson. Then he continued to tell his story, switching back to the first person. "That's how I got hired at a small-town newspaper, sweeping up the back room."

Mary Catherine's ears perked up, remembering her father's print shop. Every evening, the floor had been covered with shards of lead from the linotype and strips of newsprint sheared from the machines that folded the newspaper.

"I absolutely loved sports," the county superintendent was saying. "I told my boss, the editor, that I aspired to write sports stories like Red Smith. He told me to start writing about high-school games—baseball, football. He offered to work with me, and he promised me, 'When your stories get good enough, I will print them in the paper. Maybe I'll even give you a by-line.'" Dr. Rosander paused in his reminiscence, his blue eyes piercing and his voice deep and close.

Students gazed at him with rapt attention, struck that the school chief had once been like them.

"That editor was a very tough taskmaster and worked me very hard!" the county superintendent told them with a wry laugh. "Five days a week, I swept the print shop, and five days a week I worked on writing stories. Every day, he marked up my draft with red pencil. It hurt."

The students gave their teacher a sidelong glance, knowing what it was like to get their English papers marked up with a red pen.

"It took me a full year before the editor said I was good enough to be published in the paper," Dr. Rosander smiled with triumph.

He narrowed his eyes, pointing his finger didactically. "You need to know that my grandparents had little schooling, and my parents did not have a high-school education. So their goal was to see that all nine of their children learned English and graduated from high school. That was as far as they could dream."

The students from Mexico and Vietnam looked up. Their parents also had been forced to leave school—to work in the fields, or escape the communists.

"But this editor had bigger dreams," Dr. Rosander said. "He wasn't content for me to graduate from high school. He had graduated from the Columbia University School of Journalism." He swallowed hard, fighting back tears. "He gave me confidence that I could go to college. When I left my boyhood home, I went to the University of California at Berkeley. And today I am county superintendent of schools—a job my parents didn't even know existed."

The room was absolutely silent, except for a loose window shade batted by the afternoon breeze from the sea.

"It was that newspaper editor who taught me carefully and gave me the courage to go on to college," Dr. Rosander said, turning slowly to face Mary Catherine. "Today, I have met his daughter, who is doing the same thing for you."

— LIMBO —

Mrs. Swanson faced her last class before graduation. The grant proposal had been submitted, but she had not heard back. If approved, she would move to the county to disseminate the AVID program to other schools. If denied, she would not return to Clairemont High in the fall.

Either way, today was her last day of teaching.

She gazed at the faces flushed with excitement for summer vacation. The seniors with tears in their eyes as they signed each other's yearbooks. Should she tell them? The ones bound for college would keep in touch, but the younger kids would return and find her missing. She had recruited them and made them promise to stay in AVID for four years, and now she was the one dropping out. *How could she let them down?*

"Mrs. Swanson, Mrs. Swanson!" insistent voices were calling her. She stood mutely before them, trembling within. Her rage against the system was replaced by an overwhelming sense of loss.

She had been a teacher for 20 years. She dreaded not knowing if ever again she would walk through a classroom door. Because she did not know, she could not say anything to the kids. All she knew was that when the younger students came back in the fall, another teacher would be in her place. Because she could not tell them why she was leaving, they would feel abandoned.

The final bell rang.

"Mrs. Swanson, see you next September!"

She nodded silently. Pressed against the royal blue door as their bodies swept past her, Mary Catherine struggled not to betray a maudlin display of emotion. She would not lay her problems on their shoulders. A stabbing guilt impaled her, twisting her painted smile into a grotesque grimace.

One by one, they straggled out the door. She waved until her hand hung motionless in the air, holding onto the last rays in their sunlit hair.

That final Friday at Clairemont High, Mrs. Swanson and loyal tutors Debbie, Lisa, and James packed up. Her entire teaching career fit into 26 legal-sized cardboard file boxes. Everything was color-coded: orange for curricula, blue for college outreach, and so on. When the bulletin boards were empty, the bookshelves clean, and the collegiate banners taken down, she took one last look. Then she left the room where she had transformed students' lives and had been transformed by them.

Outside, the liquid ambar trees were green. The lunch court was virtually empty. The institutional green walls were as lonely as a prison walkway. She turned in her keys at the office, then checked in her audio-visual equipment. It was 11:30 A.M.

In a Clairemont tradition, the faculty celebrated the end of the school year by breaking bread and drinking wine and beer at a local restaurant. This year, they met at the Windsock, a barnlike bar and grill cheek by jowl beside the airline runway at Lindbergh Field. Under the roaring jets, they attempted to make jovial conversation, amends for misunderstandings, and romantic passes. There was much boisterousness and laughter as the teachers let loose. Then they got down to the program: Gifts were presented to retiring teachers.

Jim Grove, who had retired two years before, joined Mary Catherine at a semi-circular booth. She smiled numbly at her ally and mentor. *I'm not really with it,* her eyes spoke across the table. She felt sadly disconnected. A misfit.

"You're not your usual buoyant self," Jim whispered.

She shrugged, dodging his inquisitive gaze. She did not feel pain. She did not feel relief. She did not feel anything. She was in limbo.

On the long drive home, she passed below the mesa where Clairemont High stood. She did not look up. She did not look back.

Her son, Tommy, was home for the first day of summer vacation. Mary Catherine and Tommy had always been close. But the onset of adolescence mysteriously distanced them. She knew how to deal with ornery teenagers at school, but it was not so easy when her own son mocked her silently.

Early the next week, she called Jack Tierney at the County Office of Education. His booming voice lifted her spirits. "You're a free woman!"

"Yes, I suppose so," she said uncertainly.

"Jerry thought you were terrific," Jack said. "He'll move Heaven and Earth to get you over at county."

Mary Catherine had the sinking sense that Dr. Rosander was more committed to helping Ed Jacobs's daughter than rescuing AVID from oblivion.

"Any word from Sacramento?" she asked.

"I've heard there's an opening for an editor in the communications department," Jack said, sidestepping her question.

"Editing?" Her stomach shrank. Proofreading papers was the teaching task she least enjoyed. At least the students' essays were imaginative, stimulating. Editing bureaucratic jargon blurred her eyes.

Her unenthusiastic tone, she realized years later, might have tipped Jack off to her difficult position, because he said: "I'll check up on it."

"Thanks," she said, holding onto the phone as if it were a railing. She heard a dim drum beating funereally:

Limbo at school,

Limbo at home,

Limbo on the telephone.

Limbo, limbo, limbo . . .

As the weeks passed, she began to relax into the rhythm of summer. The school bells stopped clanging in her ears and she began to sense subtle changes: the leaves unfolding, the water trickling in the sunlit garden, the growing strength of Tommy's limbs. She lay in a hammock of timelessness, suspended between the breakneck pace of teaching and the ambling gait of a free soul, wandering. For the first time in her life, she had no definite future. No immediate demands. No responsibilities beyond the circle of her family. She smiled with wicked pleasure: *I could get used to a life of ease!*

In the third week of June, her soul was awakened from limbo.

"Mary Catherine?" Jack boomed over the phone from the County Office of Education. "Grant came through! Half your salary paid by the county, other half by the grant. You've got to replicate this thing."

Her heart rejoiced: *AVID has a second chance!* A whole new life was opening before her as the gates of responsibility closed behind. A tremendous challenge faced her. Jack thundered in her ear: "Report for work July first."

The real challenge in education
is not to come up with a sensible new idea.
The toughest challenge for an educator
is
to break down the barriers
that threaten to block or destroy
the implementation of a good idea
at every step of its development.

—Mary Catherine Swanson

PART THREE

DISSEMINATION

1986–1998

— TRAILER DAZE —

"Disseminate AVID throughout the San Diego County Schools."

This was Mary Catherine's one-sentence assignment from the State Department of Education. The rest was up to her. The job was dauntingly simple. As simple as Johnny Appleseed, planting seeds of learning in frontier soil. But how to purify AVID's essence into a seed? And how to protect the vulnerable new hybrid from indigenous weeds, predatory bugs, exposure to the harsh sun, and funding drought?

Many teachers dream of propagating their best teaching techniques, but most are mercifully spared the agony of stuffing a lifetime of teaching skills into a mimeographed curriculum handbook. Few watch their efforts survive past the seedling stage before being scythed by budget cuts or poisoned by pesticides.

On the first of July, 1986, Mary Catherine reported to work at the County Office of Education. She knew only two people: Superintendent Jerry Rosander and Jack Tierney, manager of research and development. Martha Tower, who'd been instrumental in helping AVID receive the Tanner Grant, was moving to the University of California at San Diego.

The County Office of Education shimmered in a sunlit campus of modern buildings overlooking Mission Valley. Mary Catherine was assigned an office in Room 701. But the addresses on the buildings only went from 100 to 600.

She finally found 701—a metallic trailer baking in the July sun. Her new office was in the middle of a parking lot allotted to a fleet of county-owned vehicles. The white trailer seemed as isolated as a one-room schoolhouse on the prairie. She felt like a new teacher showing up on the first day of school, but this time her only students were ghosts.

The rickety steps were broken and, when she unlocked the door, the room gave off the stale odor of a tomb.

Tottering on high heels, she toted 26 file boxes up the steps, threw open the door, and stacked them in a space seven paces long and five wide, crammed with three banged-up desks and three chairs, but no file cabinets or partitions. After the light and activity of her AVID classroom, she felt like she was entering a prison cell reserved for rebels condemned to solitary confinement.

There were no phones in the trailer. No restroom. No insulation. No fan or air conditioner. The closest toilet was in a unisex bathroom in the nearby "Hope Trailer," housing a crowded outreach program for severely disabled children. It meant a long wait, but at least there were people to talk to.

She stood in the suffocating trailer and wondered: *How am I going to get a program going without a phone, a file cabinet, a secretary? In this cell, how am I going to keep my sanity?*

At 10 A.M., she went to Jack Tierney for help. In nearly every bureaucracy there exists a big-hearted individual who is willing to help a newcomer and, in this case, it was Jack. He showed her how to requisition a phone and office supplies. He even volunteered his secretary, Xana Ivory, to help part time until a secretary was hired for Mary Catherine by the grant.

Xana was not pleased to be sent from Jack's beautiful office to a steamy trailer, but she put a good face on it. Xana knew the ropes. She would become Mary Catherine's first tutor in the art of effectively managing a large bureaucracy.

Mary Catherine gazed at the cardboard boxes resting on the floor. Each file in the boxes contained a story, an exercise, a discovery, an example of a student's work, a statistical record. These were the living and breathing testaments of six years of AVID classes. Now they were reduced to mute boxes of papers taking up valuable space.

Mary Catherine had to organize her materials to reflect, accurately, the materials, observations, and statistical data she had painstakingly collected. Yet if she *only* categorized the voluminous contents of these boxes, she might never gain the imaginative space to discover within the conflicting chaos and order of her former classroom a unified theory of learning. AVID, she believed, held a philosophical key that could unlock the doors of children's minds. It provided a discipline and structure to teach children how to survive in a hostile world.

A heavy stamping of feet shook her from her daydreams as a violent force rocked the trailer back and forth and, for a moment, Mary Catherine feared the trailer was being sucked into the black funnel of a twister. The door flew open and a lumbering creature, almost superhuman in size, crashed through the threshold, bumping into the ceiling and walls. A deep voice announced the arrival of her new roommate. This Paul Bunyan of a man was the new science coordinator for the County Schools. He was going through a divorce, she learned, overhearing his end of their post-connubial shouting match over the phone. Later, he would slam the door so hard that a window actually shattered, allowing a bit of fresh air into the trailer.

Mary Catherine stacked her file cabinets into a Great Wall to keep barbarians from the gates. Head down, she found a protected place to organize the materials from the past and conjure up AVID's future.

If I am going to disseminate AVID, I need to answer two questions: What is my approach? What materials will I need?

The silence was unnerving. How could one think about anything important in this infernal trailer? She was used to being interrupted every five minutes in the AVID classroom and could not concentrate on one thought. The sudden lack of ringing bells, student melodramas, and constant interruptions nearly drove her to distraction.

For the first time, she had to create a coherent framework and build a logical system of implementation. This would require enormous concentration, and she didn't know if she were up to the task, but she looked forward to it.

As a classroom teacher, Mrs. Swanson had always stayed after school, working 10- or 12-hour days without looking at the clock. In the claustrophobic trailer, cut off from kids and everything she loved, she watched the second hand crawling. For the first time, she could not wait to leave work. But she was trapped—her husband had the car.

"Tom, if you are one minute past five o'clock to pick me up, I am going to go crazy!" she whispered on the phone. "Please, don't be late."

— AH HA! —

Classroom teachers rarely have the opportunity to reform public education, and few succeed in replicating their successes in other classrooms, let alone in other school districts. In 1986, the chances of a high-school teacher in San Diego creating a classroom-based education reform movement that would spread across the United States and encircle the globe was almost nil. Yet this was what Mary Catherine Swanson would accomplish in the next decade and a half.

In telling her story, Mary Catherine makes one thing clear: She never set out to change the face of public education. Rather, she faced obstacles and found ways to overcome them. This sounds modest, but in fact it is how she worked, with determination, creativity, and outbursts of laughter, but never tears. At least, not in public.

To effect change, one needs a power base. In education, there are at least five power bases: institutional, economic, political, temporal, and research. Teachers may have the power to affect lives, but not to change the system.

On the most basic level, individual teachers do not have institutional, economic, or political power bases within the school system from which to launch education reform. Principals follow the superintendent's agenda, teachers' unions are primarily interested in protecting salaries and benefits, and school boards represent community and business interests. Finally, education research is generally conducted by universities or foundations, and classroom teachers don't generally have access to research from which to shape education reforms.

While she was at Clairemont High, Mrs. Swanson did not have a power base on any of these levels. But she *did* have the power of experience. When they counted it up, she and Jim Grove discovered that they had nearly half a century of combined teaching time—a vast base of practical expertise.

At the County Office of Education, Mrs. Swanson had a small base of funding and political support. She also had access to systematic educational research. It was a joy to escape from the trailer and spend hours in the county's large professional library for teachers. There she discovered authors like William Glasser, whose learning theory complemented her classroom experience. Glasser analyzed the needs of students. His research revealed that students gained a deeper understanding when they worked together than when they studied alone. That was what collaborative learning was all about in AVID.

Ah ha!

She read reports that confirmed the role of the teacher as mentor and facilitator. *That's exactly what we were doing in AVID.* Her job as an AVID teacher was to bring in as many resources as she could so that tutors could use them to teach and kids to learn.

Ah ha!

Emerging from her research, Mary Catherine discovered a basis for her education theory. *A teacher should only do what a teacher, uniquely, can do.* In AVID, she had learned to delegate many tasks so that she could focus on the unique functions—creative lesson planning, one-on-one sessions with students, and organizational strategies—that had the greatest effect. While tutors took over routine tasks, she saved herself for problem solving.

She discovered the work of Uri Treisman, a professor of mathematics at UC Berkeley. Dr. Treisman asked: Why do Asians typically do better in calculus than whites, Hispanics, and African Americans? His research revealed that it was not an innate characteristic, but that Asians succeeded because of their study habits. They worked together on homework—*collaborative learning*. Mrs. Swanson was amazed that Dr. Treisman also used writing as a tool for learning—writing, inquiry, collaboration. To her joy, he succeeded on the post-secondary level, as AVID did in high school.

She had many *Ah has!* Her reading confirmed that what she had created with Jim Grove's help was cutting-edge stuff. It was supported by research. They just hadn't known it.

At the County Office of Education, Mrs. Swanson had a foothold. Now the onus was on her to turn those 26 file boxes into an AVID curriculum.

That first summer, she had no grand design, no road map—only a clear vision of what students needed and a strong will to move mountains that blocked their path. She had taught kids that *"We shall overcome"*—not somewhere, someday, but right here, today.

She had better hurry. By September, AVID had to be up and running in 12 schools. How could she possibly do it alone?

— LISA IS THE GLUE —

Lisa was living in a little cottage across from the lettuce fields in Salinas, Northern California, and was working at the Western Stage Theater. It was *East of Eden* country, and she was in love with melodrama.

At age 24, she had turned down an offer from Stanford University's prestigious teacher-training program that offered a master's degree in education. Instead, she had begun to pursue her Broadway dream and had taken a job as stage manager in this dusty farm community.

One evening in July, she received a phone call. Lisa instantly recognized the caller's voice.

"Help! I'm trapped in a trailer!" Mrs. Swanson cried, half in jest, half in desperation. "I've got to put together an AVID program for the fall. Could you help me write a handbook?"

You want me? Lisa still felt guilty for shooting her mouth off to the reporter and nearly destroying Mrs. Swanson's career. After seeing the way the school district had humiliated Mary Catherine, Lisa had decided teaching was not the career for her.

"We need to go through all those file boxes and write an AVID curriculum," Mary Catherine was saying.

The "we" was a sign of her mentor's trust. How could she abandon Mary Catherine? On the other hand, how could she leave the Western Stage?

"I really need you," her mentor said.

"I'll be right down," Lisa promised.

A few days later, she packed up and drove south, crossing half the length of California. An hour north of San Diego, she got off the freeway and headed toward Olivenhain. The hilly countryside, dotted with avocado trees and vineyards, looked like Tuscany, with homes sequestered beneath shade trees.

Lisa breathed deeply in the air of peace and solitude. Mary Catherine greeted her with head thrust back and arms spread wide. They hugged. No longer teacher and tutor, but surrogate mother and daughter, partners in a bold new enterprise.

"I've made up the guest room." Mary Catherine led her into the house. Lisa found herself in a cozy bedroom with French doors opening to a private garden. The house was filled with books. In the backyard, a sheep grazed. Tommy was rearing a lamb for his 4-H Club. She felt like a part of the family.

Lisa started working the next morning. There was a primitive Apple IIe computer at Mary Catherine's home and a typewriter in the trailer. There was a lot of cutting and pasting to do, and Lisa was the glue.

Sometimes she worked at the house, using the writing program on Tommy's computer; other times, she went back and forth to the County Office with Mrs. Swanson. By day, Mrs. Swanson wrote the AVID handbook. Lisa worked on the introduction. At meals, they chewed on AVID ideas. At night, they talked AVID philosophy. In their separate beds, they dreamed AVID. On waking, they performed the AVID catechism, or, rather, struggled to create one. Lisa would ask questions, provoking Mrs. Swanson to translate the program in her head into words set down on paper. In dialogue, they organized the material catalogued in the filing boxes into sections of a handbook:

- Course outline: What is AVID?
- Program description
- Objectives
- Evidence of need
- Evidence of effectiveness
- Adaptability: How AVID would fit in other schools
- Responsibilities of everyone on the team
- Step-by-step approach to implementation
- How to recruit students
- Teaching philosophy and tutoring role
- Counseling
- Parental involvement
- Faculty involvement
- Campuswide impact
- How to evaluate the program
- Gaining public support

The work was incredibly strenuous: long hours, little sleep, constant hassles, lack of outside help, punishing deadlines, unbelievable glitches, insane demands. Yet it was fun. Mrs. Swanson loved logical thinking. Organization gave her aesthetic pleasure. The lessons she had taught her students in essay writing—brainstorm ideas, create an outline, write a powerful thesis, back it up with evidence, expand the scope, deepen meaning, edit, revise, rewrite, rewrite!—gave structure to this immense work. They worked one on one and brought in more team members to work collaboratively. Nonstop work, work, work.

They fell into bed exhausted every night and awoke before dawn. To keep their spirits up, they sang a refrain from the song "Happy Talk" in the musical *South Pacific*.

If you don't have a dream . . .
How you gonna make
a dream come true?

But would the dream come true?

— AVID HANDBOOK —

It was a blessing in disguise to be in that trailer, because nobody knew Mrs. Swanson was there. The phone hardly ever rang and nobody disturbed her. Once she had adjusted emotionally to the quiet, she could concentrate more deeply on organizing and writing.

Folders opened their wings and flew into logical places in the outline. Colored files opened magically. Materials slipped into their proper places. Student writing models that had been buried for years sprang back to life. The models were each reproduced in the student's original handwriting, for which she needed to get copyright permissions. The 16 Writing Domains that she had worked so hard to create with UCSD fit perfectly in the new AVID curriculum.

She had written this handbook with her body and soul, day by day, in the countless acts of teaching. And now she was finally writing it down in words, sentences, chapters, and sections.

Not that the words sang poetically. No, she recognized the flaws in conception and execution. So she insisted on writing on the cover, for all to see:

Working First Edition

She enlisted Sam Bristol, a former tutor, to design the cover. He took an antique diagram, "Kepler's Cosmic Mystery," that illustrated the integration of all parts of the universe, as a template. Then Sam took the AVID logo, designed by a former Clairemont student, Natalie Zhu, and placed the AVID triangle in the center of the cover's universe.

"We were unifying curricula, faculty, community, parents, and tutors with students at the center," Mary Catherine recalls with a smile, glowing faintly with memories. "It was a major work: to take what was in my head and create a philosophy of teaching and a step-by-step approach for implementation."

It was major, indeed. In two months, she wrote a 100-page implementation strategy. Lisa wrote a beautiful introduction. Sam edited, sitting three inches from Mary Catherine, cramped on a table in the trailer. Hundreds of curriculum pages were revised. A giant work of cut and paste. The book was printed on an ancient computer printer. The letters were so light they were hard to read. Reams were hand-punched on a three-hole punch.

By September, the entire *AVID Handbook and Curriculum Guide* was finished. It was over 500 pages long and 3 inches thick, but the 3-ring binder was divided into sections and marked by thumbnail indexes that were clearly organized for a teacher's convenience. A new AVID teacher did not have to master the entire handbook in order to begin instructing an AVID class. Instead, the teacher was given a sequential guide to a year-long series of lesson plans and student exercises for each grade in high school, a guide that set clear goals and expectations, but allowed for flexibility and creativity. Accompanying the lessons were realistic examples of essays, Cornell notes, and assignment schedules that had been created by actual AVID students.

This book became the AVID "bible," but it was not treated as gospel. On the contrary, it was a work in progress, open to new insights and improved exercises. The binder could be snapped open and pages inserted, removed, or replaced. Since 1986, the *AVID Handbook and Curriculum Guide* has been edited, revised, expanded, and reissued in a dozen editions. But its fundamental philosophy and organization remain intact.

The handbook addresses issues of importance not only to teachers, but also to administrators, tutors, students, and parents. It shows teachers how to organize, shape, teach, support, and motivate an AVID class, from recruitment through graduation—and how to involve colleagues in the creation of an AVID Site Team. Administrators use the handbook to gain an overview of AVID's organizational structure and philosophy and to learn steps to implement a new AVID program in a school system. Tutors use it to learn how to mentor students by challenging them to ask questions, *not* by giving them the answers. The handbook provides students with practical exercises that help them schedule assignments, prepare for tests, study in groups, set goals, brainstorm ideas, and organize essays. It suggests social functions to bring parents and guardians into the classroom, and it offers ways for families to create a home environment that fosters learning.

Dog-eared copies of the handbook can be found in AVID classrooms; new copies are available from the AVID Center in San Diego. Generations of AVID teachers have contributed to the evolving handbook. Fourteen years after its creation, the *AVID Handbook and Curriculum Guide* stands as a masterwork—a blueprint for educational reform in the twenty-first century.

— TOE IN THE POOL —

In the midst of this all-out creative effort, Mrs. Swanson was called away on a mission of proselytism. Every summer, the San Diego County Office of Education hosted a retreat for school superintendents, held at a resort in Palm Springs. The desert in July is hellish, and there was no place on Earth that Mrs. Swanson would rather avoid. But, to disseminate the AVID program throughout San Diego, she would have to win over the superintendents of districts large and small. San Diego County is immense, stretching roughly 65 miles north from the Mexican border to Orange County; 56 miles east from the Pacific coast to the desert of Imperial County. The San Diego Unified School District is the largest in the county and the seventh-largest in the United States. It is also the most urban district in the County of San Diego.

The retreat attracted superintendents from smaller rural and suburban districts, serving a diverse array of students. But the honchos had one thing in common—they were all men.

Mrs. Swanson showed up to discover that she was the only teacher, one of the few attendees under 50, and one of the few females. She had a terrible cold. The only respite from the heat was a kidney-shaped swimming pool. After the meetings, the "Supes" stripped off their ties. Sporting tropical shirts, they lounged with margaritas, telling off-color jokes in the shade of plastic umbrellas.

In their fishbowl offices, these men were constantly assailed by testy board members, taxpayers, teachers, parents, reporters, religious fanatics . . . the California menagerie. The guardians of political correctness policed their every move. No wonder they enjoyed cutting loose once a year.

One well-lubricated superintendent sat down by the pool and launched an attack on his teaching staff. His scatological comments had his cronies crowing with delight.

Mary Catherine was no prude. She could laugh at a joke, slap her sides, and stomp her feet. But she could not bear hearing an egotistical bureaucrat talking down teachers.

Mary Catherine had come to test the waters. She discovered that some of the men who ran school systems had tremendous egos and that they showed little respect for the professionals who taught students. Some were particularly demeaning to women. She removed her toe from the pool and withdrew from the group.

Driving back to San Diego, she wondered: *How am I ever going to convince these administrative "edu-crats" to adopt a teacher-centered program?*

— THE PITCH —

In the fall of 1986, Mrs. Swanson prepared her first campaign. Its goal: to convince a dozen schools to try out the AVID program. She set out to meet with district superintendents on their turf. This time, she must hold her nose and jump into the water up to her neck.

She needed an insider to help her get a foot in the door, and she needed statistics to build a case for need. Was there a fundamental inequity in public education? Did a particular district fail to provide opportunities for all students? If she could establish inequity, then the superintendent might be eager to find practical ways to reduce the achievement gap. AVID's record would sell itself.

Jack Tierney threw her a lifeline. As director of the County Office's Department of Evaluation, Dr. Tierney had access to data from every district in San Diego. The problem was that the data were too generalized to reveal the gap in school performance between whites and minorities.

"I think I can help you," Jack smiled, eyes twinkling in his ruddy face. Within a few days, his office disaggregated the districtwide data by ethnicity and gender. What emerged was an appalling portrait of the inequities in public education. District by district, school by school, the evidence of need was compelling.

"Thank you, Jack," Mary Catherine said almost apologetically, because she had a further request. "Could you help set up meetings?"

"Happy to call those good ol' boys for you," he assured her.

Armed with hard data and the *AVID Handbook and Curriculum Guide,* Mrs. Swanson ventured forth from the trailer into the lion's den. Or, rather, dens. There were 17 secondary districts in San Diego County, and she visited each one.

Once she got into a superintendent's office, her fear left her.

"Are you committed to provide equal education to all students?" she asked.

"Of course!"

"Look how your district is doing in comparison to others," she said, flipping through her notes to a chart.

"Not bad," he smiled with self-satisfaction.

"Now look how your students *of color* compare to the Anglos in your district."

The suburban superintendent's face fell. It was abundantly clear that each district was failing to live up to expectations. She had the superintendent's attention now.

"I have some research I would like to share with you," she said, tapping the chart. Then she flipped to the latest achievement scores comparing schools in San Diego Unified. "Clairemont has a high minority population, but its test scores are at the top," she pointed out proudly.

"I see," the superintendent nodded slightly, raising his eyebrows. "What, Mrs. Swanson, do you think accounts for that?"

"This," she said, plopping the three-inch thick AVID handbook on his desk. "At Clairemont, we created a program called AVID that challenges every student with rigorous curricula and provides strong academic and social support," she explained.

"What does this AVID stand for?"

"*Avidus,* which means 'eager to learn.'" She talked about determination, individual responsibility, group support. "Achievement is not an accident. It is the result of a focused process of learning based on writing, inquiry, and collaboration. The AVID curriculum was developed in my classroom by dozens of students, tutors, and teachers. The program begins with recruitment and ends with college admission. A step-by-step implementation guide is described in this handbook. The curriculum is laid out, week by week, grade by grade, for four years. Here are models of student work, exercises, binder checks, tutoring lessons. It's common sense. It works."

She shoved newspaper reprints before the surprised superintendent's eyes. The headlines caused them to nearly pop out of his head.

"Ninety-three percent go to college?"

"Yes, and most of them are still enrolled."

He leaned back in his chair and lifted his chin. His gaze was respectful and curious, as if he had just seen her for the first time. She seized the moment.

"I've received state funding to implement this program in your district, if you are interested."

"How much will it cost?"

"Staff development will cost you nothing. You will have to pay college tutors minimum wage. We have no extra budget for teachers' time."

"Well, this sounds interesting," he acknowledged. "Of course, I can't make any decisions today. But I'd like you to talk with our principal."

"When?" she pressed. "School is about to begin."

"I'll call him right now." He scribbled a name on a piece of paper.

"Thank you," she smiled genuinely as she passed him a heavy white binder containing the handbook. "This is for you to keep." As she turned to go, he stood up and extended his hand.

Then she drove immediately to the high school. Once she was in the principal's office, she pulled out the specific site data for that school. It was interesting to see the reactions: dismay, anger, disbelief. She came to realize, after several meetings, that the more dedicated the principals were to helping all their students, the more eager they were to confront the data, without rationalization or denial or self-incrimination, as a helpful tool. The weaker principals, in her judgment, either made up excuses for the school's poor performance or, worse, saw themselves as victims of a the changing student population and blamed the students. When principals avoided taking personal responsibility for their schools, was it any wonder that teachers cast blame and students avoided responsibility?

When principals showed genuine interest, Mrs. Swanson invited them to bring motivated teachers to visit the AVID classroom at Clairemont High. Now she was getting close to the people who mattered most—teachers. If she could get a few good teachers into an AVID classroom and let them feel the excitement of tutors planting seeds in young minds . . . what trees might grow?

— ROAD TO AVID —

Oceanside is the northernmost beach town in San Diego County, a palm-lined picture postcard of the 1950s. Yet in the mid 1980s, Oceanside was closer to South Central Los Angeles, Vietnam, and Mexico than Norman Rockwell's America. It borders Camp Pendleton, which was the staging area for the U.S. Marines during the Vietnam War. After the fall of Saigon, it became a massive refugee camp for tens of thousands of IndoChinese boat people.

The complexion of the Oceanside schools changed radically in the 1980s, as they absorbed the children of African American soldiers, Hispanic farm laborers, and Southeast Asians. Many spoke no English. Some came from preliterate cultures. The principal of Oceanside High was suddenly dealing with students from trouble spots around the world. Faced with language, cultural, and economic barriers, many of the children were going nowhere.

When Mrs. Swanson paid a visit to Oceanside High, the principal became excited by the program's potential. He talked up AVID to his faculty. If they were interested in visiting an AVID class at Clairemont, they had to apply to his office. He rented a minibus and brought 15 teachers down the coastal highway to San Diego.

In the AVID classroom, they were greeted by Grant Hopewell,
Mrs. Swanson's successor. Thirty-eight years old, with a salt-and-
pepper mustache and a yellow pullover, Mr. Hopewell was a quiet-
spoken, very caring English teacher. He was selected as her successor because of his strong mentoring skills and his incredible
commitment to students. He did not have an insincere bone in his
body. That day, he was relaxed and warm. His "soft and fuzzy"
personality contrasted with Mrs. Swanson's academically demanding mien, and the feel of the classroom reflected his character. Yet
the AVID curriculum, structure, and routine were functioning like
clockwork.

In an essay, "The Road to AVID," Mr. Hopewell would later
write:

> Imagine an educational program where students succeed.
> Picture a well-equipped classroom of smiling, engaging ethnic
> minority and economically under-represented students dis-
> cussing the moral dilemmas of *Julius Caesar,* or considering
> the socio-economic landscape of Germany, circa 1930. And
> imagine a cadre of 45 high-school seniors graduating from one
> program with college acceptance letters in hand to such pres-
> tigious institutions as UC Berkeley and Stanford University.

When he came to Clairemont as a substitute teacher, Mr.
Hopewell wrote, he could not imagine such an exciting teaching
and learning environment. In his prior teaching assignments,

> I had learned to adjust my teaching style to accommodate
> lackadaisical students, busy parents, and, more often than not,
> neutral school administrators who were too preoccupied with
> issues other than what was going on in the classroom.
> Nothing sinister colored my desire to teach, but I was almost
> without purpose.

"Teaching AVID," he wrote, "changed all that."

Now the teachers from Oceanside High crowded into the classroom. The AVID students did not appear to be ruffled by the

intruders; this was not the first group of observers, nor would it be the last.

A dark-haired young man was working with a peer tutor on an English essay. The student's name was Gustavo Escobedo, the brother of Máximo and Jaime. The Escobedo brothers had become an AVID tradition.

Now, handsome Gustavo, who made the girls swoon, was listening to his friend Luis give him advice on his essay. Luis was one of the most extraordinary students in that AVID class, according to Mr. Hopewell.

"A quiet tenth-grader with a penchant for reading anything and everything, Luis symbolized everything good as a Clairemont High School student," Mr. Hopewell wrote. "He listened intently to my mini-lectures and took copious notes. He had his hand in the air all the time. He questioned everything, from Cassius's motives in *Julius Caesar* to the proper use of a verb."

Oceanside teachers observed the two students working collaboratively on Gustavo's essay. Clearly, Luis was pushing Gustavo. The influence of one student on another could be more powerful than a teacher's, Mr. Hopewell explained quietly to the visitors.

Later, in "The Road to AVID," Mr. Hopewell would quote his students. "'This year a role model I can't forget is Luis,' Gustavo wrote. 'He really made me work very hard. . . .'" And Luis described AVID's impact: "'I need a commitment that I can relate to, so I can continue my persistence.'"

Persistence. Determination. Individual responsibility. These invisible forces were very much present in the AVID classroom, made visible through examples of student work proudly posted on the walls, quantified in achievement scores. How were these values passed on to students?

"'The AVID teacher lends a helping hand, and I'm not saying it just to get an A. It's a fact. The teacher is a friend, an advisor, everything,'" wrote Gilda. Her younger colleague, Ana Maria, wrote: "'The perfect high school is the kind that has patient tutors and teachers.'"

In summing up his experience, Mr. Hopewell wrote:

A circle of learning has developed around the students and me. I am no longer the focus or center of the classroom, but I am providing radii of direction and structure, honesty and concern. A cadre of college-bound, under-represented students from the AVID program makes this metaphor very real. The Carnegie Forum on Education and the Economy suggests, "The product of the schools of the twenty-first century must be a *citizen of the world.*" Those citizens are here today. Come meet them; they're in AVID!

The visiting teachers were impressed, and the tutorial groups seemed to evince the most fascination. Teachers could not believe the level of conversation, as students argued passionately about Shakespeare or disputed chemistry formulas. In fact, after watching the intensity of a Socratic seminar, some teachers were confused.

"Which class is this?" asked one teacher.

"The AVID study group."

"I thought it was a Seminar class!"

Mr. Hopewell couldn't resist a devilish smile. Outside of the room, so the students would not hear, he whispered to the visitors, "Two years ago, these AVID students were making C grades in remedial classes."

Testimonials from students were genuine and unrehearsed. "My goals this year are to master my reading and writing skills and expand my vocabulary," said Gilda.

Marco Antonio chipped in, "I just came to the U.S. last year. It's like a dream here. We don't have things like AVID in Tijuana."

The AVID classroom was visually exciting. The bookcases were filled with rows and rows of well-thumbed paperbacks, and collegiate posters were prominently displayed. The spirited classroom evoked hope, opportunity, and camaraderie.

"How do you get so many kids from so many ethnicities to work together?" an Oceanside teacher asked.

"This," Mr. Hopewell smiled, holding up the blue AVID binder. "They have to check each other's binders, trade notes, edit each other's papers, study together for tests. Many of these kids never had real, personal contact with kids from other groups. But in AVID, they depend on each other for their individual success. In a way, I think of the AVID binder, holding all their assignments, as a metaphor for a program that binds students together."

Finally, visiting teachers asked Mr. Hopewell, "Isn't this a lot of extra work?"

"I may be here a little longer after school," he replied. "But I get the rewards of working closely with students and seeing lives change."

On the road back to Oceanside, the teachers were energized. After experiencing the camaraderie in AVID, they felt bound together as teachers and learners in a new adventure.

When they returned to their school, there was unanimous approval to bring AVID to Oceanside. "If you want to apply, put your proposal on my desk by next Wednesday," the principal told them.

That week, his desk overflowed with requests. Not all could become AVID teachers, but the spirit was already touching many classrooms. Oceanside became one of the first three schools outside of the city of San Diego to adopt AVID.

Mr. Hopewell taught AVID for four years, sending dozens of Luises and Gildas to college. The road to AVID, he wrote, gave him the most fulfilling experience of his career. Suddenly, in his fifth year, he became gravely ill, making it impossible for him to continue teaching. As his students pursued their dreams at Berkeley, Stanford, and beyond, he moved home to his mother's care and died within a year.

— FIFTEEN MINUTES —
OF INFAMY

While school districts in the county grew interested in AVID, the administration of San Diego City Schools remained aloof. Before leaving Clairemont High, Mrs. Swanson had attempted to interest the City Schools in submitting AVID for the state Tanner Grant, funds to be used to prepare programs for under-represented students. But the Ed Center had its own proposed project for which it submitted an application, and Mrs. Swanson was supported by the county. After she won the grant and the City Schools lost, it may have been too much for some administrators to accept that their plan had been bested by a high-school teacher's project.

Yet Mrs. Swanson took seriously her responsibility to disseminate AVID to schools *throughout San Diego County*. She had spent great effort to meet with 16 superintendents of outlying districts, and she could not avoid trying, once more, to approach the central administration of the City Schools.

From some quarters at the Ed Center, she was viewed as an upstart teacher who had made an end run around the City Schools to get her program funded. And now she was coming back to try to sell them on an idea these seasoned administrators with Ph.D.s had already rejected.

Mrs. Swanson called her friend Martha Tower for advice.

"Meet with the four area assistant superintendents," Tower urged her.

It took courage for Mrs. Swanson to make the appointment. Returning to the Ed Center, she was tense. She brought fresh copies of the handbook and curriculum guide.

The meeting took place in an atmosphere of cold formality. Four administrators faced one ex-teacher. As area supervisors, they were the overseers of the schools in their geographic bailiwicks. The woman in charge of Clairemont High, who had always backed up Mrs. Chipp in disputes with Mary Catherine, was joined by two other women and one man.

Mrs. Swanson explained the parameters of the state funding. The Tanner Bill authorized the County Office of Education to disseminate AVID, but did not provide funding for districts to pay for teacher training or tutors. However, costs were low in comparison to the documented benefits of student performance and college acceptance. She had developed a strategy for implementation that was outlined, week by week, month by month, lesson by lesson, for each of the four grades of high school. It was all in the handbook.

"I offer my services to the district," she proclaimed. "I am available for teacher training and support."

The group did not ask one question, nor offer one word of encouragement. When Mary Catherine presented the supervisors with the fruits of her labor, the newborn *AVID Handbook and Curriculum Guide,* they showed no interest.

After her 15 minutes of infamy spent pleading her case before their critical eyes, she felt numb from stress. One of the supervisors, a tall, large-boned woman, said: "We do not need your help in our schools, thank you."

Mary Catherine was dismissed like a truant student. Intellectually, she knew she had done the right thing. She told herself: *They're being small. There's no way I can win with these people. I've got to move on. . . .*

But the sting of rejection still hurt.

— INCUBATION —

Independent of the central bureaucracy, Mrs. Swanson had managed to interest four other English teachers within the City Schools to try AVID in their high schools. The schools had large populations of urban poor: Lincoln High, in Clarence's old neighborhood; Madison; Point Loma; and San Diego High. The teachers received approval from their principals to move forward, but the Ed Center was not directly involved.

Mrs. Swanson helped these pioneering AVID teachers start programs beginning in the ninth grade. Before the Tanner Grant, she had had little time to get involved.

As the 1986–87 school year began, AVID suddenly experienced 15 minutes of fame. Late in August, Mary Catherine got a call from the State Department of Education in Sacramento asking her to arrange for State Superintendent of Public Instruction Bill Honig to visit Clairemont High School on the opening day of school. Tall and bespectacled, with the zip of a battery-powered bunny, Honig was California's top elected official in public education. He chose Clairemont High, from all schools in the state, to spotlight excellence, specifically AVID's successful preparation of disadvantaged students for college.

From her trailer at the County Office, Mary Catherine prepared the way for the Education Czar's triumphant visit to her old school. The opening-day ritual was performed in the Clairemont library. On stage with Honig were the top educators in the City Schools: the superintendent, Mrs. Chipp, and the members of the board of education. With wounds still fresh from her departure from teaching, Mary Catherine sat in the audience.

Honig praised AVID to the sky, and the media carried his message to television stations and newspapers across the state. Gesturing to the local school chiefs on the stage, Honig gave credit for AVID's success to the superintendent who had little involvement with the program, to the principal who had virtually run her out of the school, and to the board of education that had rejected her requests for funding. They basked in the praise, their faces brimming with self-congratulation, and they fell all over each other in extolling AVID's virtues.

Although Mary Catherine was in plain view of the educators on the stage, not one of them publicly recognized AVID's founder during the entire ceremony. Mary Catherine sat stoically in the shadows of the TV lights, overwhelmed with conflicting emotions. She felt thrilled for AVID students, tutors, and the new AVID teachers who were in the audience; stunned by the hypocrisy of her former boss, who basked in acclaim for the infant she had tried to strangle in the cradle; cut to the quick by the callous omission of any credit for her and Jim's roles. It was not the first time Mrs. Swanson had been publicly humiliated for bucking the system, nor would it be the last. If her opponents thought she was in this struggle for glory, they were sorely mistaken. She became ever more determined to fight for AVID kids and for the program to grow and mature, no matter what was thrown in her path. She learned an important lesson: There is nothing you can't accomplish if you are willing to let others take credit.

That fall, AVID programs got underway at five city schools: Clairemont, Lincoln, Point Loma, Madison, and San Diego High. By February, three more schools in San Diego County joined the AVID family. Mrs. Swanson went to the schools and helped the new AVID teachers set up, recruit ninth-graders, and choose site teams. She was rushing around the county, but the teachers were on their own in their classrooms.

The new *AVID Handbook and Curriculum Guide* was a great help. But a teacher could not run an AVID class by the book any more than a novice sailor could use a sailing primer to navigate a 22-foot boat across the Pacific. AVID teachers needed curriculum instruction, coaching, and group support, not only from Mrs. Swanson, but from each other.

It was not enough to disseminate AVID. Mrs. Swanson had to create a teacher training and learning environment to nurture new AVID teachers. The County Office of Education was an incubator of innovative ideas. But the claustrophobic AVID office in the trailer was too small to host meetings. The county superintendent offered the boardroom as a meeting place; Mrs. Swanson scheduled eight meetings at one-month intervals during the school year.

The first meeting brought together a highly motivated group. They looked at each other with shy expectation, like distant cousins at a family reunion. It was good to come in from isolated schools where each was innovating a program to this elegant boardroom where they were joined in a common purpose. The atmosphere of the meeting was very much like that powerful combination found in Mrs. Swanson's classroom: rigor and support.

The first two hours were devoted to a full immersion of AVID teachers in cutting-edge research. Mrs. Swanson passed out reprints of papers from leading academic journals. She wanted to expose teachers to the brightest minds in education reform, far-sighted thinkers like William Glasser, Uri Treisman of Berkeley, and Jim Cummins of Harvard.

"How does Glasser's research on group learning apply to our teaching practices?" she asked.

The teachers were forced to think "outside the box" of classroom teaching as they knew it, to engage in critical analysis of how they interacted with students, and to search for innovative ways to break out of the lecture mode. By understanding how learning goes on in adolescent minds and social groups, they could harness peer pressure as a spur to academic achievement.

"You mean AVID students adopt a group identity where it's cool to *study?*" one teacher asked incredulously.

"Yes, they become close-knit, supporting each other during conflicts at home," Mrs. Swanson replied.

"Then AVID's like a *good* gang?"

Teachers laughed, but the insight was breathtaking. *Ah ha!*

"I don't like the word *gang,* for obvious reasons," Mrs. Swanson said after the laughter died down. "But there's a significant difference between a social clique, based on culture or gender or money, and the teenagers from diverse backgrounds who hung around my classroom during lunch break and after school. Here were kids from Mexico, Vietnam, and southeast San Diego who probably would have gone through school in the same remedial classes, never knowing each other. But in AVID they were thrust into advanced classes, rubbing elbows with Seminar students from privileged homes, and *my kids* had to study hard and help each other. They had to stick together to survive academically, and this created a kinship of common interest, not color."

"So AVID is not only a college-prep program?"

"Yes, we found that rigor, instead of driving kids apart, brought them together," Mrs. Swanson explained patiently. "One of the byproducts of studying together is learning to understand one another and to see each other as individuals. This is what integration is all about, but it's not happening at most schools."

"Then in AVID we are about building a pluralistic classroom for a democratic society?"

Mrs. Swanson clutched her throat. "Oh, my. You just said the most beautiful word."

"You mean *democratic?*"

Mary Catherine acknowledged the importance of public education as the foundation of democracy with a nod, but this is not the word that had touched her so deeply.

"You said 'we'!" she exclaimed. "Not 'you,' or 'they.' *We* is the identity that AVID creates. It begins with us: teachers. *We are. We can. We will.*"

On this inspirational note, she plunged them into the praxis of the AVID curriculum. The next two hours were devoted to *how* to create an AVID classroom. During each meeting, Mrs. Swanson took one piece of the curriculum and went through it, section by section. She asked the teachers to turn to the sample of Cornell notes, then she passed out note pages labeled "Learning Log."

"The best way to learn how to teach Cornell note taking is for us to take Cornell notes here," she said. "Take good ones, because we're going to exchange them and ask each other questions."

There was a muffled sigh among the teachers, evocative of the loud groans of students in her classes. How she missed Bernice's groans and mumbled imprecations already! For a moment, she saw again Clarence, Máximo, Kouang, and Angelina's faces. Then a strange thing happened: The teachers lined faces' grew smooth and she saw them young and fresh as college students again.

Teachers as learners, students as teachers. In learning a new curriculum, the devil was in the details. She showed them how to organize binders and check them each week.

"Fold the covers back like wings and shake the binder," she said, demonstrating. "If any loose pages fall out, students lose a point toward their AVID grade."

"But you can't treat high-school students like third-graders, with stars and stickers," a teacher protested.

"I know it seems juvenile, but it works. By expecting kids to organize their binders, we are really helping them organize the chaos of their lives." The point system was designed, she explained, to give AVID students credit for going through the disciplined acts of time organization, goal setting, and study that were often missing from their backgrounds. "My kids got As in AVID if they worked hard and kept organized, and this gave them heart to get Cs and Ds in advanced classes. Eventually, the discipline paid off in higher English and math grades. Self-confidence grew from accomplishing things they'd never thought possible. Now, turn the page and we will review the point system."

Ugh! Teachers lacking stenographic skills wondered: *Will she ever slow down?* After forcing them to suffer mental stress and writing cramp at AVID boot camp, she invited them to lunch *chez county cafeteria*. Jaws crunched. Glucose poured into bloodstreams. Caffeine rekindled heartbeats. Breaking bread, they loosened up. Then they rolled up their sleeves.

The afternoon was reserved for sharing problems from their classrooms. "I wish it were easier for us now than it was at the beginning," Mrs. Swanson said. "But you're describing the same kind of resistance that I faced every step of the way." *And still do!* she thought. "What keeps me going are my kids. Who is education for? Schools are not for teachers. Not for principals. Not for bureaucrats. If a teaching technique benefits kids, then it should be done."

Complaints turned into problem-solving sessions. Here, the teachers worked together, offering suggestions and moral support. Mrs. Swanson let go and watched them advise a teacher how to confront an angry parent, and it reminded her of the confrontation with the biology teacher who went from accusing AVID students of cheating to supporting the program.

The monthly meetings of AVID coordinators repeated the evolutionary development of AVID, stage by stage. Then the teachers returned to their schools, carrying the seeds of AVID with them.

— GROWING PAINS —

Two weeks after Mrs. Swanson was rebuffed by top bureaucrats at the San Diego City Schools, she received a phone call from the president of the district's board of education. Marjorie Ford, a powerful and independent-minded African American who represented an inner-city neighborhood, was frustrated by the lack of progress of under-represented students in city schools.

"Mary Catherine, you are no longer an employee of the school district, and there are some things I can now say to you," Marjorie said. "I would like to meet with you tomorrow. Could you come to my office after hours?"

The lights were out in most of the Ed Center's offices when Mrs. Swanson arrived. She passed the locked doors of the area administrators and headed to the board suite, where the lights still burned. In San Diego, the day-to-day running of the schools was left to the superintendent and his staff, but policy and budget were controlled by elected school board members, who rotated in the president's chair.

"I wanted to meet with you privately because, quite frankly, some senior staffers have forcefully opposed AVID," Ford began, cocking her head toward the corridor. "They are unhappy because AVID has outshone their programs, and they have worked against you behind the scenes."

Mrs. Swanson was doubly astonished. First, she could not believe that the school board president was speaking so openly. Second, Ms. Ford confirmed Mary Catherine's worst fears of political backstabbing within the entrenched bureaucracy. *So this is what was going on. It wasn't all in my head!* As the school board president described the situation, it became clear that she was displeased with the district's remedial approach to educating minorities. AGP was moving too slowly to reduce the achievement gap.

"Now I am going to actively support AVID at the school board level," Ford said, concluding the meeting mysteriously. She did not say how, and Mrs. Swanson left the meeting happy to have found an ally, but without a clue as to the board president's ambitious agenda. Instead, Mrs. Swanson imagined a slow expansion of AVID into a few more classrooms, where teachers volunteered to teach AVID classes.

Behind the scenes, a power struggle was going on between Ms. Ford and her allies, who were advocates for change, and other more conservative members of the board of education, who resisted new academic strategies. The board presidency revolved every year or two, and Marjorie Ford saw an urgent need to address fundamental inequalities in the system, improve achievement scores, and raise expectations, especially for minority students. Mrs. Swanson's documented successes at Clairemont High made adopting AVID a tempting solution.

In December 1986, at the urging of its president, the board of education voted to implement the AVID program in all 17 comprehensive high schools in the City of San Diego. This was a mandate from the board, not a request for volunteers, and it caught Mrs. Swanson unaware. She appreciated the support for AVID, but feared that a rapid expansion would provoke opposition from principals and teachers. The board was adamant that all schools should gear up immediately. It was nearly winter break, and AVID classes were supposed to be up and running by the end of January. This was a prodigious task and, further complicating matters, Ms. Ford did not solicit Mrs. Swanson's input on how it should be done.

Harry Truman was once asked how it felt when President Roosevelt died. Have you ever had a load of hay fall on you? Truman replied.

After years of opposition, Mrs. Swanson had the unenviable responsibility of having the school board's mandate fall on her shoulders. The bureaucrats with whom she now had to collaborate believed that she had gone over their heads, and the principals resented that AVID was being forced upon them.

Like Truman, a former haberdasher from Independence, Missouri, Mary Catherine came from a small town where people had to do what was expected without complaint. She would have preferred to disseminate AVID slowly in the high schools, to persuade principals and teachers to make the choice of adopting AVID on their own, rather than being forced into it. She would have preferred to see how the original group of AVID coordinators fared, to build team spirit among committed educators, to monitor quality, and to make modifications in the handbook and curriculum guide. She would have preferred that Marjorie Ford had not overturned the hay wagon without contemplating who might get crushed.

But Mary Catherine did not have time to shout or duck. As the staggering weight came down, she looked up through the haystack and saw stars. *What an opportunity to bring hope to kids!*

She shouldered the responsibility and started running. In January 1987, Mary Catherine visited all 17 high schools in San Diego. She helped teachers set up AVID programs in 13 new schools. She even helped them recruit kids. She worked with half a dozen principals who were excited by the program and with an equal number who resented having AVID rammed down their throats.

From the original 12 coordinators, AVID grew to 29. Soon, there was not enough room in the boardroom at the County Office of

Education. The tenor of the meetings changed. A number of teachers who felt they had been dragooned into AVID sat mutely through the discussions and dodged out as soon as they could escape.

Mrs. Swanson learned an important lesson. AVID could not be forced on a student, a teacher, or a school. It depended on participants making a choice to take the risk of becoming involved. There could be no advancement *without* individual determination.

— PUNKY —

AVID needed an ally within the Ed Center. To Mrs. Swanson's relief, she found that support from the director of curriculum. Kermeen "Punky" Fristrom was a former Seminar teacher, a man she respected deeply and whom she called a friend.

Punky had seen AVID grow and he supported it. A strong, square-shouldered man who wore orthopedic shoes and walked with a limp, Punky had overcome physical disability to help coach generations of football players at Point Loma High. As an AP English teacher, he had won the respect of students by his high academic standards and his warmth of character. He had joined Mary Catherine in her quixotic quest to improve the teaching of writing in secondary schools and colleges. He had a keen mind and sense of justice, and he fought for the underdogs.

Unlike his friend Mary Catherine, however, Punky knew how to fit into a bureaucratic hierarchy. He had plenty of savvy and used his power to change the system from within. He became AVID's godfather and protector.

Punky agreed to administer the AVID program at the City
Schools. This took courage and not a little work to accomplish on
top of all his other duties. Punky saw the promise of the AVID curriculum and liked Mary Catherine's spunk.

Punky's involvement was a coup for Mrs. Swanson. Now AVID
had support from the school board and from the director of curriculum. This was a tremendous step up from her days fighting
Mrs. Chipp at Clairemont High.

Immediately, Punky warned her of an impending budget crisis.
The program simply didn't have enough funding to pay for its
rapid expansion. Tutors and materials cost money, and the district
was running short. There was a statewide emergency. The
California tax revolt, enshrined in Proposition 13, was slowly
strangling the system of public education. In this climate, programs that addressed the intense social challenges facing schools—
to assimilate children of the underclass and new immigrants into
the American dream—were chasing fewer dollars. And most dollars
were targeted for specific purposes. The Tanner Grant did not
authorize a single dollar for tutoring.

"If AVID is to survive in the City Schools, we need other
sources of funding," Punky warned.

But what sources? Private foundation grants for public-school
programs were almost impossible to find, as Mrs. Swanson had discovered at Clairemont. The school district was no longer able to
receive local property taxes; it all had to go through the legislature
in Sacramento before returning to San Diego. Due to the 1980s tax
revolt, California's per-pupil spending plunged to forty-second in
the nation, virtually destroying the system that had been built in
the '50s and '60s. Begging for dollars ran against the very principles of individual responsibility and self-sufficiency that AVID
students were taught.

How could AVID legitimately earn money to sustain itself?

The question was a form of revelation, for it liberated Mrs.
Swanson's thinking. Instead of being powerless, AVID *did* have
intellectual assets that it might be able to exploit for its survival. Not
on the street, but within the public sector. AVID had know-how.

AVID teachers could train other teachers. The curriculum was a treasure trove. Why give it away?

Punky Fristrom located a budget item that authorized monies for teacher training. The new crop of AVID teachers was desperately in need of training. The monthly meetings at the county offices were not enough to insure quality of instruction and the boardroom was too small.

She wondered about the possibility of creating an AVID summer teaching institute.

AVID was growing. In the 1987–88 school year, the program nearly doubled to 36 schools, all in San Diego County.

In the summer of 1988, there was a big breakthrough. Mrs. Swanson spoke at an educational colloquium in Los Angeles. The director of curriculum for Riverside County approached her after the speech.

"Could we adopt AVID in Riverside?" he asked.

"I never thought about it," Mrs. Swanson said, taken aback. "We're based at the San Diego County Office of Education, and I don't know if they would approve of my going outside the county. But I'm partially supported by state funding. I'm sure willing to try!"

So one summer morn she left her home in Olivenhain and drove in the opposite direction from Clairemont High, heading east and north. The radio announcer called Riverside the "Inland Empire." It was beautiful foothills country, burnt brown and green—when you could see it through the smog. She met with the Riverside educators and they decided to start the first AVID program in the school with the lowest test scores, Ramona High.

Counties are fiefdoms, jealously guarding their autonomy. Therefore, it was an extraordinary step for the San Diego County Office of Education to allow Mrs. Swanson to help set up AVID in Riverside County. She did the legwork, but the support of her home office was vital. For the first time, AVID spread beyond San Diego County.

This established a precedent for the program to grow across political and geographic boundaries, while remaining centered in San Diego.

The staff development meetings now drew AVID coordinators from 100 miles away. The network of teachers and schools demanded organization. Mrs. Swanson had never taken a course in management. Instead, she used the skills she had learned as a teacher. Organizing students in study groups taught her how to organize teachers into a network. Her job was to provide rigor and support. She didn't have all the answers for teachers any more than she had to kids' questions about algebra. She relied on the teachers to help each other, as the students had worked together. She provided teachers' curriculum models, as she had provided students' AVID binders. More experienced AVID teachers became trainers for new AVID teachers. The new organization was her old AVID classroom writ large.

Yet the experience of teaching was far more satisfying, emotionally, than was her new job. How she missed her kids! They were in college now, spread out from UC Berkeley to a theological seminary in Mexico City. She kept in touch with them when they came home for vacations. Many a time she was awakened by a call in the middle of the night when a lonely kid on a faraway campus needed advice.

AVID was not a panacea. The problems their families struggled with in barrios and immigrant households followed AVID students to college. The rigor of the University of California was particularly challenging to first-generation students, and there was no equivalent of AVID on most college campuses. So AVID students created their own ad hoc support groups. Angelina, Máximo, Joe, and other AVID students congregated regularly at a certain table in the SDSU library, studying and hanging out together socially. Dozens of AVID alumni returned to high schools as AVID tutors and many went on to become teachers.

Clarence made the varsity football squad at the University of Utah, and every time his team played SDSU, he made a point of meeting with Mrs. Swanson before or after the game.

"Mrs. Swanson, it's not easy being one of the few of my people at Utah," Clarence confided.

"Think of all the opportunities you have," Mrs. Swanson replied.

"I was so lonely at first, I wanted to quit and come home," Clarence said with a shy smile. "At football camp, I used to dream of M'Dear's cooking and Mama's voice soaring on Sundays. You know, I prefer our little church choir to the Mormon Tabernacle."

"How are your sisters?" Mrs. Swanson asked.

Clarence shrugged. "Okay, I guess," he said.

Sensing his disappointment, Mrs. Swanson didn't press him for details. "What about your friends from Lincoln?" she asked. "What are they doing?"

Clarence looked away. "I run into them sometimes back in the neighborhood. It seems like they're either hanging around, or strung out, or locked up, or dead." He turned back, his eyes searching. "I used to envy them, sleeping late and partying. How I hated being tired all the time. But now I appreciate it that you made me work so hard. I even use Cornell notes!" he laughed. "I don't know where I'd be now without AVID."

"You would have made it anyway!" she said. "But thanks for saying so."

Angelina was the first in her Honduran family to break out. She enrolled at San Diego State and thrived academically. Yet Angelina was not content to escape into the ivory tower—leaving her sisters vulnerable at home. She rented her own apartment and brought her sisters to live with her. To support them, she worked at a legal advocacy organization and still managed to remain a part-time student, majoring in English. Studying, working, raising siblings. Life was incredibly difficult for Angelina and dozens of students like her.

Máximo lived at home, studying art at SDSU but not really relating to the American university. He took time off from college to earn some money, and Mrs. Swanson was concerned about his future. Then one day Máximo called with fantastic news: He had been accepted to the small, but prestigious, Art Center College of Design in Pasadena, where he studied graphics and packaging design.

Meanwhile, his sensitive brother Jaime, who had won a scholarship to study chemistry at UCSD, shocked Mrs. Swanson by dropping out of college after his freshman year. Unbeknownst to her, Jaime had experienced a spiritual awakening at a Catholic retreat and decided he wanted to become a priest, not a scientist. Jaime entered a Catholic seminary in Mexico City, arriving days before a devastating earthquake toppled buildings. The selfless way that people risked their lives to rescue victims from the wreckage further strengthened his faith in the miraculous power of love. He completed his seminary studies in Mexico City, then returned to San Diego, where he studied theology and philosophy at the University of San Diego.

Kouang raced through UCSD's grueling physics and engineering programs, graduating with a bachelor's degree in three years. Then he skipped the master's program, going straight for a Ph.D. The unexpected problem was that he was offered scholarships to doctoral programs at Harvard, Yale, MIT, Cal Tech, and UC Berkeley.

"Mrs. Swanson, where should I go?" he asked his AVID mentor.

Mrs. Swanson replied, "Kouang, these are all excellent universities. But what about your personal and family considerations?" Kouang thought about his mother, who had sacrificed for her children and now needed her son. "I'll take Cal Tech so I can visit her on weekends," he said. Mrs. Swanson cheered him on to achieve his goal of becoming a rocket scientist.

Not all of her AVID students had stellar academic careers in four-year universities, but their college retention rate was 89 percent. This indicated that AVID not only helped students get *into* college, it effectively prepared them to handle the course work and gave them determination to follow their own stars.

— FIRST SUMMER —
INSTITUTE

The downside of rapid growth was non-stop toil for Mrs. Swanson, as AVID's first summer institute approached. The idea of an intensive, week-long summer teaching institute had been percolating for a year. There simply was no other way to pass on AVID's curriculum and philosophy to a large number of teachers. The cost would be defrayed, in part, by funds earmarked for teacher training and curriculum.

Invitations were sent out in the spring. The program offered eight "strands": administration, counseling, AVID implementation, English, history, science, math, and foreign languages. An auditorium was rented at the University of San Diego, across the road from the County Office of Education.

To Mrs. Swanson's surprise, 450 teachers signed up. From the San Diego City Schools, Punky Fristrom found funding to send four teachers from every high school. He also offered help in providing math and science trainers.

The job of preparing thick notebooks full of reading material for all the participants fell on Mrs. Swanson. Each teacher was to receive individual site data for his or her school. The notebooks were divided into sections: general sessions, staff development, site team, schoolwide reform, special interests, program information, and AVID transparencies.

The data sheets were typed by Bev Wilk, "the fastest secretary in the world," who had a deep voice and a wry sense of humor. Bev had been working at the County for a long time—long enough to be skeptical. To escape the tedium of proofreading, she amused herself by writing sarcastic comments about the text in the margins, knowing no one else would ever see them.

"Would you mind proofing AVID's data?" Mary Catherine asked her.

"I can't wait," Bev growled. As her eyes scanned the page, Bev muttered a running commentary, like the bassoon lurking in Prokofiev's "Peter and the Wolf." She would read a line of text, then write in her comment:

AVID students take notes in all their classes and have weekly binder checks.
You've got to be kidding!
AVID tutors never give their students answers, only ask deeper questions.
Really? How nice.
AVID students work collaboratively, sharing knowledge and building relationships.
You bet!
In conclusion, 93 percent of AVID graduates go to college.
Come on! Who would believe that?

Bev placed her copy of the data sheets on the desk and went off to smoke a cigarette. While she was gone, a harried helper ran it over to the printer to be reproduced. Hundreds of pages later, three former AVID students began collating the sheets by hand. Mrs. Swanson fed them pizza and soda pop. The pages were arranged sequentially around tables. Students attired in grubby sweatshirts and gym shoes literally ran around the tables picking up sheets, one after another, and compiling each notebook.

Three dizzy days and several pizzas later, 450 notebooks were stacked neatly. A job well done. Preparations went on to decorate the meeting hall. A few days later, one of the coordinators picked up a copy and began reading the data.

"*'Come on! Who would believe that?'*" she asked.

"What?"

"I'm just reading some weird margin notes. I quote: '*You've got to be kidding!*'"

"Let me see that," Bev yelled. "Oh my God, we printed the wrong copy!"

When Mrs. Swanson saw Bev's acerbic comments, she could not help bursting out in laughter.

"What are we going to do now?" the coordinator cried. "There's no time to reprint all these pages."

"Order a case of White Out!" Mrs. Swanson shouted. "And more pizza!" Around the table they flew, brushing White Out liquid 450 times on each of a dozen offending pages. Until the pizza ran out.

The first AVID Summer Institute began with a keynote address by Henry Gradillas, the former principal of Garfield High School in the barrio of East Los Angeles. A Garfield High math teacher named Jaime Escalante had achieved amazing success in preparing under-represented students for the Advanced Placement test in calculus. In fact, so many Garfield students passed the test that the national Educational Testing Service accused them of cheating. They took the exam again and all passed. A *Washington Post* reporter, Jay Mathews, had discovered this small news item that piqued his curiosity: *How did this teacher inspire his students to achieve far above expectations?* Mathews visited Escalante's class and observed the Bolivian-born teacher's intense teaching methods. Mathew's powerful book about Escalante captured national attention and was later made into a Hollywood movie, *Stand and Deliver!*

As Mrs. Swanson listened to Gradillas, she mused about the similar cheating scandal that had occurred at Clairemont in 1980, when her AVID students were accused of cheating on the biology test. Ironically, the unreported Clairemont incident had taken place only a year before Escalante's students faced censure. In both cases, the determined students had proved themselves capable of achieving to the highest. The system was forced to recognize their worth.

Yet the two teachers' methods appeared to be dramatically different. In the movie, Mr. Escalante, played by actor Edward James Olmos, was shown hectoring and even shaming his students into working beyond their perceived limits. Mrs. Swanson had always avoided ridiculing her students in public; instead, she would search a difficult pupil's sometimes dismal record for one good thing to praise. Both methods produced impressive test results, but Mrs. Swanson believed that, in the long run, it was better to build up students' strengths rather than to harp on their weaknesses.

There was another difference that she did not realize at the time, but that would distinguish their efforts over the next two decades. Mr. Escalante's success was specific to one teacher, one classroom, one school. His example inspired millions of students and teachers with hope, and for this America owed him a debt of gratitude. But his personalized method would not be widely replicated. Mrs. Swanson's teaching style was less dramatically charged, and certainly less publicized, but she was gifted with the ability to work beyond one classroom, one school, one system.

To reform education, it was not enough to be a great teacher. To cause change, one must be able to organize a movement.

For his insistence on rigor at Garfield High School, Gradillas had been reassigned to the district office as asbestos inspector. He, too, knew how difficult it was for an individual to challenge the bureaucracy.

Gradillas's impassioned speech brought the audience to its feet. Now that they were inspired, it was time to focus on the nitty gritty. The plenary session broke up. Teachers headed to working sessions, the heavy binders under their arms.

The August sun turned the mission-style buildings of the Catholic university into kilns. The clay of teachers' minds was fashioned into molds and fired. Miraculously, they emerged, blinking, from sessions with unique patterns glazed on their consciousness. Or, glassy-eyed, they burned out.

In her address, Mrs. Swanson talked about one of her former students, Nog Trung. She spoke of the Vietnamese refugee's strength in coming to the United States and knowing no English. Mrs. Swanson related the story of how Nog had persevered through AVID with great determination to finally pursue a career in teaching. Nog was a first-year teacher attending the institute.

As she spoke, Mrs. Swanson felt the power of storytelling to convey AVID's message. It was easier for an audience to relate to one student's story than to comprehend statistics for a hundred students.

The first AVID Summer Institute culminated with a closing speech by Uri Treisman, a professor from UC Berkeley who had revolutionized the teaching of mathematics to under-represented students at the university level, for which he had received national recognition. Mrs. Swanson had first heard Dr. Treisman speak at an education conference two years before, and she would never forget it. He spoke a million miles an hour, cracking jokes one moment and revealing his insights the next. He made ideas crackle in the air.

In his 1986 lecture, Dr. Treisman had asked why some Asian students from economically impoverished homes—*kids like Kouang,* she thought—did better in math than kids who grew up in the barrios and ghettos of American poverty. It was an old debate: nature versus nurture.

Dr. Treisman's point was that study habits, not brain sizes, were the crucial factor that distinguished successful calculus scholars. Kids who studied together around the kitchen table; who studied for a purpose, either out of gratitude for their parents' sacrifices in bringing them to America, or to make their way in the New World;

kids who used writing to learn—these kids displayed the habits of mind that Mrs. Swanson had instilled in Máximo and Clarence, Angelina and Kouang.

After the lecture, Dr. Treisman was introduced to Mrs. Swanson. He smiled, thrusting out his hand warmly. "Are you that teacher in San Diego who treats all kids as if they're gifted?" he asked, causing her to blush.

In the two years since they had met, the Berkeley professor had made a profound influence on Mrs. Swanson's thinking, and they became fast friends. Dr. Treisman's research with university students confirmed her own intuitive belief in the importance of challenging students with rigorous curriculum—and giving them academic and moral support.

Now, Uri's speech became the culminating moment of the first AVID Institute. Not a teacher left that room without feeling awed by his research and inspired by his passion. More significantly, through his writings and teaching methods, Uri Treisman made a lasting mark on the democratization of higher mathematics—a major achievement—without sacrificing excellence. In 1987, Dr. Treisman was awarded the nation's highest accolade for educators, a Dana Medal "for leadership in post-secondary education."

— OUT OF OUR LEAGUE —

In March of 1991, Mrs. Swanson received a letter informing her that State Superintendent Bill Honig, who had slighted her back in 1986, now wanted her contributions to be recognized by one of America's premier education foundations. Without consulting Mary Catherine, Honig had nominated AVID's leader and two other California teachers for a Dana Medal. No secondary teacher had ever been the recipient of a Dana Medal, which was generally given to university presidents or renowned professors from Ivy League schools. The previous year, First Lady Nancy Reagan had been an honoree at the Dana Award ceremony held at the Plaza Hotel in New York.

Mrs. Swanson stared at the letter in disbelief. *Nominating a former high-school teacher? What was Honig thinking of!* A tireless advocate for school kids, Honig had addressed the AVID Summer Institute in 1990. After his speech, in a hurry to catch a plane back to Sacramento, he had gobbled his salad and then absentmindedly gobbled the salad of the man next to him. *Had he gone crazy?*

Bemused by Honig's letter, she sent a packet of information requested by the Dana Foundation in New York City. She dismissed it as a "flash in the pan" and quickly forgot about it.

In August, 800 teachers and administrators attended the 1991 AVID Summer Institute held at the University of San Diego. One of the participants in the audience was Bart Largomarsino. He was deputy superintendent of schools in a system that was run by the Department of Defense for military dependents at bases around the globe. He had called Mary Catherine, asking if he could come to the institute. She had thought he wanted a vacation in San Diego. Why would anyone from Washington, D.C., want to attend an AVID Institute?

Mrs. Swanson was running the institute with a team of AVID teachers and volunteers. It was like being ringmistress of the Barnum & Bailey Circus, only she managed to keep a dozen seminars running without cracking a whip. In the middle of this year's plenary session, she received a frantic call from her office.

"It's the Dana Foundation. They want more information," her secretary, Peg Marks, cried. She reeled off a long list of requests: recommendations, data, sources, evidence of achievement, academic degrees, and a biographical profile. Mrs. Swanson strained to hear above the din in the next room. The prospect of fulfilling the list of requests seemed worse than helping 32 AVID students collect recommendations, grades, and college board scores in order to mail their college applications in by the deadline.

"They want copies of everything you've published in academic journals."

"Published?" Mrs. Swanson laughed. Obviously, the Dana requests were aimed at professors with long lists of publications. "Peg, I once wrote an article in *Teacher* magazine, back in 1984. That's it."

Every couple of hours that day, Peg would call in a new request for information made by the Dana Foundation. Mary Catherine would rack her brain for the location of the file containing the data. "I think it's at the back of the cabinet under the handbooks in the trailer."

"I found it!" Peg shouted. "Now, where do I find the annual report for . . ."

"I don't know!" Mrs. Swanson hurriedly hung up, rushing to introduce the closing speaker. *We're out of our league,* she thought.

After the conference, a man came up to her and introduced him-self as Bart Largomarsino.

"Mary Catherine, you have a thousand teachers here who say AVID is a good thing," he said with a glint in his eye. "How can you keep it from us?"

"Where are your schools located?" she asked.

"Germany, Italy, Spain, Japan . . . pick a continent," he answered. "Our kids move around a lot. Come in all colors and backgrounds. Great kids, if you can get them focused. They need that rigor and support you talk about. They sound a lot like AVID candidates."

She listened to him imagine out loud. He kept using the acronym DoDDS, which she finally discovered stood for Department of Defense Dependents Schools. Could AVID get involved with DoDDS? *It sounded odd. Exciting and daunting.* All the while she was wondering: *How am I going to run AVID programs around the world from the San Diego Office of Education?*

In October, Mary Catherine got another call from the Dana Foundation. *Oh, this is absurd,* she sighed. *What obscure data do they want me to dig up now?*

"Congratulations!" It was Phyllis Carruthers, program officer for the Dana Foundation. "I wish to inform you that you are a 1991 recipient of the Dana Award for Pioneering Achievement in Education."

Mrs. Swanson was dumbfounded. Her heart was beating so hard she could barely hear. The woman continued talking about the other winners. "Derek Bok, the retiring president of Harvard, will be the Dana honoree. . . ."

Mary Catherine remembered her father kidding her when she brought home her report card. *I know what you got. Zero, zero, zero!*

". . . a $50,000 cash award . . ." Ms. Carruthers was saying.

"How wonderful for AVID!"

"The award is for you individually," Ms. Carruthers corrected. "Minus taxes, of course. Now, logistics. Prepare a speech. There will be an award ceremony at the Plaza Hotel."

Where Zelda and Scott Fitzgerald swam in the fountain? Mary Catherine had been to New York once when she was 15. The idea of giving a speech there was inspiring *and* terrifying.

"We will host your family," Ms. Carruthers concluded before ringing off. "It's a black-tie event."

Mrs. Swanson's mouth was dry, her heart pounding. Her mind flew back to classroom days. *Clarence rushing onto the field against Lincoln High. Angelina lifting her eyes from* Don Quixote, *imploring. The Escobedo brothers beaming like a row of votive candles lighting their parents' faces at each others' graduation ceremonies.*

"You're not going to believe this," she told Peg.

"The Dana Award?" Peg exclaimed.

"We won! Thanks to your diligence!" Mary Catherine's heart was overflowing with gratitude to so many people, beginning with Jim Grove.

While Mrs. Swanson called her family, Peg informed the County Office of Education.

"Amazing!" her husband cried at his executive desk—quite an exclamation from a banker.

She reached her father at the *Kingsburg Recorder.* Ed Jacobs crowed, "If your grandfather were alive, he would be proud because this award is for education."

Her parents were coming. Tommy, a sophomore at UCLA, wouldn't miss it. Her mother-in-law wanted to come, and so did her sister and two sons. Mary Catherine called Ms. Carruthers at the Dana Foundation and told her, "There will be eight family members."

"Eight? I'm sorry, Mrs. Swanson. The foundation is only able to pay for immediate family."

She blushed, apologizing. That night she and Tom agreed that they would treat the rest of the family to the trip. They booked rooms at the Plaza. *The Plaza Hotel! What will I wear?*

The County Office of Education put word out to the media. By the next morning, Mrs. Swanson was besieged by requests for interviews by radio and television reporters from national networks and local affiliates. Dirk Bender was *not* among them. She awakened the second morning to a front-page headline in the Metro section of a San Diego newspaper:

```
          Teacher Wins
   Nobel Prize in Education
```

Uri Treisman called to congratulate her. He said he wanted to be with her at the ceremony. She tried to explain her wonder and the excitement of bringing her family.

"Mary Catherine, I have to tell you I took my mother and stepfather," Uri said. "The ballroom was filled with philanthropists and college presidents. My parents were seated at a table with rich people. My stepfather turned to the poshly furnished man at his right and said, 'I know what I do for a living. I collect garbage. Just what do you do?'" The dam burst and Mary Catherine rode on a flood of laughter and tears. She was trying to grapple with the enormity of it. She felt awed, nervous, frightened.

To ground herself, she went shopping and bought two knit suits.

Speech! She was very nervous about addressing an august audience. So she went about it the only way she knew: as a teacher. She turned it into a creative lesson plan, a 20-minute talk illustrating AVID's philosophy and accomplishments. Instead of using an old-fashioned overhead projector, Mary Catherine, the computer "whiz," programmed the data into a new-fangled computer that projected graphic images electronically on a screen. She prayed the gadget wouldn't break down as she addressed the bigwigs.

— DODDS —

Once again, a fateful coincidence guided AVID's path. Two days before the award ceremony in New York, DoDDS hosted a meeting of superintendents in charge of military dependent schools around the world. Out of the blue, Bart Largomarsino called, congratulating her for the Dana kudo.

"On your way to New York, why don't you swing by D.C. and talk to us folks at DoDDS?" he suggested. "We'd like to take a close look at AVID."

So it was that Mrs. Swanson traveled ahead on an extraordinary trip to the East Coast. Tom would bring their family to a rendezvous in New York. She zigzagged across the country, passing through New Orleans for a conference, en route to the nation's capital.

In other circumstances, she might have been nervous addressing the DoDDS group. But this no longer seemed intimidating in comparison to the upcoming Dana lecture. So she was relaxed and very much on mark when she presented AVID to the skeptical educators. As usual, she had done her homework. Assessment data revealed that kids in DoDDS schools were performing below expectations. Their demographic profile was highly diverse. As expected among dependents of enlisted soldiers, many students came from families without a college-going tradition.

Then she clicked her mouse and the computer flashed AVID's results on the screen. The gizmo worked! As she quoted statistics from San Diego, she was overcome with *deja vu*. A man's intense gaze was boring into her from the audience.

I don't believe my eyes! she thought as she spied her old boss. *It's Tom Goodman.* The educator, whom she hadn't seen for years, looked as shocked as she was to see one another in Washington, D.C.

Goodman had been the San Diego Schools superintendent in 1980 when AVID was born. In 1982, Goodman had supported Mrs. Swanson's efforts to build collaboration between high schools and universities by authorizing $5,000 to pay stipends to graduate students and professors who taught at Clairemont High. He never supported AVID directly, but AVID had not yet received much attention when Dr. Goodman abruptly left the district and Dr. Payzant became superintendent. Under pressure from the court's desegregation order, Payzant had expanded the district's proscriptive AGP initiative, and the rest was history.

Later, Goodman became superintendent of the Santa Clara County Office of Education and invited Mrs. Swanson to come there and disseminate AVID throughout Santa Clara County. But she did not accept his offer because she felt that her loyalty must be to Clairemont—and she had not yet reached the end of her rope with Mrs. Chipp. Ironically, Dr. Goodman offered Mrs. Swanson the same job in Santa Clara that she later took at the San Diego Office of Education. After Goodman left Santa Clara, she lost track of him.

I always wondered where Tom Goodman had ended up, Mary Catherine mused while delivering her talk. *How very odd that he's landed at DoDDS.*

"I see Dr. Goodman, my old boss, is here," she said to the audience with a surge of nostalgia. "Under his leadership in San Diego, AVID got its start."

Goodman, who had landed a plum post as superintendent of the Mediterranean district, beamed. That night he graciously attended a dinner party that was given in her honor at a restaurant overlooking the Potomac.

Mary Catherine left Washington with a contract from DoDDS. AVID was going global.

— PLAZA HOTEL —

Next stop: New York. Flying over the fabled towers of Manhattan, Mary Catherine thought of that fateful day, 26 years before, when she had gotten the scholarship to Columbia. She wondered what her life would have been like had she turned down Tom and taken the path of journalism. Deep down, she had a wistful feeling: *What would it have been like to live on Broadway? Could I have gotten a job with the* New York Times? Her generation was torn between the stay-at-home moms and the careerists, and she was lucky to have found a calling that gave her both a career and family. It was nice to be coming to New York as a celebrated educator and to share this event with her family.

At the Plaza Hotel, she was ushered into a phenomenal room overlooking Central Park. The leafless trees and snowy paths shimmered beyond the window.

The Jacobs–Swanson clan arrived in an airport limo. Ed Jacobs pointed out the sights, regaling them with stories about his salad days at Columbia more than a half century ago. Walking through Central Park, the San Diegans' suntans glowed like candles, with frosty clouds puffing from their lips in the wintry evening.

Exhausted, they retired early. But Mary Catherine lay in bed, too excited to sleep and anxious about her presentation the next day.

In her hurry to get ready for her talk the next morning, a piece of dental floss caught between her teeth. Unable to dislodge it, she felt like a rube and rushed to catch a taxi. To her horror, the cab became ensnarled in a traffic jam. Luckily, it managed to arrive just in time.

She composed herself. The room was filled with Dana Award winners and former winners. Uri was nowhere to be seen. It was daunting. *What would I tell my students to do?* She could hear Clarence whispering in her ear. *Don't let them psyche you out, Mrs. Swanson. Just think of us kids when you talk.*

They marched into a conference room, and she was put at the head table. The other winners were medical researchers, a college president, and a famous social psychiatrist. They seemed confident. She tried to smile without showing her teeth. Her skin prickled in her knit suit.

She searched the room for her family. Her son, Tommy, was sitting next to his grandfather. Her husband caught her eye and smoothed the worries from her heart with his comforting gaze.

The program began. The winners were introduced in the order that they would speak. She came last.

First came the medical researchers. They had created a formula to save starving babies. The lights dimmed. A powerful documentary video portrayed their work in Africa. The audience burst into applause. Mary Catherine was deeply moved.

Second, an impressive figure rose to the lectern. J. W. Carmichael was a professor of biology at Xavier University in New Orleans. He had pioneered a program that prepared African American college students for medical school. Using charts and graphs, he presented impressive data. Though small in size, Xavier produced more African American graduates who went on to become physicians than did the entire University of California system. The applause was strong. Mary Catherine felt awed.

Third, Dr. James Comer stood up and spoke without the use of notes. The bespectacled professor of psychiatry from the Yale

Medical School was a national figure in education reform. The eminent professor spoke of the separate world in which he had grown up as a black child. "Colored" schools were inferior in brick and mortar to their white neighbors, but their spirit of excellence burned bright. Growing up in a closely knit community, he could not escape from his teachers, who shopped at the same grocery store and attended the same church. This kind of neighborhood involvement was now missing, he said. To fill the void, Dr. Comer advocated that schools create a governing body of teachers, students, and parents. Comer model schools had begun in the ghettos of New Haven and had spread across America. His speech ended with a tribute to his mother, who had raised her children to become college-educated professionals. The applause was thunderous from all parts of the room, especially from several tables filled with members of Comer's entourage.

As Mrs. Swanson was introduced, dozens of guests stood up and quietly filed out of the room. The exodus emptied the Comer tables. With a sinking heart, Mrs. Swanson rose to give her talk. Apparently, a teacher was not as interesting as the other speakers.

The exodus turned into a flood. As the group passed her father's table, he leaned over and whispered loudly, "Those damn people! What's the matter with them walking out on my daughter!"

Mrs. Swanson was absolutely mortified by his outburst, but she could not control her father's tongue. He remained fiercely protective of his daughter.

"Well, I appreciate that a few of you stayed," she began disarmingly. "I'll try to make your time worthwhile." Once the first AVID slide was projected on the screen, she knew she could do it. Her talk was logical, succinct, right to the point. The program explained itself. The data backed it up.

The small group listened intently. At the conclusion, she got a warm hand. The applause of her family meant more to her than she could have imagined. Afterward, a Dana staff member told her, "Your talk was given like a true teacher."

She was who she was. And proud of it.

Next morning, the day of the banquet, the Swanson family pretended that they owned Manhattan. Breakfast at the Plaza. A walk through Central Park. Lunch at Tavern on the Green. Tea in the Peacock Room.

Back in their rooms, Mary Catherine found two bouquets of flowers from her friends and colleagues at the County Office.

The banquet was formal. Her Dana escort arrived and took her arm. A small chamber orchestra was playing as they entered a gilded room. A waiter offered champagne. Fearing she might have to give a thank-you talk at the end of the evening, she shook her head no.

One by one, her escort introduced her to the philanthropists and distinguished members of the Dana board of directors. New York society was everything she had imagined it to be—and less. Less haughty. Less stiff. Less condescending. Yet also less connected to the harsh realities of her own students.

It was more lavish, more sophisticated, more "social register" than Mary Catherine had imagined. She was more grateful than she could express. Yet she also felt more removed. Almost numb.

She was escorted to a balcony overlooking a ballroom. One by one, the award winners were formally announced to the socialites below: "Mary Catherine Swanson, founder and director of Advancement via Individual Determination." She gazed down at the applauding faces, blurred pink and glowing in the gilded ballroom.

She was whisked to an elevator and stepped out into the lights and cameras of a surreal photo shoot. Television and news photographers jostled for positions, but no questions were allowed. Presiding over the media event was the poised figure of David Mahoney, chairman of the board. While cameras clicked, Mary Catherine's family was being seated with Charles Dana III, grandson of the lumber magnate for whom the foundation was named.

Suddenly, a curtain opened. She discovered that she was on a balcony overlooking the ballroom. The honorees were escorted in single file behind the head table, raised on a dais. She came second in line. Her hands were sweating.

The orchestra struck up "Pomp and Circumstance." She heard her name being announced, but she didn't listen—could not even entertain what was happening. She found herself seated between eminent men. To her left was Derek Bok, the president emeritus of Harvard University. On her right was Charles Dana Jr. Everyone was much older than she and seemed a bit pompous. She was aware that she was the only teacher.

Bok barely deigned to speak with her. But Charles Dana was fascinating company, regaling her with a story about a family Christmas long ago. "Before Christmas, we took our boy window-shopping at F. A. O. Schwarz," he said.

'Dad, I want Santa to bring me that trainset.'

Santa brought him the whole window!"

The dessert arrived. "They serve this blasted tiramisu every year," he growled, jabbing his spoon into the quivering sweet. "I hate it!"

The award ceremony was ready to begin. The waiters retreated. The clamor of glasses and laughter died down. All eyes were on the dais.

The first Dana winner, Dr. Carmichael, was called forward to receive his gold medal. The inscription praising his efforts on behalf of African American medical students was read aloud. As she listened, Mary Catherine twisted her linen napkin. She didn't know if she was supposed to give a brief thank-you speech. She had prepared one: *I dedicate this award to my students, in the name of all teachers. . . . Or should I simply say thank you?*

Carmichael took the medal in his hands and bowed. *No speech!* she thought with relief. Then her name was called and she somehow made it across the dais. She saw her family sitting in the front row.

David Mahoney, chairman of the board, read aloud the Dana citation:

Mary Catherine Swanson has created an imaginative way of restructuring the school day to give academic support to thousands of students who are often overlooked by our education system; students who are now going on to college and succeeding.

In one sentence, the judges had condensed her work. *Restructuring time. Strange, she had never thought of AVID's mission so temporally.* She was grateful that they used the word *imaginative.* She did not know where her ideas came from, except that she would go to bed frustrated over a problem, would dream of relentlessly absurd situations and surrealistic chase scenes, and then would awake with a simple solution. Creativity, for her, was using logical reasoning, putting concepts together from different fields, *imagining* the solution. The fun was trying things out and seeing if they worked. Creating lesson plans was like sculpting curious and magical creatures out of clay. The art of group learning was in the collaboration, where minds working together created something none could have achieved alone. *Learning is not a product of an industrial process!* she silently protested. *It takes work and discipline, but it is an ineffable grasping of a little piece of truth from the dross.*

The ineffable vanished and she was left holding a gold medal.

When she sat down, the elderly Mr. Dana said, "Give me that award." He opened the velvet-lined wood case. On the front of the medal, the likeness of Julius Caesar was placing a laurel wreath on the head of a Roman hero. Dana flipped it over. On the obverse was a *bas relief* portrait of his father, Charles Dana Sr.

Mary Catherine finally allowed herself to relax, listening to Derek Bok's speech. Then the dinner was over, and she rejoined her family. Amazed by the opulence, her mother, Corrine, whispered, "Mary Catherine, what do these people do for a living?" Her son, Tommy, joked, "Mom, now that you're famous, do you think you could help me get into Harvard?" Mary Catherine laughed, "You're not going to need me."

Flying home to San Diego, she watched her son in the next seat studying for exams at UCLA. To her dismay, he never used any of AVID's study skills, but managed to get excellent grades. Rock music blasted from his earphones and, every few minutes, he would look up from his textbook and shake his fists.

"Tommy, whatever are you doing?" she asked.

"When I understand a course concept, I celebrate!" he smiled. "I know it's *mine.*"

After landing in Los Angeles, Tommy parted for UCLA. The Swansons missed their connecting flight to San Diego and took an exhausting 75-mile bus ride from Los Angeles. At midnight, Mary Catherine felt as if Cinderella's coach had turned into a pumpkin. The trip ended ignominiously at 2 A.M. in a deserted shopping center on a freeway exit seven miles from their home. Too tired to savor their memories of the ceremony, Mary Catherine and Tom dragged their luggage to a gas station and called a cab. The taxi driver took one look at the bedraggled couple, bundled up in winter overcoats, and commented that he had picked up people before at this time of night, but never with suitcases. It was a long way from the Plaza Hotel, but Mary Catherine was glad to be home.

— KENTUCKY —

Mrs. Swanson received a phone call in 1992 that would define AVID's destiny as a national reform movement. Up until this point, AVID had been a program that spread haphazardly, usually by word of mouth. It operated in several districts in the state of California and in the DoDDS schools abroad. But it had not yet gained a foothold in other states of the Union.

The long-distance connection was poor. Over the static, Mrs. Swanson heard a man's voice rumble, "Mary Catherine, it's Tom Boysen."

Until recently, Boysen had been the San Diego County superintendent of schools. He was hired by the State of Kentucky to clean up its poorly performing public-school system. Kentucky's schools had been declared unfit for students by the state supreme court. The ruling provoked the passage of sweeping education reforms mandated by the Kentucky Education Reform Act. As Kentucky's new education czar, Boysen was under the gun to raise low student performance. The nation was watching this bellwether experiment.

"I want . . ." Tom's voice became unintelligible.

"Tom, I can barely hear you," Mrs. Swanson yelled into the phone.

"I'm calling from a car phone in a rainstorm in the hills of eastern Kentucky," Boysen shouted. "I want AVID to come to Kentucky!"

She was startled by the urgency of his call but, on deeper consideration, nothing really surprised her anymore. Her first thought was not *if* AVID could be transplanted to Appalachia, but *how* to do it from her base in San Diego.

"I'll have to ask Harry Weinberg's permission," she said. Dr. Weinberg was Boysen's far-sighted replacement as the San Diego County superintendent. A tall, plain-spoken former history teacher with a compassionate heart and a penchant for philosophical questioning, Dr. Weinberg believed in the county as an incubator of ideas. Rangy and quick to smile, he looked a bit like Johnny Appleseed.

"Sure, go for it," Dr. Weinberg answered her request when she called him next.

Commissioner Boysen was a man with a mission. He wanted to deploy AVID in Kentucky's worst schools.

"That's not a good idea," Mrs. Swanson said, defending AVID's traditional focus on "kids in the middle," who responded to rigor and support—not adolescents with behavior problems. The last thing that she wanted was to promote the unrealistic expectation that AVID was a panacea for endemic injustices, which went far beyond the schools. Appalachia's woody hollows harbored some of the most stubborn pockets of poverty in America, where children suffered from malnutrition, lack of health care, illiteracy, and violent feuds within communities. She did not want to set the program up for failure and not serve students well.

The administrative challenge was to maintain AVID's standards in a distant region of the United States and to run it from the San Diego County Office of Education, where she was a paid employee. Her workload already demanded 10- to 12-hour days, without taking on any new challenges. *How can I possibly take on Kentucky? Help!*

Superintendent Weinberg suggested that AVID create a not-for-profit entity for expansion outside the county. And, for a non-profit corporation, it was necessary to have a board of directors made up of community and business leaders.

Mrs. Swanson had few connections in the business community beyond Tom's banking contacts. She had no business experience. She had never taken a business course in college, was not always accurate performing mathematical calculations, and had never considered herself qualified to handle complex financial matters. Each month, she gave Tom her paycheck and he conducted all the family business.

She was daunted by money matters but was determined not to let her limitations prevent needy children from benefiting from AVID's curriculum and social supports. She would follow the AVID example and find the equivalent of a tutor.

"Do you know anyone who could give me business advice?" Mrs. Swanson asked her boss.

Harry Weinberg introduced her to Tom Page, head of the San Diego Gas and Electric Company. The utility was under fire from consumer groups and was beholden to its shareholders. Page's chair was a hot seat, but he believed fervently in rigorous public education as fundamental to the survival of democracy and the free enterprise system. Unlike many business leaders who become honorary board members, Mr. Page became directly involved. He wanted to inspect an AVID classroom. Mrs. Swanson showed him the program at Valhalla High School, which his own children had attended.

On the long drive back to Mrs. Swanson's office, Mr. Page remarked about a Latina student they had met in the AVID class. She worked six hours a day at a major department store and still managed to take Advanced Placement classes. The hard-nosed businessman was even more impressed by the data. Bottom line: 93 percent of AVID students attended college, a statistic that held up as the program expanded. Of those, 60 percent attended four-year universities, 40 percent two-year colleges.

Mr. Page agreed to become a founding member of the board. Yet there was no actual non-profit corporation to speak of; it was still a glint in Mrs. Swanson's exhausted red eyes. She needed practical help in setting it up. Little did she know that help would come from a protégé of her old boss, Dr. Tom Payzant.

President Clinton summoned Payzant from his post in San Diego to a federal job in Washington. He was appointed assistant U.S. secretary for elementary and secondary education. Public education in the United States is the primary responsibility of state and local communities, unlike other Western democracies that have national education programs. Still, the former superintendent's new job was a tremendously important responsibility for setting education policy and funding pioneering education programs.

From the banks of the Potomac, he wrote Mrs. Swanson a warm letter of congratulation for the Dana Award. She appreciated it not only as a gesture, but because she respected his progressive commitment to improving education for America's youth. It was now possible for her to laugh at her own hijinks, and those of her bureaucratic opponents, in the struggles she had endured as a teacher and to appreciate the testing that had helped her forge a stronger program. She was able to forgive, if not forget.

— SCHOOLS OF — THE FUTURE

Back in San Diego, in the late 1980s, the San Diego City Schools, led by Board President Bob Filner, had appointed a blue ribbon panel to propose progressive education reform measures in San Diego. A tall, young idealistic easterner named Ron Ottinger was hired as the superintendent's planning assistant in charge of school reform. His job was to provide technical support and to keep the citizen committee on track. The goal of the "Schools of the Future" commission was to propose structural reforms that would make each school more responsive to the needs of its particular community. In fact, the superintendent was aware of the problems of the centralized bureaucracy—the arbitrary rules that stifled creativity and thwarted innovative teachers like Mrs. Swanson—and the committee set into motion a process to democratize and decentralize the schools, giving more power to administrators, parents, and teachers at each school site. Or so the commission proposed.

This was part of a fluorescence of reform efforts being tried out by local school districts across the United States. Education reforms were following two separate paths: structural reform and curricular reform.

Structural reforms in school governance, as advocated by Dr. James Comer and others, stressed the connection between the school and the community. The school site became the locus of change, through a democratic process bringing different constituencies—administrators, teachers, parents, and students—to work together. Structural reforms, it was hoped, would "empower" schools to better serve the needs of their students.

Curricular reforms focused on rigorous standards, testing results, and accountability. The focus was on performance at all levels: students, teachers, schools, and the entire system. Evaluation was the key to measuring progress or stagnancy. Students were held accountable to pass tests before advancing; teachers were held accountable for the knowledge measured by test scores of their students; administrators were held accountable to improve schoolwide performance.

Mrs. Swanson was a pioneering advocate of curricular reform, but within a supportive social framework. She was all for high standards and academic rigor—she demanded that AVID students take the hardest and most advanced classes. But she parted company with single-minded reformers who demanded high standards without providing support for learning. When she started AVID, she naively believed that exposing kids to great classes and expecting them to achieve would be enough. Yet she soon realized that students who were struggling with socio-economic issues—difficulty learning English, chaos at home, low self-esteem, violence in the neighborhood—needed a supportive community of tutors, peers, and a caring teacher to help them. They needed to *learn how to learn* and to be taught the "hidden curriculum" of how schools worked in order to be successful.

Which reform would prove more effective: structural or curricular?

The answer to the big question hanging over education policy would not emerge for a decade, when the data would indicate a winner. In the meantime, the Schools of the Future Commission chose the path of structural reform, which ran into the lethargy and opposition of the bureaucracy. Mrs. Swanson was a lonely voice advocating rigor and support in the curricular-reform camp that was beginning to gain steam nationally. And Ron Ottinger was groomed by his mentors to run for the school board of the San Diego City Schools.

Ottinger had studied the research and discovered that large class size impeded the ability of primary students to learn to read. He ran on a progressive platform of reducing the size of classes for kids at the beginning of elementary school—and won in 1992.

As a school-board member, he could no longer work as an employee of the City Schools. Through the informal education network, Ottinger was offered a job by Harry Weinberg at the County Office of Education. There, Dr. Payzant's former protégé found himself being interviewed by Mary Catherine Swanson for a part-time position in AVID. The program was growing by leaps and bounds, and she needed help to get a hold of the organization.

When Harry Weinberg suggested she interview Ron Ottinger, Mrs. Swanson was not looking forward to it. As they met face to face, the hard-knocks educational reformer from Kingsburg and the dark-haired young man from Washington, D.C., were a portrait in contrasts.

Ron Ottinger was raised in the Eastern Establishment. His father had been a liberal Democratic U.S. congressman from New York City. Ron attended private school at St. Albans in Washington, D.C. He graduated from Amherst College in Massachusetts.

Yet this scion of a New York political family had a strong social conscience. After graduation, he worked as a community organizer in Brooklyn and later with protégés of Cesar Chavez in California. Mary Catherine had come from a Central Valley farming community where citizens decried Chavez's tactics. Ron came from a family where service to community was the highest vocation. After toiling in the fields of organizing, he came to believe that hope for social change began with children, and the best way to improve a child's chances in life was by improving public education. A man of contradictions, he became passionately committed to educational reform—even though he had never set foot in a classroom as a teacher.

Mrs. Swanson had come to the same conclusion about social change. She was suspicious of top-down reforms that rang true in sound bites on TV, but that did not have a practical application. She was a born teacher, and she believed that classroom teaching was the highest calling. When she was a young bride just starting out in teaching, she had told her husband that she loved teaching so much that she would have been willing to do it for free. Disseminating AVID had brought her professional recognition, but it was a personal sacrifice that she made every morning to drive past her former classroom to the sterile administrative headquarters of the County Office of Education. She only did it because she knew she could help more children there than by teaching her own class. But she promised herself that, before retiring, she would return to teaching AVID.

As the adamant teacher's teacher faced the energetic new schoolboard member, they felt a curious rapport. What struck Mary Catherine, beyond Ron's obvious intelligence and education, was his compassionate heart and willingness to pitch in.

"If you want me to open your mail or answer phones, I'll do whatever we need to do," he said eagerly. She liked his using the word *me*. It showed he was already identifying as a member of a team. Ron had the politician's ability to talk comfortably with anybody and had a keen eye for strategic planning. These were two qualities she desperately needed for AVID to grow in the political world.

As a board member, Mr. Ottinger was aware of the scuttlebutt about Mrs. Swanson back at the Ed Center. The new deputy superintendent, Frank Till, was up front about the mood at the City Schools. They didn't like the fact that a classroom teacher had created an effective program and had showed them up.

But Mr. Ottinger was his own man. He was impressed that Mrs. Swanson had created a policy board for AVID in the County Office. She brought together superintendents, representatives from secondary schools, and faculty members from the University of California and San Diego State to look at the status of student performance and other key policy issues. He had sat in the meetings back in 1988. It was a powerful experience, seeing strong educators hash out key policy issues.

"It was a major deal, getting these reform-minded folks together in one room, focusing on kids and their college aspirations," Mr. Ottinger reflects now. He was impressed that Mrs. Swanson presented data on college completion rates by ethnicity. "She wanted to be held accountable for measurable results. She had an ability to think big. And she was very determined. She embodied AVID for me. When you think of individual determination it starts with her story at Clairemont High." He bursts into laughter. "I can't recall many battles Mary Catherine has lost!"

She knew she had lost many skirmishes, if she had won some battles, and had learned from her mistakes. Her personal War on Poverty, Ignorance, and Despair was just entering a crucial stage, and she needed to build an organization that could sustain itself.

"Ron, I'd like you to join AVID," Mrs. Swanson told him warmly after a meeting they had attended together. "I know you can only work part time, you've got responsibilities at the school board, and you want to be with your young family. But we have an important mission: to set up a non-profit organization."

"I don't have much experience in that field," he admitted, anxiously cracking a smile.

"Neither do I!" she cried.

They laughed together: he, throwing his head back; she, clutching her sides. It was a dynamic professional relationship sealed by laughter.

The not-for-profit corporation was established in 1992 and was named the AVID Center. The original board of trustees included Mary Catherine; Ron Ottinger; the head of San Diego Gas and Electric Company; a businessman; a bank president who was a business acquaintance of Tom Swanson; a retired member of the county board of education; Professor Uri Treisman; and a very special former AVID student, Clarence Fields, now working at the Xerox Corporation.

Ron, Mary Catherine, and Uri were the only educators on the board. It was heavily stacked with business leaders, whose expertise was invaluable. Tom Swanson was not a member of the board, but served as Mary Catherine's financial adviser.

Later, Gary K. Hart, California's legislative champion of public education joined the board. Known as "Mr. Education," Hart had served as chair of the education committee in the state senate. Mary Catherine had a special respect for him because, while he was "Mr. Education" in the state capitol, he also taught U.S. history at a high school in Sacramento. He wanted to feel the pulse of students.

At Sacramento High, Hart had heard teachers talking about a program called AVID that sent 93 percent of its graduates to college. Intrigued, he flew down to San Diego to visit Mrs. Swanson. She gave him a copy of Professor Hugh Mehan's pioneering research book, *Constructing School Success*, which had recently been published by Cambridge University Press.

Dr. Mehan and a team of UCSD researchers had observed AVID classes, analyzed data, and interviewed AVID students and teachers. In the book's introduction, Mehan explained that he had become weary of writing negative critiques about the failure of American education to provide opportunity to children in poverty— a failure which he blamed, in part, on systems that "tracked" poor students through poor classes to menial jobs and sent privileged students to college. Searching for a positive "untracking" model, Mehan discovered that one already existed in AVID.

The book was both complimentary and critical. It praised AVID's "hidden curriculum" that taught minority kids how to operate effectively in schools and lauded AVID's "social scaffolding" that supported kids to overcome obstacles of poverty and alienation. Yet the book was critical of what Mehan perceived as an uneven application of AVID programs in varying school populations.

Mrs. Swanson had her own rebuttals, but she respected Mehan's independent judgment and respected Senator Hart enough to let him draw his own conclusions.

In turn, Hart was impressed that she had given him Mehan's book, and this established credibility for AVID. Yet the lawmaker did not want to proceed solely on the conclusions drawn from a book. He wanted to see AVID in action, and he followed through by observing AVID classes at Valley High School in Sacramento. The more he saw, the more impressed he became.

After years on Capitol Hill, Senator Hart grew tired of legislative gridlock and opted to fight for better schools by leading the Institute for Education Reform at California State University. In 1996, he joined AVID's board of trustees.

AVID now had a powerful ally with political influence in Sacramento.

Notwithstanding these early organizational efforts, the AVID Center lay largely dormant, a paper entity with possibilities but lacking a clear vision and strategy. AVID was expanding faster than its capacity to deal with growth.

The program was invited to Virginia by the Newport News superintendent of schools, Eric Smith, in 1993. The district was located in the Newport News region near historic sites from the American Revolution and the Civil War.

More than a century after Lincoln's Gettysburg Address and the Emancipation Proclamation, the legacy of slavery still divided white and black children in the Newport News schools. Newport News, Virginia, was historically, geographically, and culturally removed from AVID's roots in San Diego, although these contra-coastal communities both harbored large military installations. Could the AVID program help the descendants of slaves and masters learn to study together? Could it help children of military families and teenage outcasts derided as "trailer trash" gain dignity by achieving in rigorous academic classes?

The first AVID colony on the East Coast lay downriver from the Jamestown Colony, which began in 1607 with a beautiful New World dream and met a tragic end. Would AVID Colony suffer a similar fate?

The AVID board of trustees saw the mortal danger of AVID in the wilderness. No matter how valuable the program, it could not survive without a firm economic basis.

The trustees strongly suggested that AVID develop a business plan. Since neither Mary Catherine nor Ron had an inkling of how to create one, they followed the AVID example and hired two "tutors" to mentor them through the process. Helen Monroe was an independent consultant who had helped build the San Diego Community Foundation; Rod Tompkins was a savvy adviser from a mortgage company. They guided the educators through the intense process of self-evaluation and strategic planning necessary to transform the paper entity into a dynamic AVID Center.

The groundwork had been prepared by AVID's National Dissemination Board. Led by Uri Treisman and funded by the Dana Foundation, the board had met annually since 1992. Its goal was ambitious: to look beyond the pressing problems of the moment and to plot AVID's path into the future. Board members asked the right questions: How can AVID expand without compromising quality? Which districts are best suited to adopt the program? What administrative framework is required—and how would they pay for it?

The provocative sessions forced Mrs. Swanson to think "outside the box." But the group met too infrequently to provide practical answers. There was no alternative but to spend the time and effort to complete a comprehensive plan.

Mrs. Swanson fell back on her penchant for research and discovered a seminal dissemination study by Public Private Ventures in Philadelphia. The authors had observed several social-reform models, such as the Head Start Program, and had distilled their lessons. Two models seemed especially applicable to AVID. The first was a "concept" model: A concept was formulated and tried out in a specific location and, if it worked, the concept was disseminated. The second model was a "franchise" model. Once a social program was developed, others could "buy" a franchise and replicate the program.

AVID combined aspects of both concept and franchise models to create a hybrid. The AVID teaching and learning structure was outlined in the *AVID Handbook and Curriculum Guide,* and was taught in the AVID Institutes. Yet the concept alone was not enough to sustain AVID programs in far-flung parts of the world. A network was needed to provide ongoing support, evaluation, and improvement. But how to convince schools to pay for it?

This question provoked an argument on a transcontinental flight between Mary Catherine and Ron Ottinger.

"You need to have a way to keep districts connected to the hub," Mary Catherine asserted. "We have to charge a networking and consultation fee."

"I wouldn't pay for that as a school-board member," Ron argued.

Indeed, some educational programs only charged a one-time fee for providing the concept, materials, and first-time implementation and training. Once the program was set up in a new location, the school was on its own. The one-time charge appealed financially to school districts that were wary of having to pay annual fees.

"Out-of-the box programs might start out well, but without continuous communication and updating they peter out quickly," Mary Catherine contended. "Then the whole investment is lost." AVID was not a cookie-cutter program; each region, student population, school, and classroom demanded constant adjustments. Flexibility was the AVID way. But too much flexibility would inevitably water down the program until it was no longer AVID. "I am convinced that we must maintain close contact through a strong network," she said, crossing her arms. "Without one, AVID will die."

"You win, on principle," he said. "But before we ask for network fees, we've got to be sure they are justified. What does AVID cost, Mary Catherine?"

"I could tell you a figure I think is close," she said. "But we've never really broken down the costs at every level."

"We've got to find out, don't you think?"

The job of determining costs at every level—classroom, school, district, region, national headquarters—was mind-boggling. Each state had a different funding formula; New Jersey, for example, spent about twice as many education dollars per student as did California. Each district had its own methods of distributing funds and accounting for expenditures. Then there was the question of determining hidden costs of preparation time, travel expenses to institutes, and percentages of a teacher's salary.

After an intensive analysis, they created a framework that put the heaviest costs up front. These included the purchase of the AVID curriculum, a one-time expenditure. To set up a program, a school must send a team of teachers, usually eight in number, to a summer institute. The fees for the institute were the same, roughly $350 per teacher for a week-long program, but travel expenses depended on distance and hotel costs.

The first year a school participated in the AVID program was the most expensive, typically $7,000 per school. In the second year, curricula was inexpensively licensed and, during each subsequent year, costs dropped dramatically. A mature AVID program would still require updating, monitoring, additional training, and communication. Annual fees to support these functions, they estimated, would amount to one-seventh of the first-year cost—about $1,000 per year. For an initial freshman class of 35 students, the first-year cost of $7,000 would amount to $200 per student. By the fourth year, this cost would be amortized to $50 per student.

"Fifty bucks a year per kid, with a 93 percent college-admission rate—amazing!" Ron exclaimed. "I think school boards would buy that."

That would remain to be seen. The total cost of the program was actually higher because each school district was responsible for paying the salaries of teachers and tutors. The tutors' salaries were low, by teachers' standards, but Mrs. Swanson believed that AVID tutors should be paid the same rate as college tutors.

The benefits of educating a new generation for college far outweighed the costs, but it would still be a hard sell.

The business plan required far more than a budget. It called for the development of an AVID structure in each region and state. The state organization would have three responsibilities: funding, staff development, and technical assistance. Should the staff come from the San Diego office? Mrs. Swanson decided that they would be hired in each state so that they would know how their systems operated. Yet they would come for training and meetings in San Diego. The network would be international, but each state and DoDDS program would be connected back to the AVID Center.

But, as yet, there *was* no AVID Center.

Mrs. Swanson found a charming Victorian house that had been salvaged from destruction and relocated to Heritage Park, near San Diego's Old Town. She leased space in the wood-frame building, called McConaughy House. "AVID Center" was painted on a shingle posted outside the door.

The center needed a staff. Changes at the County Office of Education suddenly left Ron Ottinger without a job. He was hired as the first employee of AVID Center. Mary Catherine would keep her job at the County Office of Education. That way, she would keep in touch with the day-to-day operation of her organization in San Diego, staying current with changes in the schools and the new challenges for AVID. She took on a part-time position at AVID Center, dividing her time between the County Office, on the bluffs overlooking Mission Valley, and AVID Center on the valley floor a few miles away.

The business plan was adopted in 1996. The document was an inch thick, a blueprint for a global organization with a hub in San Diego. In 16 years, Mrs. Swanson had moved from a classroom at Clairemont High to a trailer at the County Office of Education to the AVID Center at McConaughy House. Her desk of simulated polished cherry faced a second-story bay window overlooking an emerald green park. She could almost see AVID's future rising in the western sky at sunset.

— AFFIRMATIVE —
PREPARATION

Hurricane-force winds of change were blowing the roofs off America's schools, exposing decades of decay. A new elitism threatened the egalitarian foundations of public education. Fierce critics demanded that schools be overhauled or, if this failed, be closed. Innovators lobbied for experimental new charter schools, home schooling, and school vouchers subsidizing private and parochial education. Opponents of affirmative action ripped minority-preference admissions programs from the University of California. California voters overwhelmingly backed a proposition to dismantle bilingual education; but another proposition to ban undocumented students from attending public school, though approved by voters, was overturned in the courts.

The juggernaut was overwhelming: one wheel uplifting, the other crushing.

Mrs. Swanson hailed higher standards. She opposed closing schools, but rather believed in opening the doors to rigorous and supportive academic programs like AVID. She feared what vouchers would do to public schools, undermining the foundation of America's pluralistic democracy. She thought it was not only unconstitutional but morally reprehensible to deny education to any child, especially those who were marginalized. With a deluge of immigrants in public schools, she appreciated the difficulties facing English learners and their teachers. She believed teaching English was of paramount importance but policy should be set by educators. Of all these changes, the most immediate and stunning changes resulted from the dismantling of affirmative action.

In one year, African American admissions to UC medical schools plummeted and hardly any blacks were admitted to law schools at the University of California.

This change affected the AVID program most directly, but had negligible negative impact on AVID students. They were admitted to college not because of affirmative action, but because they had met or exceeded the entrance requirements. AVID was an affirmative *preparation* program. As racial preferences for minorities were eliminated, affirmative preparation became all the more crucial for first-generation students to be admitted to college.

Finally, the rush to raise standards had impelled several states, Texas among them, to require that students pass standardized tests in order to graduate from high school. The AVID program provided a curriculum and support system that enabled students to master academic disciplines, enabling children who had been left behind to gain and retain the skills and knowledge required for graduation.

In the world of higher standards and diminished preferences, AVID was more vital than ever.

— AVID RECAPITULATED —

The evolution of AVID from conception to replication took six years, from 1980 to 1986. In the next 12 years, AVID grew exponentially in size and scope, reaching tens of thousands of students across the United States and around the globe. AVID had evolved from its single-class origins at Clairemont High but its genetic code remained remarkably unchanged. Each new AVID class would repeat, roughly, the stages of development experienced by Mrs. Swanson's first class; each new AVID teacher would encounter incredible challenges and setbacks. With remarkable frequency, new AVID classes would replicate the successes of the first AVID students at Clairemont High: 93 percent of AVID students went on to college from 1980–1999.

Ontogeny recapitulates phylogeny.

Yet this simplistic metaphor failed to capture the uniqueness of each person's struggle, failed to comprehend the incredible diversity of AVID. A new generation of students was testing the program's ability to grow and adapt. As AVID approached its twentieth anniversary, its founder faced her own struggle for emotional and professional survival.

Keep AVID students in the public eye.
Schoolwide change occurs when beliefs
that certain groups of students are bound to fail
are proven wrong, and both teachers
and students see the unlimited possibilities
for students to advance and achieve.
Success breeds success.

—Mary Catherine Swanson

PART FOUR

ONE TO THE POWER OF FOUR

1999–2000

— A DAY IN HELL —

The close of the twentieth century became the most tumultuous period in Mrs. Swanson's life since the crisis at Clairemont High had forced her to leave teaching. 1999 was a year of personal tragedy and professional triumph.

In January, all the stars aligned for AVID's success. A new governor was elected in California. He appointed Gary Hart, the former chairman of the state senate's education committee, to the cabinet post of California secretary for education. The new secretary, who was a fervent AVID supporter, resigned from the AVID governing board to head up the governor's education-reform effort.

For the first time in the 19 years since AVID's birth, Mrs. Swanson had a powerful ally at the center of political power in the state capitol. Coincidentally, the new chairwomen of the education committees in both the state assembly and senate were also AVID supporters.

After two score years of financial struggle, AVID gained a secure source of state funding. It looked like some good years lay ahead.

But in April, Mrs. Swanson was stunned by bad news.

Awakening before dawn on a chilly, pre-millennial morning and driving 45 minutes in freeway traffic, Mary Catherine arrived at her desk promptly at 7 A.M. There was a message waiting for her to call the Atlantic division.

She lit a gas log in the fireplace of her cozy, second-story office at AVID Center in the Victorian McConaughy House. Her eyes were puffy from lack of sleep, and she had worn a crimson blazer to brighten her day.

She picked up the phone and called Hortense Watson, AVID's Atlantic director. AVID had expanded to 13 states and 13 foreign countries, and there were more than 50 regional directors. The Atlantic division was in charge of 130 programs in 6 states, with 10,000 AVID students. AVID was expanding, and each new district presented a new challenge. It was a tough job to get these programs off the ground while maintaining high academic standards. Hortense had been active in AVID since 1990, first as an administrator and now as Atlantic director. Mrs. Swanson depended on her to run AVID's expanding East Coast operation.

The Atlantic director's voice, three time zones ahead, was bright as the midday sun. "I've been offered a fabulous position and I just can't turn it down!" Hortense gushed. Hortense could not hide her excitement, talking a mile a minute about her new opportunities: a wonderful job, big title, better pay, no travel. Mrs. Swanson listened with a sinking heart.

Hortense paused, breathlessly, while Mrs. Swanson struggled to overcome her shock. She seemed to be waiting for Mary Catherine to offer her congratulations, as if her sudden departure from AVID would not cause major disruptions for the organization. Reeling, Mrs. Swanson could not offer her congratulations—not now, the disappointment was too fresh, the weight pressing down on her too heavy. To offer phony words would betray her disappointment.

Already Mrs. Swanson's mind was racing ahead, searching for a replacement. William Billingsly, the assistant regional director, was the natural choice.

But when Billingsly got on the line, he chirped on about his own good fortune. Mrs. Swanson closed her eyes, cringing as the other shoe dropped. "I've landed a job with Hortense!" he crowed, blathering on about his benefits. Neither administrator expressed regrets that they were leaving AVID students in the lurch. The entire Atlantic division had only three employees: two administrators and a secretary. In two months, there might only be a secretary left. Ten thousand students, dozens of teachers, and countless dreams were left hanging in the balance.

Mrs. Swanson set the phone down and stared out the bay window reflecting mental images of her AVID students. She was still receiving a public-school educator's salary, and she naively believed that the satisfactions of helping children outweighed a bigger paycheck. *Had the Atlantic directors used AVID as a stepping stone?* she wondered. This made her stop and take stock of her own professional beliefs vis-à-vis personal values.

The evening before all this happened, Mary Catherine and her husband had each worked a typical ten-hour day, grabbed a quick dinner, and made a call to a humble neighbor who had been their gardener for 13 years and was now ill. Alejandro Santos lived with his wife, Filomela, in a tiny rusting trailer at the end of a dirt road. At age 39, this hardworking, iron-muscled man started having vision problems, piercing headaches, and trouble staying balanced. Suddenly, he was no longer able to work. Like millions of other working Californians, he had no health insurance and didn't qualify for Medicaid. The Mexican gardener had many American clients, but when he stopped working the *gringos* forgot about him.

Weeks ago, when the Swansons had first heard about Alejandro's condition, they had taken him to the hospital and asked their doctor to examine him. The CAT scan was costly, but the doctor held out hope that, with brain surgery, Alejandro might survive. The procedure was to drill a hole in his cranium and insert a shunt to drain fluids, releasing pressure from the brain. The operation would cost thousands of dollars, and the Swansons gave him $8,000.

Alejandro was grateful, hopeful. But the first surgery failed, and the second after it. The third time the surgeon went in, a blood vessel was severed, causing permanent brain damage. He was brought back to the trailer, where Filomela struggled to take care of him.

On the evening of their visit, the Swansons bumped up the dirt road. The trailer was so small that the front door nearly slammed into the rear wall. Filomela led them to the bedroom, which held a single bed, with barely a foot between the mattress and the walls. Mary Catherine saw a figure lying under the covers. His head was shaved in patches. Saliva drooled from the corner of his mouth. His once handsome face, with high cheekbones and skin the color of the red earth he had made bloom, was shrunken and withered. He looked like a small forest creature who'd been caught in a trap made of twisted sheets. His *manos* that had cut and chopped and dug and watered their garden for a decade of revolutions around the sun were hidden beneath the bedclothes.

"Alejandro . . ." they greeted him, pressed against the wall.

The dilated pupils revolved toward them and his jaw worked, but his lips could not form the words. Mary Catherine reached beneath the covers and took his hand. He held on with a clawlike grasp, his thumb digging into her flesh, fingers silently imploring her to lift him out of the white bed, a living coffin.

"Is there anything we can do?"

Alejandro gurgled unintelligibly, desperate to be understood. Filomela shook her head, a young wife, childless, caring for this man-child. *What will her life be like?* Mary Catherine wondered. Alejandro was unable to walk to the bathroom, unable to feed or clothe himself, a tormented creature. The doctors said he would never recover and might live indefinitely in this condition. A forsaken man, he was of no use to anyone, a Mexican *bracero* without arms or hope.

Yet Filomela would stand by her husband's bedside.

Now, back in her office, Mrs. Swanson was thinking about this tragedy and the meaning of commitment. *What pushes some people to make tremendous sacrifices, while others abandon a cause for personal gain?* she wondered. *Where is the depth of character? Are people just out for what's best for them? Are we so selfish that all we look for is what promotes us?*

"Loyalty. . . . We have a lot to learn from Filomela," Mary Catherine sighed, turning back to her desk.

The phone was ringing again. She cringed, fearing another bombshell from the Atlantic division. Instead, the switchboard operator passed through a call from the governor's office. It was her old friend, Gary Hart.

"I've got a request," he said without hesitation. "Can you find me a high-school principal who is willing to testify on exit testing before the state senate education committee?"

The proposed exit test was an examination that high-school seniors must pass in order to graduate. The governor was behind it, and his educational reform package was racing through the legislature. After decades of decline in the California public schools, politicians had jumped on the bandwagon of educational reform. They wanted to make a high-school diploma stand for something by requiring that all seniors pass tests in order to graduate.

But some teachers and community leaders questioned whether the test would be a fair measure. They protested that any standardized test given in English would be biased against students who were not proficient in English.

Mrs. Swanson had complicated feelings. She had always believed in challenging AVID students to perform to the highest levels—and they had performed beyond all expectations. But she remembered the district's old Achievement Goals Program (AGP) that had turned teachers into drill sergeants. Would exit tests promote a return to rote learning?

Mrs. Swanson trusted the secretary of education's instincts and appreciated his trust in her.

"When is the hearing?" Mrs. Swanson asked.

"Tomorrow morning."

She racked her brain for the right candidate. Education had become so politicized that many principals, for their own protection, feared speaking their minds. She called a couple of candidates, but were told their schedules were full. *But it's the secretary of education!* Mrs. Swanson wanted to shout. The answers were polite but firm: No.

Mrs. Swanson set down the phone. It was the second frustration of the day, and she hadn't even tackled the budget due that afternoon. She had a crisis on her hands and a request for help from a political ally. At such moments, she usually did two things: She called her trusted allies for advice, and she searched the darkness for a window of opportunity.

A flurry of phone calls went out to other principals with AVID programs. She consulted with her communications director and put in a call to the president of the board to discuss the abrupt resignations. Later, she sat down at the computer and wrote an e-mail informing AVID staff of the resignation of the Atlantic division directors.

It's a day from hell! she laughed to herself, repressing tears.

She received a series of calls and again consulted with her tireless communications director, Rob Gira, charting a new course of action. From this office she ran a vast network of AVID directors and coordinators. California had 600 AVID schools alone, each following curriculum guidelines she had composed in the lonely isolation of the trailer.

For Mrs. Swanson, AVID was not only a job, nor even a profession. It was a cause. And it was this sense of mission by which she judged colleagues and employees who weren't necessarily as devoted as she. Her determination was the *D* in AVID. Mrs. Swanson set high standards for her staff, perhaps beyond what ordinary humans, like the Atlantic division directors, could live up to.

The danger for AVID was that its charismatic leader would become so identified with a program that it would be difficult to separate personality from policy. When she retired, who could carry on the AVID spirit? Mrs. Swanson had anticipated this problem by bringing young people aboard.

But the morning's resignations were deeply disconcerting because the exit of key staff, drawn by the promise of money and title, revealed the uncertainty of the future.

Would AVID survive?

Amidst imponderable questions, Mrs. Swanson became deeply thoughtful. The red blazer that armored her for battle opened to reveal glimpses of a deeper soul that day. The faster she went, the slower she spoke, giving emphasis to words like *loyalty, devotion, friendship, commitment.* She was moved by things that were invisible to outsiders and that could not be quantified by statistics. These forces might be called the traditional values, or spiritual qualities, that ennobled ordinary human beings.

These values, like the components of AVID, were not new. They were practical and enduring. Yet they could not be quantified. AVID was an opportunity for a teacher to develop a relationship with students. It offered an opportunity to recover from burnout and to feel, once again, the satisfaction that teacher had known when he or she first began teaching. Mrs. Swanson could point to the curriculum and tools and studies, but the essence of AVID was human. Its humanity was both a strength and a weakness, like the people who helped others and those who received help.

Before noon, Mrs. Swanson got a call from Riverside County. A principal involved in AVID was delighted to testify in Sacramento. Mrs. Swanson briefed her on the political intricacies, saying, "I'll be honest. They want someone to speak up for high graduation standards." Mrs. Swanson was in her lobbyist mode, an advocate.

Ron Ottinger, AVID's board president, called, and they talked about finding replacements for the Atlantic division. When she hung up, Mrs. Swanson reflected about the meaning of loyalty. Two years before, when Ron was AVID associate director, he had come into her office with tears in his eyes and told her that he had to leave because of family issues that had nothing to do with AVID. She appreciated his honesty and directness, a marked contrast to the behavior of the Atlantic directors. Mary Catherine knew that, wherever Ron went, she would be able to call him and he would listen and offer the best advice he had. Later, when things got settled at home, Ron came back to work for AVID as associate national director.

Mrs. Swanson raced to accomplish what she needed to before the day exploded. She had the budgets to finish in the afternoon. But before that, she had a lunch meeting with Barbara Stone, a dear friend and colleague from Clairemont High.

We go back a long way, Mary Catherine reflected. Back when she had been teaching *The Scarlet Letter,* a class discussion had turned to antiquated laws and excessive punishments, like putting scofflaws in stocks.

"Mrs. Swanson, isn't it true that it's illegal in California to have sex in anything but the missionary position?" a student asked provocatively, giggling.

"Yes, just as it is illegal to spit on the sidewalk," Mrs. Swanson answered, quickly ending the discussion.

But later a parent complained that Mrs. Swanson had been advocating certain sexual positions to her class, and the vice principal called her in to his office.

"Why on Earth are you telling your students to use the missionary position?" he asked.

"A student asked the question, and I merely reported the law of the state," she answered.

"That's ridiculous," he answered dismissively. Just then, a new teacher named Barbara Stone passed within hearing range. The vice principal gruffly called her in to settle the dispute. "That business about the missionary position is nonsense isn't it?" he asked.

"No, because once I got ticketed for it!" she replied, shrugging. The shocked vice principal had regarded Barbara as the darling of the school because she had graduated as Clairemont's valedictorian five years earlier.

That was the beginning of a 20-year friendship between Mary Catherine and Barbara. The two irrepressible teachers worked together at Clairemont and kept in touch when Mrs. Swanson moved to the County Office and her friend moved to the desert. And now Barbara was back in San Diego. She had breast cancer and was beginning to receive radiation treatment.

The Atlantic division was hanging fire, and Gary Hart had found someone to testify. Mrs. Swanson looked at her watch and fielded a final telephone call before lunch. It was J. Anne Lookabill, the AVID director in California. J. Anne had been trying to set up a meeting for Mrs. Swanson with the powerful new chair of the state senate budget committee. She needed to make AVID's case for $7 million in state funding at the highest political level possible.

"Sorry, I can't get through the brick wall of his staff," J. Anne apologized. "He's not in his office, he's not in Sacramento, nobody knows where he is."

Disappointed, Mrs. Swanson put up a good front. "Don't give up until you reach him," she said, hanging up with a sigh: *Lord knows how.*

The day from hell was only half over, and the budget loomed for the afternoon. But first, Mrs. Swanson was keeping her lunch appointment with her friend. Hurrying to the restaurant, she expected Barbara to look emaciated.

But the woman she met was the same old Barbara, full of wit and spunk. The only noticeable change was that Barbara had lost her hair and was wearing a gray wig. They picked up their relationship as if they had seen each other yesterday. Barbara was frank about the chemotherapy treatments she was receiving. Some days, she was so tired that she didn't have energy to walk from her bedroom to the living room. The doctors had pronounced her treatment successful, but she volunteered for radiation therapy at a clinic in San Diego.

"I'm sacrificing this one year to gain the rest of my life," she explained.

Mrs. Swanson could not imagine what the radiation treatments would do to her friend, but Barbara refused to mope.

"Last week, I ran into one of my students," Barbara grinned. "He'd shaved his head. So I tapped him on the shoulder. When he turned around, I lifted my wig. 'Look, we match!'"

Mrs. Swanson squealed with girlish delight, causing diners' heads to turn. It was the only unladylike thing about her, this irrepressible gush of joy that burst like a broken water main, spouting a geyser of hoots. For a moment, her problems and disappointments were reduced to giggles.

Laughter kept these kindred women going when others would give up. They embraced with tears running down their cheeks. Barbara returned to the clinic, Mrs. Swanson to the office.

A call was awaiting her from Sean Helms, the principal at Van Buren High School. He was concerned that some teachers were trying to keep AVID students out of advanced classes. In passing, he mentioned that, this afternoon, Van Buren was playing in the regional soccer championship match.

"There goes the state senator by my window," he continued, changing the subject.

"Who?" she asked, nearly choking.

"The senator. He's here to watch his son in the soccer match."

"Sean, I need to ask you a favor. I've been trying to get an appointment with him for a month. I'm willing to meet at the soccer field. Anywhere!"

"Fine." Sean promised that she could speak with the budget chief on the sidelines.

Mrs. Swanson was floating in air. She did not usually put her fortunes in the hands of Providence, but how else to explain such coincidences that had kept AVID going for nearly 20 years?

Coincidence, she reflected, gazing through the window into the sunlit haze. She remembered Jerry Rosander revealing that her father had mentored him in high school, and it had opened the doors for AVID. Jerry had since retired. She wondered where he was.

Coincidence—or commitment? she pondered, remembering today's disappointing news from the East with a pang. *How can the Atlantic*

*directors be so glib, boasting about their high-paying foundation jobs?
Does their commitment to AVID kids mean nothing?*

She turned her attention to the eye-blurring budget figures on
the desk before her. *How did she get into this—an English teacher
whose husband handled their family finances?* From the first few dollars sneaked out of the school's general fund, she had kept AVID
afloat. Now the budget was $5 million. Yet she still could not afford
to let AVID go even one dollar in the red.

How she hated performing these administrative tasks! She
yearned to be back in the classroom once again.

The phone rang. It was the regional director from Cherry Creek
Schools in Colorado, asking Mrs. Swanson to lead a staff development conference in April. AVID was new to the Rockies, and
school administrators were coming to have a look-see about adopting the program. She accepted the invitation to visit Colorado in
April.

At 3 o'clock, she was nose-deep in numbers when the phone rang
for the umpteenth time. *Wasn't anyone screening her calls?* She
wanted to let it ring off the hook, but at the sixth ring she picked
up the infernal receiver.

"Hi. This is Joe Canon," said a voice from out of the blue.

A boy's face popped up in her mind's eye. Crooked teeth and a
gaunt face. She knew instantly who it was.

"Joe," she said, astonished that he would call after all these
years. Joe was a member of the first AVID graduating class of 1984,
a tall, shy, and rather unpromising student who had slouched in his
seat. His hair had always been in his eyes. She had taught him for
four years, longer than most teachers would ever know a student,
and had helped him boost his grades from Cs to Bs—hardly ever an
A. Joe wasn't a troublemaker, nor had he been a leader. She'd once
visited his run-down house, perched atop a concrete wall on a narrow, triangular street corner in a bad neighborhood. Inside, the TV

was blaring and countless siblings occupied every inch of the tiny three-room house. "How do you study here?" she had asked Joe. "Mrs. Swanson, I go to the library every night," he'd said, which earned him credit in her book. But she had never been able to light a fire under him.

That was 15 years ago, and she hadn't heard from him in more than a decade. His brother, Walter, who was also in AVID, once told her that Joe did something mechanical and had gotten a job in the Midwest. Joe had married at 18 and struggled to support a wife and child while attending San Diego State University. She had doubted that he would ever graduate from college. He was not one of the students with whom she had kept in touch.

"Mrs. Swanson, I knew you would be there," Joe said with a gush of emotion.

"Joe, the last time I saw you you were a waiter at the San Diego Yacht Club," she replied. "Your brother later told me you had two children and were living somewhere in the Midwest."

"Wow! You know everything. Just like you did when I was in high school."

"No, I don't. I don't know where you are now."

"Well, Mrs. Swanson, that's the reason I'm calling you." Joe filled in the blanks. He had graduated from San Diego State University with a degree in mechanical engineering. Recently, he'd brought his family to Arizona. He was an engineering consultant, working with his wife out of a home office.

"I'm calling you because my son is entering Kino Middle School," Joe said. "When I went to enroll him, I discovered they didn't have an AVID program."

Mrs. Swanson listened, warmed by the fire in his voice.

"So I asked to see the principal," Joe said, "and I told him, 'Mr. Durango, I can't imagine my son going through school without AVID. Back in San Diego, there was no way I could have gone to college without AVID.'" The principal had listened, asking questions about the program. Joe told him, "I know I can find my AVID teacher and she will help you get an AVID program."

Joe had followed up his meeting with a letter.

Dear Principal Durango,

When I was a freshman in high school, I was lucky
enough to be involved in a very special program. The
program was designed to help students who dream of
going to college but have very little hope of ever
getting there. I was a member of the very first AVID
class in 1980. Consequently, I was accepted to San
Diego State University in 1984. It was a dream come
true for my family and me. I was the very first Canon
ever to attend college.

The program was the brainchild of Mrs. Mary Catherine
Swanson, an English teacher who has since gone on
implementing the program in other school systems. I
am sure that Mrs. Swanson would be more than happy to
speak with you about AVID.

Next year, my son will start seventh grade. I believe
that he and many other students can greatly benefit
from a program such as AVID. Frankly, I cannot fath-
om what school would be like without the kind of push
and support that AVID gave me.

Sincerely,

Joseph Canon

Joe had wanted to enlist Mrs. Swanson's help, but didn't know
her phone number. First, he called Clairemont High School, but
the clerk had no idea who or where Mrs. Swanson was. Next, he
called the human resources department at the City Schools and the
clerk looked in the directory, but found no name. He did not know
that Mrs. Swanson had resigned in 1986, before moving to the
County. In desperation, he asked the clerk to look into the archives.

A veteran overheard the conversation and broke in, "Wait a minute. I know who she is." She looked in her personal directory and gave Joe the number of the AVID office at the County and that secretary had patched the call in to Mrs. Swanson.

"Of course, I'll help you, Joe," she said. "Send me the letter and I'll send you the AVID information folder."

"I knew I could count on you!" With astonishment and gratitude, Mrs. Swanson and Joe bid each other good-bye.

At the end of a damnable day, Joe had given her reason to continue. That was why she put up with the administrative junk and personnel crises and financial turmoil. She marveled at the depth of character and commitment on the part of this former student who had seemed so unprepossessing in her class. With a flush in her cheeks, she realized that there was no question in his mind that he could call her 15 years later, knowing that she would know who he was without him having to introduce himself. He could tell this principal that Mrs. Swanson would do something because he knew she would do everything she could to help his son get a good education, a chance at college.

The sharp contrast between the two calls, bracketing the morning and afternoon, brought Mrs. Swanson a glimpse of understanding: *What counts is a personal commitment. When Joe needed me, he knew I would be here, ready to help his son. This is what AVID is really about: students and teachers who make commitments to each other, sharing struggles and victories together.*

The sun had set and the employees had left AVID Center. Despite the gas flame in the fireplace, the office felt suddenly chilly. Mrs. Swanson shuddered in the lonely isolation of responsibility, complaining bitterly to herself: *When AVID needed the Atlantic directors, they weren't there. They didn't even have the decency to tell me they were sorry.*

She would never understand why others did not take AVID as seriously as she. This was the burden of a founder who must, one day, contemplate turning AVID over to a new generation. She worried: *What must I do for AVID to survive as a living institution after my retirement?*

Mrs. Swanson was a doer, not one to wallow in problems. Her subconscious was already coming up with a plan, listing names of candidates to replace the departing Atlantic directors. At 8 o'clock on this wintry night, 13 hours after she started work, the light burned bright in her Victorian office.

— A DEATH IN —
THE FAMILY

In April 1999, Mrs. Swanson was scheduled to give a presentation to educational leaders in the state of Colorado who were considering adopting AVID.

On April 13, her mother, Corrine Jacobs, broke her hip. Her father was dazed and confused, unable to cope. Torn between the conference and her family, Mary Catherine chose to cancel the speech and be with her parents in Kingsburg.

The AVID conference went ahead, drawing interest from districts across Colorado. AVID students demonstrated how a study group created a school-within-a-school where each student belonged and nobody felt left out—a refuge for kids to stay connected. Visiting teachers and parents seemed enthusiastic, but a hard-nosed administrator asked, "How can my district justify spending money on a program like AVID?"

The answer came, indirectly, a few days after the conference, when the Columbine High School massacre occurred in nearby Littleton, Colorado. Shocked and frightened Americans asked:

Why has our culture bred such alienation and anger in students? How can we afford *not* to build community in schools?

In her parents' home in Kingsburg, Mary Catherine watched in horror as the Columbine nightmare unfolded on television. As she cared for her parents, she keenly felt the needs of children, holding in her middle-aged hands the fragile threads of life stretching from birth to death. Her mother's health crisis subsided long enough to bring her mother to a nursing home and to arrange home care for her father before returning to San Diego.

Back at work, the dangers facing public education seemed all the more pressing. Mrs. Swanson rededicated herself to AVID's mission, transforming alienating classrooms into safe havens where students share with teachers and parents a strong sense of purpose and belonging.

In June, Mary Catherine was preparing to deliver the most important policy speech of her career. She had a long-standing invitation to deliver the keynote address to thousands of educators attending a prestigious national education-reform conference in Seattle. For a year she had been preparing her speech, entitled "What's Needed in Education Today," and she was excited to deliver it on June 18. A day before flying to Seattle, Mary Catherine got the call from Kingsburg. She canceled her speech and rushed once again to Northern California.

On June 17, Mary Catherine's mother passed away. After the heart attack and a broken hip, Corrine Jacobs was finally at peace. Now Ed Jacobs, whose mind had been deteriorating for months, suffered a complete mental breakdown. With his wife of 59 years gone, his entire world shattered. He became psychologically disoriented, his memory failed, and he lost all sense of time. Each minute was an agony for him, and the idea of waiting several days to bury his wife was unbearable. Mary Catherine and her sister decided to bury their mother the next day, before the small-town cemetery closed for the weekend.

The family laid Corrine to rest on June 18, Ed Jacobs's eighty-eighth birthday. Mary Catherine wrote the eulogy, but was too grief-stricken to deliver it. The minister who knew her parents was out of town, so another minister who barely knew them delivered the eulogy. That same day, in Seattle, Dr. Stephen Weber, president of San Diego State University, took Mrs. Swanson's place on the dais and delivered his own speech.

The next day, June 19, Mary Catherine and her husband loaded up a car and moved her father from Kingsburg to San Diego County to live with them in their home. Suffering terribly, he struggled out of his seat belt more than a dozen times during the drive. He was totally disoriented, a rebellious child. They did their best to care for him in their home.

After a few weeks, it became obvious that he was too severely impaired to remain in the house while they were out working. The doctor confirmed Mary Catherine's worst fears. Her brilliant father had Alzheimer's; one moment he could function, the next he suffered "severe dementia." There was no way to take care of him at home. After much torment, they found a board-and-care facility where her father could have his own apartment and have round-the-clock care. It was located near their home, three blocks from Tom's office at Fallbrook National Bank.

— ULTIMATE JOURNEY —

A month after burying her mother, Mrs. Swanson was booked to address three AVID Summer Institutes on two coasts within 15 days. The schedule was grueling. Monday, July 26, she would open the AVID Institute in Northern California. Tuesday, she would fly to Virginia. Wednesday, she would give the closing address to the Atlantic division. Ten days later, she would address 1,800 conference attendees in San Diego. These gatherings culminated AVID's nineteenth year, and she could not afford to cancel her appearances.

She was emotionally drained. Her father was terribly depressed in the retirement residence, but he needed virtually 24-hour care, which she could not provide. She could not bear leaving him. Yet she looked forward to meeting AVID teachers and hearing their stories.

On July 26, she began the bicoastal journey. At Asilomar, near the coastal highway between Monterey and Santa Cruz, she spoke about a subject dear to her heart: "AVID Is a Catalyst for Social Change." Then she hopped in a rental car and drove two hours to the San Jose airport. She caught a flight to the east, with a stop in Georgia. But in Atlanta the plane developed mechanical problems. They sat on the runway for two hours, then rolled back to the gate and unloaded. At 1:30 the passengers re-boarded the plane. As it headed for takeoff, there was a violent explosion. Sparks flew. Mary Catherine thought the engine had fallen off. The pilot taxied back, refusing to fly the plane.

A third flight was to leave at 7:30 P.M. But, before they took off, severe thunderstorms closed the Atlantic airport. The flight was canceled.

A fourth flight was scheduled for 10:50 P.M. They were bringing in a second flight crew from Cincinnati. At 11:30 P.M., the boarding agents announced bad news. Time had run out for the second crew. They had been on duty too many hours. They could no longer legally fly.

No more flights until Wednesday morning, the day the AVID Institute was closing.

Mrs. Swanson rushed to the ticket counter to get her travel voucher. She arrived too late to be put on the first plane out. She was booked on a flight leaving at 8:30 A.M. It was scheduled to arrive at 10:00 A.M. Her speech was to be given at 11:15.

Atlanta airport hotels were full. She was given a voucher to sleep at an inn and was directed to a shuttle. She had to cross three lanes of traffic to reach the shuttle. After midnight, it was 90 degrees Fahrenheit, 98 percent humidity. The shuttle never came.

She waved down another motel shuttle and begged the driver to take her to the inn. He agreed—for a $20 tip. After dropping off all the other passengers, he let her off and drove away. The inn had a chain-link fence around it. There was no parking lot. No lights. The office was closed.

She saw a sign: "Check In Room #104."

She walked down the darkened corridor. Inside room 104 she saw three men in their mid-thirties. They were standing around a makeshift desk, looking eager for female company. They looked her up and down. She had no luggage. Just her handbag. Her clothing was sweat-stained. Her curly blonde hair was plastered to her forehead.

"Let's party!" cried one, winking at her.

She scowled back. The "desk clerk" took her voucher and gave her a key. The room was on the second floor of another wing. She had to walk down a darkened walkway and take an elevator to the third floor. There was no bellboy to walk with her.

"Hey, let's find a bar!" the men shouted.

Averting her eyes, she passed them, striding into the darkness. The men followed her, cracking jokes and laughing. She was angry, hot, sticky, exhausted, and more than a little frightened. She reached the elevator, pushed the button and waited. The men came behind her. She smelled alcohol on their breaths. Her heart pounded. She had nothing to protect herself, just a purse and her presentation materials. When the elevator door opened, she let them pass. Turning heel, she almost ran back to room 104.

"Do you have a security guard?" she asked the two desk-less clerks.

"No." They eyed her strangely.

"I'm not going to that room by myself."

One of them escorted her to her second-story room. It gave off a stale smell. The air conditioner wouldn't go on. She took a cold shower and rinsed her underwear. The rug was filthy. She sat down on the toilet seat and wrapped towels around her feet for booties. The seat made a popping noise and she jumped, terrified of falling in. Then she started laughing, wildly, at herself.

She still had to call Barbara Smith, the new director of the Atlantic division, to ask her to pick her up at the airport. One problem. There was a lock on the phone beside the bed. She couldn't call the desk clerk. So, she got dressed in her clothes, *sans* wet underwear, and walked down to room 104. It was 2 A.M. and she had to wake up at 5 A.M. to take the shuttle.

She was really ticked off now.

"I have to make a phone call and there's a [bleep]ing lock on it!" she cried.

"That's because you didn't leave a deposit for the phone," the clerk replied, grinning. The inn required a credit card or cash. She stormed back to her room and returned with a card. Finally, she reached Barbara. It was 2:30 A.M.

"Barbara, there was a 6:30 flight, but I wasn't far enough up in the line to get it," she apologized. She gave Barbara a description of her checked baggage and asked her to meet her at the gate.

Then she called Tom back in California. His voice sounded low. He told her about a crisis at the bank.

"Where are you?" he asked.

She started to tell him, but decided not to. He had enough on his shoulders at home, and, if she started talking, she feared she would lose control. Then she would be in deep trouble. *I have to stay strong,* she thought. *I'll call when it's over.*

She couldn't sleep. Her underwear was damp. She put on yesterday's sweat-soaked Levis and a shirt, checked out of the wretched inn, and caught a shuttle to the airport. Many people were waiting at the boarding gate for the plane. She sat down next to an elderly lady and gentleman.

"I have an incredible story to tell you," the lady said. "Last night, we stayed in this so-called 'inn.' During the night, we heard knocking at our door. My husband opened it and there were two young boys, ages nine and seven.

"'What are you doing?' my husband asked.

"'Mother locked us out.'

"My husband went down to room 104 and asked the men, 'Please take care of these two kids.' They just shrugged. So we asked the kids' names. They knew where their room was: two doors down from ours. We all marched down there and knocked on the door. The mother opened it. She had on a big wig, tons of makeup, gold jewelry, and this short, white outfit with gold trim and high, high heels. There were two men in the room. They looked real irritated that the kids were at the door.

"You know," the lady told Mrs. Swanson with her voice full of disgust, "where my husband and I stayed last night was a house of prostitution!"

So that's why there was no check-in desk, Mrs. Swanson thought. *Those men must have thought I was a hooker.*

The plane touched down 10:05. Barbara was waiting at the gate. They found the luggage and rushed off to the car. Speeding down the highway to the site of the meeting, they looked for exit 186A.

"It's taking me a lot longer than when I came," Barbara confessed, hunched over the wheel. She was new to Virginia. They passed Exit 171, then 169.

"We're going the wrong direction!" Mrs. Swanson wailed. The dashboard clock said 11:00. Barbara U-turned at the next exit and pushed the pedal to the floor. They called ahead on her cell phone. "We'll be there in ten minutes!" Barbara cried.

They screeched into the hotel entrance. The meeting was in session. People were dressed formally. Mrs. Swanson rushed to Barbara's room, threw on dry underwear, hose, a dress, and dry shoes. Five minutes later, she walked into the ballroom, handed the multimedia operator the script to her presentation and walked onto the stage. He uploaded the disk while she was being introduced.

After 29 hours without sleep and no food since lunch in San Jose, she blinked at the audience, dissociated in time and space. Then she spotted three AVID students sitting in the front row. She remembered why she had come, and the words came to her lips.

"It is my distinct honor and pleasure to introduce three extraordinary AVID students," Mary Catherine said, smiling at two teenaged girls with pony tails and a slightly built black boy with large eyes. "They attend an extraordinary AVID demonstration school led by an extraordinary administrator in an extraordinary school district. Newport News was the first school district east of California to adopt the AVID program, a trail-blazing effort that catalyzed the expansion of AVID to 13 states and 13 foreign countries. I am very proud that Russ Archer, principal of Powhatan Middle School, a national AVID demonstration site, was recently honored with the Administrator of the Year Award in Newport News—a signal honor for a principal. We are delighted that Russ is joining us today.

"The great accomplishments of educators in the Atlantic division—and extraordinary devoted educators like the 800 participants in this conference—were overshadowed by the most horrific education story of the year, perhaps of the century. The tragedy at Columbine High School awakened Americans from complacency. We now are painfully aware that American children are at risk because of affluence, divorce, and family tragedy, *as well as* from drugs, poverty, and racism.

"What role can AVID play?

"As you listen to the following three stories, I want you to ask:

"Why didn't Tyrone, whose mother died, fall apart and seek company in a gang?

"Why didn't Vera, whose parents divorced, develop low self-esteem and drop out?

"Why didn't Crystal, who comes from a stable family, rebel against her parents and join a group like the Trench Coat Mafia?" Mary Catherine let the questions sink in, then plunged ahead. "These are their stories."

Tyrone

Tyrone was a precocious African American 13-year-old, small of frame, straight of stature, with acutely aware eyes. His nightmare began when he was nine.

"Ty, get up!" his brother, Byron, had cried. Tyrone sat up in bed. It was dark and he did not know if he was awake or dreaming. Byron pulled him out of bed. "Hurry! Something's wrong with Mom."

In a daze, Tyrone stumbled down the hall. A comforting glow came from his parents' bedroom, drawing him toward the warmth of his mother's sleeping form in a pink nightgown. But the stark tableaux Tyrone beheld was anything but comforting. His mother lay rigidly on her back, her neck twisted to the side, face contorted, mouth gaping. He could barely recognize her. "Mama?" he cried. "Mama!"

Tyrone's father bent over his wife, huffing into her mouth and crying, "Honey! Wake up!" Then his father reared back, pressing down with his palms and rhythmically pumping her breast bone, desperately trying to resuscitate her.

Tyrone stood in his Superhero pajamas, the pajamas she'd bought him, and prayed for Spider Man to fly off his pajamas and rescue her. He had never before seen his father cry, a strong man made powerless. Boots clattered up the stairs. A rough hand grabbed Tyrone's shoulder and yanked him back.

"Go downstairs," a paramedic yelled. "Now!"

Tyrone obeyed, numbly standing at the bottom of the stairs. Surely he was dreaming and this nightmare would end like a TV episode. If Spider Man couldn't save her, he knew what to do. Falling on his knees, he closed his eyes: "Please, Lord!"

"Out of the way!" the paramedic thundered. Tyrone skittered back on his knees. The paramedics carried a stretcher out the door, and Tyrone saw his mother's face, covered with an oxygen mask, illuminated by the flashing red lights of the ambulance. His father climbed in the vehicle and it drove off, sirens wailing.

Tyrone and Byron were sent to the neighbors' house to wait. The flickering TV hypnotized them, and it no longer seemed real. She was a loving mother, beautiful inside and out, and only 40 years old. It was just yesterday, it seemed, that she had coached him to ride his new shiny red bicycle.

His father returned at dawn and sat Byron and Tyrone down on the couch.

"Your mother has passed away," he said.

On the outside, Tyrone showed no emotion. Inside, he cried: *Why? Why to us?*

An autopsy revealed that his mother had died of a massive myocardial infarction. She had complained of chest pains for weeks, but the doctors had said it was just heartburn or maybe an ulcer, and they gave her antacids.

Tyrone's father moved to Newport News with the boys. *How was he going to raise them without a wife and mother?* They were both bright, but he feared for their future in a new neighborhood. The church was their mainstay, but they needed someone to look after them at school.

Tyrone could barely climb out of bed in the morning. *What was the purpose?* He didn't see any reason for going to school. He was teased because he was small and wore glasses and because he got the right answers on tests. He couldn't help that he was smart, any more than he could bring his mother back. *Why live?*

A year after his mother's death, an AVID recruiter called Tyrone out of class and invited him to join a class where it was okay to be who he was.

"Your teacher says you're bright as a button," the recruiter said. "She also told me about your mother passing away. It must be hard."

"I don't care," he said.

"In AVID we care very much," she said.

Tyrone's father gave his approval. He was digging out of his own depression and had started a business as an environmental consultant. Tyrone started AVID in sixth grade, and Byron started that same year in eighth grade.

"The first day, I was kind of scared," Tyrone recalls. "I wanted to be in pre-algebra in sixth grade." He liked being part of a group. "The tutor comes and blends in with the group, trying to help you with your questions. I can relate to them because they are in college."

Their father began to notice a difference in his sons' outlook. Tyrone brought books home and read every night. He also started bringing home As and began to show some self-confidence.

One day, a big kid cornered Tyrone. "You're an AVID dork, aren't you?"

"I'm not a dork."

"You guys think you're better than everybody else, but really you're just a bunch of nerds!" the bully roared, knocking the books out of Tyrone's hands and swaggering off. Slowly, Tyrone picked up the books and went to AVID.

"I'm proud to be a nerd," Tyrone told his father.

"Keep on going, son. Strive. Don't let other people bring you down."

Tyrone participated in AVID for three years. It changed his way of learning. The tutors helped him understand the information; he soaked it in and knowledge became a part of him. In eighth grade, Tyrone achieved straight As.

He spoke to younger kids about his experiences. "It's not harder work," he explained, "especially when you get help from tutors and teachers."

After school, Tyrone began tutoring younger children whose fathers weren't around to help them. One 11-year-old was flunking math, and the teacher said he was a behavior problem.

"I don't care about no math!" the boy whined. "I don't care about nothing!"

"I used to say that, but I really wanted someone to care about me."

"Yeah, sure. You're getting straight As. You don't care."

"In AVID, we care a lot." Tyrone confided in the boy about his mother's death and coming to the new school and being teased. "We help each other."

At the next meeting, the boy told Tyrone he and his mother were living in a car and that his father was in jail.

"At least you've got your mother," Tyrone said. "I'd sleep in a car any day to get my mom back."

"I guess I'm lucky, huh?" the boy said.

Every afternoon, the boy met with Tyrone. The 13-year-old became an older brother for the homeless boy, and slowly his math grades improved. One day, the mother came to school with great news. "I found an apartment!" she rejoiced. "Are you his tutor?" she asked Tyrone. "Thank you for helping my son."

"It's nothing," Tyrone said. "AVID helped me and now I'm just passing it on."

That spring, Tyrone signed up for AVID in high school. "I'm going to college for sure," he told the AVID recruiter. "I'm going to be an engineer or a doctor." But that was not enough, he said: "I'm going to keep on my spiritual path. I want to be a family man."

Five years after awakening to the horror of his mother's death, the nightmare was over. Tyrone, Byron, and their father were thriving in Newport News—a family held together by love, faith, and support from AVID.

Mrs. Swanson finished telling the first story and asked the audience to hold its applause until the end of all three students' experiences. "Another AVID story was unfolding in Newport News at that time," she said, feeling their energy seep into her body. "It involved a relationship between two adolescent girls, one from a solid family, another whose parents divorced. This is the story of Vera and Crystal."

Vera and Crystal

It was impossible to watch Vera and Crystal chat for hours on the phone, intently quizzing each other for tests and gossiping about boys, without believing that life for these white teenyboppers was a bowl of cherries. Yet their contrasting home lives, like those of millions of American children, revealed the sharp and jagged edges of a generation divided between children of stable homes and kids shaped by custody battles who shuttled back and forth between parents.

Crystal's folks were happily married, and she did not fit the typical AVID profile of a student from a low-income or minority family. She grew up in a white, middle-class household with two parents and an older brother. Crystal's parents were aware of the dangers—alienation, drugs, loneliness—that lurked behind the facade of suburbia. They chose to send their children to a racially balanced public school, where they would socialize with kids from all kinds of backgrounds. Academically, they wanted their kids to have the best education possible.

"Which class combines social diversity and academic excellence?" Crystal's parents asked the principal of the middle school.

"AVID, definitely," Russ Archer answered. "Crystal doesn't really fit the AVID profile, but I think I could bend the rules."

"We don't want her to fit any stereotype," her mother said. "We want her to learn how to deal with all kinds of kids, because that's the diverse world she'll live in."

"AVID's a great place to meet the future being made," Russ said. "But Crystal will have to work her butt off if she's going to make it in Mrs. Reilly's AVID class."

In her sixth-grade AVID class, Crystal met another bright, bubbly, and academically competitive girl named Vera. The two teenagers became fast friends—and AVID rivals. When Crystal scored 95 percent on a math test, Vera came back with a 97 percent, and vice versa. At first, Vera feared Crystal was stuck up, and Crystal thought Vera was too competitive. But gradually they let down their guards, revealing secrets about their feelings and experiences.

Vera was a child of divorce. The "he said, she said" details of her life were private. But Vera, like many other children caught between divorced parents, felt intense stress. The economic and emotional hardships had endured since the breakup—visits to the non-custodial parent's house, outbreaks of anger and recrimination, expressions of hurt and rage—all of these factors seemed to intensify daily. One day a conflict between her parents pushed Vera over the edge.

Sobbing, she blurted out the story of her parents' fight to her teacher, Mrs. Reilly.

"Hey, Vera," Mrs. Reilly comforted her, wiping the girl's tears. "You know, when I was your age, my parents split up. I hated my old man because I thought it was his fault, and I refused to see him. He tried calling me at first, but I was stubborn." Mrs. Reilly's lip trembled. "You know what, kid? I haven't seen him for ten years. I'll never forgive him for giving up."

"I'm sorry," Vera said comfortingly. "I live with my mom, too, and she's like my best friend. But my dad always wants to see me."

"See, that's really something," sighed Mrs. Reilly. "It doesn't matter who's right or who's wrong in a family. The important thing is both your mom and dad love you."

After that conversation, Vera no longer felt alone. If Mrs. Reilly could be such a kind person, despite what had happened to her, Vera could, too. This gave Vera strength to carry on in school.

In AVID, the competition between Crystal and Vera intensified. They were each one point away from an A. One day, their binders were being checked. Mrs. Reilly pulled the covers back, like wings, and shook the binders. If a loose page fell out, that was a point taken away. It was an a small test, but the point was to teach the kids not to lose their assignments.

Crystal went first. When Mrs. Reilly pulled back the wings, a note to Crystal's boyfriend flew out, winging to the floor. Passing notes was strictly forbidden in AVID class.

"Who's this addressed to?" Mrs. Reilly asked sternly.

"It's mine," Vera lied, defending her friend. "I put it there."

Mrs. Reilly held up Vera's binder. It must have weighed ten pounds. Not a single page flew out. Her life was back in order.

"I don't know whose note this is," Mrs. Reilly said, "but I'm giving you both As for loyalty."

After that, the competition was to see who could help the other the most. Crystal comforted Vera and vice versa. They slept over at each other's houses and shared secrets of their lives. Crystal got to see a side of reality that she had never known, and Vera saw that even an intact family had its own difficult moments.

These ties paid off academically. At the end of the year, Vera and Crystal were honored for their achievements at the eighth-grade "continuation" ceremony. All four parents attended, although they didn't sit together. When the girls crossed the stage to receive their honors, Mr. Archer could not distinguish whose parents were Vera's or whose were Crystal's, nor could he tell what social category they fit into. Through AVID, the students had met, grappled, reached across boundaries, and spurred each other on.

Mary Catherine clutched the sides of the podium, gazing out at the audience.

"Let me conclude by asking, once again, those three nagging questions," she said, spotting the three students in the front row. "Why didn't Tyrone, depressed by his mother's death, fall apart and seek company in a gang? Why didn't Vera, stressed by her parents' divorce, fall into self-pity and drop out of school? Why didn't Crystal rebel against her background and join a group like the Trench Coat Mafia?

"You can find the answers in your own classrooms, where emotional support pays off in academic success. Let me leave you with my own perspective as the first AVID teacher:

"Tyrone, Vera, and Crystal are three extraordinary individuals, but their success stories are not *extra ordinary* in AVID. Each of you has had a Tyrone, Vera, or Crystal who needed support, emotionally, to perform academically. Multiply these three stories again and again, and you gain an extraordinary formula for bringing students, teachers, and families together in a triangle of infinite potential.

"A golden thread runs through the frayed fabric of American society, weaving students to each other and teachers to kids. Academic achievement and social relationships are *inseparable*. You can't raise grades if you don't support kids through the inevitable crises of growing up.

"AVID does both, and we have a 19-year track record to prove it. That is why I believe our program has substantive answers not only for children at risk from drugs, poverty, and racism, but for children endangered by divorce, family tragedy, and suburban affluence in the twenty-first century.

"Let's hear it for these three students, whose stories are multiplied again and again."

For the entire time that Mrs. Swanson spoke, Tyrone's knees were nervously banging open and shut. He was quiet and thoughtful. From the row behind, Tyrone's father's eyes shone with pride.

Vera and Crystal sat next to Tyrone in the front row. Ten rows further back, Crystal's parents and grandparents watched proudly. Vera's estranged parents were both there for their daughter.

Images of the three kids standing in front of the classroom were projected on a screen behind Mrs. Swanson. There was a close-up of Mrs. Reilly, eyes shining with pride. When Mrs. Swanson told about Vera's parents' divorce, Vera started to tremble and tears ran down her cheeks. Then the most beautiful thing happened. As Mrs. Swanson looked down, Tyrone reached over and pulled Crystal's hand toward Vera's hand. He clasped their pale fingers in his dark hands and held them, intertwined like white roses around a trellis, in Vera's lap.

Mrs. Swanson had a lump in her throat. Her mouth was dry; her heart started thumping irregularly, as it had at the Dana ceremony. She was terribly tired from the ordeal, grief stricken by her mother's death, and she felt very vulnerable. She told herself, *If I lose control now, I won't be able to finish.* She looked away from the children to the back of the room, seeing an AVID coordinator from Dekalb, Georgia. He was wearing a funny T-shirt, and just seeing him saved her from losing it all.

She asked the kids and their families to stand. "If you do these things in education, these are the results you have," she said, holding back tears. "These kids and their teachers are shining examples."

The audience jumped to its feet and gave a standing ovation.

"This is the reason we went into the profession of teaching," she nearly shouted, above the applause. "Our responsibility is awe-inspiring. There is no one who will more affect the future of this country than teachers." She paused, letting the sound lift her above her weary body, above her grief, into the realm where minds soared with the joy of learning. She exclaimed, "How proud I am to be among you and a part of our profession!"

The teachers gave a second ovation. Mrs. Swanson walked down the stairs to the audience. The kids were holding each other, parents and grandparents were hugging. She was in the middle of them all, in the middle of life.

Tyrone, Crystal, and Vera opened their programs and asked her to autograph them.

"To Tyrone," she wrote. "You are my hero," and she underlined the word *my*. She wrote the same words in Vera's and Crystal's programs. "You are my heroes," she said out loud.

A teacher came up to them, fluttering like a butterfly. "Mrs. Swanson, you must be so proud to have founded this program and seen it grow!" the woman gushed. "Oh, it must be so wonderful to stop teaching and become a celebrity. To fly all around the world, staying at fancy hotels and giving important speeches. I wish I could be you!"

She remembered the grounded flights and the motel and the louts hounding her and the prostitute who abandoned her child. "No, you don't want to be in my shoes," Mary Catherine told the autograph-seekers. "I'm the one who envies you. I miss teaching more than you can imagine."

— LIGHT OF THE EARTH —

Flying home on the final leg of her journey, Mary Catherine braced herself for AVID's 1999 Summer Institute in San Diego. It promised to be the most demanding ever.

This year, she didn't feel up to it.

Dozing 33,000 feet above the Arizona desert, Mary Catherine's mind drifted back to the previous summer institute in San Diego and to an AVID student named Buay Tang. That August, in 1998, the convention center was packed with 1,800 educators, dressed in summery clothing, who came from a dozen states and an equal number of military outposts abroad. On the stage, a score of AVID students peered nervously into the sea of faces. One by one they were introduced and stepped forward to the microphone. As they spoke about their experiences, a video camera projected their images onto giant screens behind them.

The new AVID teachers in the audience were struck by the aplomb of two middle-school girls who acted out a one-act play they had written, showing how they worked together. Then an Hispanic boy told about his unschooled grandfather who had died, and the silence that reigned among men in his family. The boy wanted to change all that and get to know his father and make him proud because he was going to be the first to go to college.

The testimonials were genuine, and the audience had responded warmly. Finally, it was Buay Tang's turn to speak. His mouth was dry and his wide cheekbones shone almost blue under the klieg lights. Tall and lithe as a sapling, he wore a dark double-breasted suit—loaned by his older brother—a red tie, black shoes, and white socks. His accent was musical, running like a child's fingers over the keys of a piano, and he sometimes landed on the wrong syllable, but his words stuck in her mind. A year later, Mary Catherine could still remember Buay standing straight and tall, eyes boring into the darkened hall, as he told his story.

Buay Tang

When I close my eyes and gaze into my last happy memory of my parents, I am no longer a 17-year-old student at Crawford High in San Diego. I am a seven-year-old boy living in our family's shady hut in Sudan, before the civil war burned our village.

My name is Buay. In the language of my people in the East African country of Sudan, this means "light of the earth." My parents gave me this name on Christmas, a time of forgiveness. Light is a symbol of God's forgiveness. Where there is *buay*, there is no shadow.

On this pleasant day, my mother is cooking *coop*. It is good, but not my favorite food. She is sitting outside on the dirt. It is a really hot day. She is wet with sweat. Her face is melting like ice. She has dimples and sometimes she tells me I have exactly the same dimples as she. She is singing a song that gives her the courage to sit next to a hot fire on a stifling day.

The only relief on a summer day is to go to the river and dive into the cold, clean water. My house is a hut covered with brown grass. It's really hot inside the big circular room where my father sits, weaving a fishing net. My father is tall, and sweat shines on his body. He has the muscular legs of a warrior. His trousers are made of animal skins and his sandals are made of elephant hide.

Our land, our life, our civilization are like the native Americans were before whites came to the New World. It is a good way of life because there is no disease and we have not invented instruments to kill each other. In order for us to survive, my father has to hunt for food with a bow and arrow. Sudanese hunters bring back meat of deer and elephant. On a happy day, they bring giraffe.

I am still a little boy, not able to run fast enough to escape from a lion. As I sit next to my father, I smell the food my mother is cooking. It feels good being with my parents. Nothing can harm me because they are there. I want my parents to live forever and raise me to a good life like theirs. Before we eat dinner, my father leads us in prayer, thanking God for the food he gives us on this wonderful day.

Two years later, my father calls me: "Buay, Buay, come here." His voice is really tight, like a bird that is singing a song of courage. He is ill with diarrhea. I am scared that my father will die. He touches my head, my shoulders, my body, and my heart. He says slowly, "You will live for eternity and be immortal."

There is a silence in the room. His eyes are bright like the sky and dark like shadow. His forehead is wrinkled from hard work in the sun. I touch his heart with both hands, and my heart is pumping like a drum that is beating in a funeral dance. I want him not to die. Tears are running down my cheeks and falling on the dust.

I go outside because I cannot do anything to help him. At this moment, I wish I can save my father's life. I walk back in and grab his hand, saying: "I'll never let you down. I will become a doctor so I can save all the people's lives."

"You may do whatever you want, my son, and be successful—but only if you have me in your heart and pray to God always."

At age nine, I make the choice to become a doctor.

One afternoon, when I am ten years old, fighting begins in the round circle of huts in our village. Light-skinned Muslim soldiers are fighting against Christians. They are both Sudanese. I don't know why they fight; I think it is because we want to be independent.

I am in my hut. I hear people running outside. Their voices are like the ocean or like a bell that is ringing. I smell smoke from the loud gunshots. I see other parents looking for their babies, but it is hard for them because it is foggy. I see some of the huts are burning like a rising sun. I huddle on the floor.

This is the moment when my parents are killed, but I cannot find words to describe it. I can only say how I feel. I am full of anger, and my heart is burning like the sun. It makes my heart melt with fear, and within me I do not know what to do. I want to tell my brothers about how I feel, but it is too late for me to tell them. There is a loud scream in my heart, and in my mind I cannot do anything. I cannot listen to any words from other people or take any advice.

My brothers save me, and we walk countless days to reach Ethiopia. During our journey, I see some disabled people and it is really hard for them, especially in places where there is a lot of water and grass. While we are walking, I hear a lot of different tribes speaking their native languages. It is intoxicating to know so many of our Sudanese people share such a common plight. While we are still on our journey, some people die because of a lack of food. Some of the people die because there are no doctors.

In order for us to survive, we have to eat the leaves and the fruit of the trees. Most of the people die because of the water that they drink. The waters are very dirty and contaminated with lethal bacteria. People are drinking from the waters where dead bodies are floating by. During this war, I feel scared and I think I will not survive. When I see a dead body floating by, I cannot drink water for one or two days and not even eat for a week. When I try to eat, the image of what I saw before comes back to me. It seems like I would be eating what I saw previously in the river. At last we arrive at our destination. I think it takes us about 21 days to get to those villages.

From Ethiopia, we travel to a refugee camp in Kenya. That is where we make contact with my cousin in America, who sponsors us to come to the United States.

When I arrive in San Diego at age 13, I can't speak English. It is really hard, because I don't understand what people are talking about. I feel really bad. Even though I am embarrassed, I keep listening to the strange sounds and trying to understand their pronunciation. I takes me a month or so to speak enough English to begin interacting with people.

By the time I reach high school, I have high expectations for myself, but there is no one who gives me the support that I need to go to college. I think I'm taking the right courses and I'm getting all As, but I discover these beginner classes are not the hard subjects I need to go to a four-year college.

One day, my reading teacher, Mr. Visconti, looks at my progress report—all As. "You don't belong in remedial classes," he says. "We need to get you in AVID."

"What is AVID?" I ask.

"AVID means Advancement Via Individual Determination," he explains. It is a program that helps kids prepare for college. In my sophomore year, I enter AVID. Soon I learn that Mr. Visconti is a generous man who gives me the support I need. I begin to take as many advanced classes as I can take and to study real hard.

After school, I go home and take a nap because there are children running around my room and I can't concentrate. So what I do is sleep until five o'clock, or until they go to bed. Then I wake up and do my homework. I study from the time I wake up until 3 A.M., or sometimes I study until morning and proceed to school.

In AVID, special tutors from UCSD and SDSU help me with English. Before AVID, I was so shy I could not speak to anyone. AVID helped me feel comfortable. Now I have a lot of friends, and I feel close to my classmates.

I am now taking advanced chemistry, advanced pre-calculus, and other classes. I need to work on my English, but I am getting help from my AVID tutors. My grade-point average during freshman and sophomore years was 4.0. Now I am taking harder classes. In my most recent progress report, I got four As and two Bs.

I want to attend public universities like UCSD or Berkeley, or private colleges like Harvard, Stanford, or Columbia, but I would need a full scholarship.

Three afternoons a week, I am working as a tutor at Crawford High School. I am helping some of the students with their homework because I know we always need each other. At night, I am taking calculus at City College.

AVID is a tremendous program for students who want to go to college and don't know where to start. My goal is to become a surgeon, so I can help my people. I want to earn money as a doctor in America to build hospitals in Sudan and pay for doctors there. When I die, I want people to know that I was one of the people who rebuilt Sudan and provided them with hospitals.

My father taught me that nothing is impossible for those who keep love in their heart and pray to God. My mother taught me a song of courage. No matter what happens, they will be with me always. My life has strengthened my belief in myself and my appreciation for people like my AVID teacher, Mr. Visconti, who have helped me in America. If we work hard and have faith, we will survive.

While Buay Tang spoke to the teachers at the institute, images of the war in Sudan were projected on screens behind him. He stood on the stage and read portions of his essay in a voice that was strong. His pronunciation, accented with his native African intonation, was strangely musical. One could almost hear the Sudanese blessing of his dying father and the bird singing the song of courage. Buay read quickly from his edited manuscript. As one of several extraordinary AVID students to present that day, he had to cut his remarks down to a few minutes.

Buay Tang received a standing ovation from 1,800 participants at the 1998 institute. The teachers in the audience were clapping for him and for the other students on the stage and for their own students back at home.

Mary Catherine had been deeply moved and struggled for self-control. As a teacher and a parent, she did not show favor to one student over the others. Every student on the stage was remarkable, standing for hundreds who would remain unknown to her. Yet Buay Tang's figure, tall and straight, beneath the images of skeletal Sudanese children, gave meaning to her deepest hope: that education could provide a path from the horrors of the twentieth century to a peaceful and hopeful future for children of poverty, hatred, and war. Buay Tang's will and determination went beyond anything she knew, and he would be an extraordinary young man under any circumstances. Yet AVID had been there, through Mr. Visconti's acumen in recognizing potential and his ceaseless encouragement, to enable Buay Tang to go far beyond any teacher's imagination.

She yearned to know about the lives of this new generation of students, as she had grown to know the intimate stories of her early AVID students. It was ironic that the greater the reach of the program, stretching across states and continents, the further away she was from kids. This was her personal sacrifice for the public good.

Sitting near her on the stage was one of her favorite alumni, Máximo. Darkly handsome as a portrait painted by a Spanish Master, he rose to speak about Mrs. Swanson's influence on his life. The boy who had known only five English words now spoke eloquently without an accent, confident in himself, with that twinkle in his eye that she had first seen in 1980. Máximo did not tell the poignant story about his first terrifying day in public-speaking class, but sketched a realistic portrait of Mrs. Swanson as a hard grader with high expectations and a big heart. She wasn't easy, he laughed, but she gave him determination to change the material circumstances of life. Máximo spoke not only for himself, but for the five Escobedo brothers who had gone through AVID and on to professional careers.

Máximo had achieved his dream of becoming an artist. Many people call themselves artists, but few support themselves through their creative work. But he was a leading graphic designer in San Diego and a proud husband and father.

After the meeting broke up, Mrs. Swanson observed a group of AVID students from two generations. Amid handshakes and hugs, she heard Máximo Escobedo congratulate Buay Tang on his courage in overcoming incredible hardships. Filled with admiration for the older AVID graduate, Buay politely asked: "Mr. Escobedo, you were in Mrs. Swanson's class in 1980?"

Máximo nodded, smiling.

"That's when I was born!" Buay exclaimed.

Máximo's face fell momentarily. Mrs. Swanson guessed why: In his mid-thirties, Máximo was still unaccustomed to being viewed as an older guy by a young man. Then Máximo laughed at himself for being time's fool. Gently, he touched Buay's shoulder. Before her awestruck eyes, Mrs. Swanson witnessed the warm hand of continuity bridge two generations of AVID students.

How have so many years passed? she had wondered last summer, not knowing if she felt terribly happy or dreadfully sad. She hugged them both.

Now, a year later, the airplane tilted vertiginously and the "fasten seatbelt" signs went on, jolting Mary Catherine from her memories. Approaching the runway, the plane barely cleared Banker's Hill, and it looked like it was going to crash into a parking structure. Then the wheels set down, and Mary Catherine felt a rush of relief that she was safely home. Tom was waiting at the gate.

Jet-lagged, wrung out, and grieving, Mary Catherine yearned for a moment of peace when she could untangle her feelings before she worked on the summer institute. She found it difficult to allow others to see her as a vulnerable, hurting human. The last thing she wanted at the end of this incredible journey was to have her personal life catch up with her in public.

Something up-close and personal was in the works. The program for the summer institute was filled with exciting events for AVID participants. But for Mrs. Swanson, after this difficult year, the crush of people and the demanding schedule was daunting.

To kick off the conference, the *Washington Post*'s education writer, Jay Mathews, was delivering the keynote speech. Mathews was the winner of the National Educational Reporting Award, and he had just published a new book, *Class Struggle: What's Wrong (and Right) with America's Best Public High Schools.*

Wednesday, Mrs. Swanson would deliver a speech just as she had given talks in Asilomar and Richmond. She knew it almost by heart, but there was always a catch in her throat before speaking in San Diego, where she had fought so long and hard for AVID to survive. At 19, AVID was the age of a college freshman. She did not often pause to take stock of time's passing, preferring rather to keep moving forward. But next year AVID would celebrate its twentieth anniversary in the year 2000.

— HARD HOPE — REVISITED

For the final plenary luncheon, Mrs. Swanson had an unusual proposal. She invited me to give a progress report on the book I was writing about AVID. Roughly once a week for the last year, I had been interviewing her, asking about the beginnings and history of AVID, and she did her best to answer. Sometimes I asked her about her background, and she spoke about the importance of her family and of growing up in a small town. It was strange what memories were unearthed, and what she had a hard time remembering. When I asked, "Why did a person from your white, small-town roots become an advocate for educating underprivileged kids from the ghetto?" She laughed and said, "Because I am a teacher, and I thought it was my job."

Afterwards, I wrote vignettes based on what she had recalled, along with profiles of AVID students and teachers. She had an idea of what I was writing, but the book as a whole was still a mystery.

Midway, she invited me to address the AVID Institute in August 1999.

"I'd like you to share reflections about AVID students and teachers," she said. "Talk about the lessons you've learned on your journey."

Those were the only instructions she gave me. It took me a long time to put my thoughts together, but an idea struck me. A few days before my talk, I asked her, "Please invite your family and people who are important to this story."

She never asked me what I was going to say, and I never showed her my note cards.

— TREPIDATION —

The weekend before the AVID Institute, Mrs. Swanson was anxious about her father's health and the wisdom of bringing a partially blind, 88-year-old widower to a large public gathering for what might be a traumatic experience. Ed Jacobs was still grieving for his wife, he had been uprooted from his world, and he was having trouble adapting to life in a residential care facility.

Yet it would be good for her father to receive attention, even from strangers. And he had never attended an AVID event, except for the Dana Award.

Her concern for her father came before all others: Her husband and son could take care of themselves. Yet it also made her a bit anxious to have her family attend an AVID function, where she wanted to be seen as an educator and participant, not as a distant and aloof figurehead.

She had delicately balanced the separate worlds of family and school all her adult life. It scared her to bring them together, even for one moment.

The weekend was devoted to family. To know what kind of man Tom Swanson was, one had only to look at what he had done for his father-in-law. Ed Jacobs's 900-square-foot apartment in the board-and-care facility had purposely been chosen because it was located three and a half blocks from the bank where Tom was president. To help his father-in-law regain some semblance of continuity, Tom had brought four overstuffed chairs and a coffee table into the lobby of the bank. Every morning at 10, Mr. Jacobs was driven to the bank. There, seated in a plush chair, he drank black coffee and talked with Tom, when he was available, and hobnobbed with other customers and employees.

This allowed Mr. Jacobs to recreate the ritual that he had maintained from 1936 to 1998. Twice a day, he would walk from his newspaper office to a community drugstore in Kingsburg. There, he would sit on a silver-colored stool covered with royal blue plastic at the soda counter. The third-generation owner of the pharmacy, Bob Ostrom, had been co-valedictorian with Mary Catherine at the Kingsburg High School graduation in 1962. There, the local movers and shakers would drink cup after cup of Swedish-style black coffee and talk about community issues. As publisher of the *Kingsburg Recorder*, Mr. Jacobs was in the midst of the local news.

One by one, Mr. Jacobs's cronies faded away like old front-page stories yellowing in the newspaper's morgue. Then the drugstore was sold to a big chain, located seven traffic signals down the road—too confusing for a man with cataracts to negotiate by car. And Corrine died.

Now, it was Mary Catherine's time to be there for her father, as he had been at her side, night after night, when she vomited as a child and lay in the hospital bed with an IV needle in her thigh. He held her little hand, as the glucose dripped into her veins, and told stories of "Mighty Midget." Returning his loving kindness was her privilege, as she struggled with complicated feelings of grief and loss attending her mother's death.

The Friday night before the conference, Tom picked up his father-in-law and brought him back to the downstairs guest room that was reserved for his visits. On that hot August night, the family went to the outdoor patio of an informal restaurant. Ed Jacobs was in love with dogs and the patio allowed pet owners to bring their canines. Mary Catherine read the menu to her father, and they sat and talked.

When they returned home, she read aloud to him from his own mother's hand-written wartime diaries, and he listened keenly. She showed him an old snapshot of his brother, a doctor, dressed in military khakis in India, circa 1944. At age 28, John had been sent to build a military hospital in India. In the photo, Uncle John was holding a monkey on his arm.

"Dad, that's John in India," she pointed out.

"That's right, John went to the war," he replied, brightening. "I tried to go, but when I was a kid I jumped off a barn roof and broke my arm and they never set it, so the Army wouldn't take me," he reminisced with regret in his eyes.

And father and daughter drifted together in the floating memories.

"Dad, you know I have this big summer institute every year. Next Friday is the closing luncheon. I wonder if you'd like to come? Jerry Rosander will be there. Do you remember him?"

Again, Ed struggled for some thread. "Yes, wasn't he the superintendent in San Diego?"

"Uh huh. Do you remember him before that?"

His opaque eyes went blank.

That weekend, her son, Tom, who disliked being called Tommy, was home from Santa Clara. To her great surprise and pleasure, he had become a remarkable high-school teacher in his own right. He had not disclosed his interest in teaching until his senior year at UCLA, when he was accepted to the master's program in education at Stanford University. After earning his degree, he got a job teaching history at Monta Vista High, where he had just finished a successful year teaching AP American history. For the past few summers, Tom had helped out as a teacher trainer at AVID Institutes.

Saturday was forever laundry day. Mrs. Swanson washed, folded, and ironed, then watered the plants. On Sunday, she and her family attended a Padres baseball game and had supper at her father's favorite restaurant, where he could pet other people's pooches, remembering his own lost furry friends. Mary Catherine reveled in these moments when her father almost became his old self. Although she'd been invited to AVID parties that night at the convention hotel in San Diego, she preferred to be with her family.

That night, on the eve of the institute, she hardly slept. At 4 A.M. Monday morning, AVID's founder lay in bed, filled with dread. Mary Catherine looked toward the week with foreboding. The fear of a hundred potential mishaps coiled in her stomach and she pushed it down, far down. She could not allow herself to show the least bit of fear, even to Tom, because she knew if she let loose she would not be able to carry on. She felt total responsibility for what would happen to the 1,800 guests. This, she knew rationally, was absurd. A committee of 30 people had made all the arrangements, and they had never done less than their best. Still, she worried about tiny things. She knew, as she walked through the convention center this week, she was going to have a thousand people stop her, shake her hand, take photos, even ask for autographs. She hated being treated as a celebrity. She was a worker and a participant, still eager to learn from her colleagues and their students.

Her son always drove separately to the conferences. When the training sessions that he led ended, he usually liked to come home early. For Mary Catherine, the institute was a 16-hour-a-day, nonstop affair, lasting for five days. Where was Mighty Midget now?

Alone in her car, she was filled with trepidation.

— SOLO —

The keynote speech on the first day always set the tone for the entire institute, and Mary Catherine had the jitters waiting for the speaker to show up. She had never met Jay Mathews and had no idea what he looked like.

"Has he checked in?" she asked the front desk.

"We can't give you that information," said a snotty clerk.

"Have you heard from Jay Mathews?" Mary Catherine asked the coordinators.

"I think so."

"Then where is he?"

Just when she was about to call for a search party, a hand touched her shoulder softly. She wheeled around. There stood an energetic, middle-aged man with a boyish grin and a baseball cap tipped back over twinkling eyes.

"Hi, I'm Jay," he almost crowed, pumping her hand. A reporter's notebook fell out of his pocket, and he swooped down like a shortstop to pick it up. He had more kinetic energy than most teenagers, which probably explained his fascination with barrio kids who surpassed all expectations and learned calculus. Jay squinted his left eye, sizing up Mary Catherine.

"So you're a Jaime Escalante with people skills," he laughed, looking around the convention hall. "I see you've also got organizational skills." His voice dropped and he suddenly looked stricken. "Something Jaime could have used before he nearly worked himself to death."

"He was a great teacher," Mary Catherine said of Escalante, who had retired from teaching. "I'm honored by the comparison."

These were the first words they said to each other, and Mary Catherine instantly appreciated Jay's candor. He was not your average education-beat reporter who mocked teachers and put down schools. Mathews had the curiosity of a man who never tired of asking questions, and he didn't have to make a name for himself at the expense of his subjects. In his 27-year career, his top assignments included opening the Beijing *Post* bureau in China and covering Wall Street. Yet he was down to earth, wearing his reputation like an old shoe. And he wanted to discuss ideas.

Mathews had written a powerful book, *Escalante: The Best Teacher in America*, which became a Hollywood movie, *Stand and Deliver*. Escalante's hard-driving teaching style was legendary, and his story had inspired students and teachers alike. Yet Jay seemed to be implying that more than great teaching skills were required in order to revamp American education: Organization was crucial, and he recognized Mary Catherine for creating an organization that replicated her teaching in thousands of classrooms, reaching tens of thousands of students.

Jay shared Mary Catherine's commitment to rigorous curricula. In his book *Class Struggle*, he rated schools according to how many kids were enrolled in Advanced Placement classes, what percentage took the tests, and how many passed. He was outraged that access to these classes was routinely denied low-income or minority students who didn't fit the collegiate profile. He wanted to find out more about AVID, how it recruited "kids in the middle," and propelled them to college.

Yet despite Jay's books and Mary Catherine's institutes, their best efforts had not convinced all 50 states to invest in more programs like AVID. The education gap, like the chasm between rich and poor, was deepening in America, and the Escalantes and Swansons were outnumbered ten to one by the forces of apathy and neglect threatening public education from within. The drumbeat of criticism attacked the very principle of public education from without. They were comrades in arms fighting the educational establishment in their own ways, yet they defended public schools as fundamental to the survival of America as a pluralistic democracy. They were outnumbered, but they were both optimists by nature. How could they not be? They believed in children as America's hope.

On the empty stage, they adjusted the sound system. Then Jay announced abruptly, "Got to file a story!" As the hour approached, the keynote speaker ran off to his room, leaving Mrs. Swanson to make sure everything was ready. There were a million details, from welcoming dignitaries to making sure the duet of AVID students was ready to sing "The Star Spangled Banner."

She was already extremely tense. Her first event that morning had been a speech to 500 newcomers. Now, at lunch, she met with 58 staff developers.

Minutes before the opening session, an aide whispered in her ear, "One of the singers hasn't shown up." She hurried out, only to find that the girl who *did* show up was terrified of singing solo. As 1,800 teachers poured in, Mrs. Swanson took her aside.

"You have sung here before and you were wonderful," she reassured the trembling teenager. "You're going to be great as a solo." Somehow, being momentarily in the role of teacher reassuring a student calmed Mrs. Swanson.

Then, from across the room, her communications director, Rob Gira, frantically cupped his hand around his lips and yelled, "Can't find Jay Mathews!"

The time had come for the opening session to begin. Punctual Mrs. Swanson approached the podium and gazed around. She could only see the people in the first few rows; before her stretched a vast expanse of humanity, but no faces. The teachers chattered like an expectant class on the first day of school. Gazing with head cocked slightly, she projected that air of authority unmistakable to any student, as when a teacher, by her glance, silently calls a class to order. The room fell still.

The spotlight shone on the lone African American student, unaccompanied, whose voice rose, tremulously: "O, say can you see . . ." She hit the high notes, transforming the song by her soulful delivery, set to a hiphop beat. Suddenly, in the middle of the second verse, she stopped. Frozen.

As she groped for the words, the audience was so quiet you could hear the chilled air flowing through the ventilation ducts. The teachers waited compassionately. Then she found the words, and the whole room swelled with her voice, thoughts bursting in air. And they saw, on the stage, the Stars and Stripes, surrounded by the flags of many nations. An anthem to America the Diverse.

As the last note died away, Mrs. Swanson hugged her. Then, addressing the audience, she explained that the vocalist had prepared to sing one part of a two-part harmony. "She had no time to prepare, but AVID students are determined. She did it as a solo!"

The teachers jumped up, applauding until their hands turned red. Among them stood Jay Mathews, she saw with relief. No other audience was so supportive. Mrs. Swanson was as proud of the AVID teachers' empathy as she was of the singer's bravery.

The institute was off to the right start.

— THRILLER —

Mrs. Swanson introduced Jay Mathews, whose professional biography read like an entry in *Who's Who*. Yet as she read off his stellar accomplishments, she wondered, *Why has he chosen the education beat?* In recent years he had eschewed the pinnacles of power in Beijing and Wall Street to write about kids struggling to learn in local schools. His career path was the exact opposite direction of the typical journalist's. *Why?*

"I feel gratitude for AVID's existence," Mr. Mathews began, humbly gazing out at the group of teachers he admired as heroes. "You are the only national organization I know of expressly organized to overcome what I think is the chief problem for American education—fear of failure on the part of teachers for their kids."

He spoke extemporaneously, barely gazing at his notes. As an objective journalist, he asked provocative questions. As a children's advocate, he offered provocative answers.

"Why is it so hard to make my argument that kids should be challenged more?" he asked. "Because teachers are the most humane people on the planet; they choose their jobs to help kids, and I am asking them to take what they perceive is a risk of hurting kids."

Mathews took issue with teachers who, in the name of compassion, lowered the standards for students. In the era of entertainment news, it was not fashionable for journalists to hold up high standards, but he believed strongly in integrity for those who report the news, and for teachers who take responsibility for their students.

"Why do I think AVID and its supporters, like me, are right and *they* are wrong?"

He described how he stumbled into education writing when he was West Coast bureau chief for the *Post*. He used to play hooky from his stodgy editors and began observing high schools. One day he saw a tiny news clip at the office. A class of students at an obscure school called Garfield High had been accused by the national Educational Testing Service of cheating on their AP calculus exam.

He went to Garfield and met Jaime Escalante. He hung out with the students from the barrio. They were like their peers in many respects, but these kids from the poorest, meanest barrio were academically motivated. Mathews was intrigued by Escalante's unorthodox teaching methods: alternately intimidating, lying, or prodding with great gentleness to keep kids in class.

"These are the three pillars of Escalantism," Mathews said, enumerating each with examples. The first was high expectations; the second, a teacher's personal relationship with each student; third, clever use of time, keeping classes open after school, Saturdays, summers.

"My great moment of revelation was when I discovered that Garfield had more AP calculus students in 1987 than all but four U.S. high schools. If Garfield kids could learn at that level, all American kids could. This blew away the basic assumptions about schools and made me want to write about them forever."

Now the teachers were leaning forward in their seats, craning their necks to hear a journalist who saw beyond the usual media cheap shots and political finger-pointing to the heart of what teaching was all about. He understood them in a way that few in the media could, and this gave force to his argument that teachers should be more demanding, not less. Students, he said, should not be underestimated but *challenged* to reach for the highest, even if it sometimes hurts.

Mrs. Swanson was listening intently, more moved than any other teacher there. His opening remarks, when he praised AVID, had left her embarrassed. But once he began speaking from his personal experience, she hung on every word, enthralled. She loved learning. This was her reward for all the tension. She could see education from a totally different perspective, that of a journalist, and see where his perspective extended her vision. Some of his incendiary quotations fired her mind.

"AP tests are pulled out like fine china for guests," he said angrily. *Yes! A good education should be every student's bread and butter, not the exclusive silver service only the rich could afford.*

He argued that kids who wanted to take the risk of enrolling in a hard class should not be kept from taking the AP exam, even if they did not pass. He railed against teachers who had a "Mount Olympus Syndrome," who defined themselves by how good their students were—teachers who discouraged B students from taking AP classes because they didn't want their students to score less than a perfect five. So the teachers wouldn't look bad.

"Those teachers did not understand that even a kid who flunks an AP test is much better off, and feels better off, than if she had not been allowed to take the test at all," he said angrily. "She has lost a one-on-one game against Michael Jordan, but she has a much clearer idea of what it takes to get to that level, and she is ready for the introductory college professor who wants to flunk her. We can tell a kid he can't take an AP course, but we cannot tell him he can't go to college. Thus, we are sending him off naked when he faces his first college chemistry professor."

When they heard the Michael Jordan analogy, the audience erupted with cheers.

Mathews now reached the core of his message, couched in the double entendre of *Class Struggle*. Through classroom struggle, a student from the lowest economic and social rung could move upward on the educational ladder. Public schools had been the vehicles for poor generations to enter the middle class. But, today, education was perpetuating the class system by systematically denying children from poor and non-English-speaking backgrounds an opportunity to compete with privileged peers. If they could compete on the basketball courts, why should they be presumed to be unable to compete intellectually? Compassion was the ultimate shackle.

"Open the gates!" Mathews cried. "Do what AVID does, the most radical thing that Jaime Escalante did. Not only open the gates, but go out and look for kids who have a spark of interest in the subject matter. Bring them in, build them up, get them ready."

Now Mathews cracked a devilish smile. "This is a generation that loves a good scare—in movies, video games, cycling, skating. Why can't we achieve the goal of encouraging every kid to take at least one *scary* course before graduating from high school? We can take the AVID model and introduce it to the whole country, a thriller movie if I ever saw one!"

Mrs. Swanson's first day was only half over. She had to attend a social function with educational book publishers and vendors. At 5 P.M., she hosted a reception for superintendents and college folk—200 invited guests. She eagerly escaped to participate in a two-hour panel discussion on the very topic Mathews had raised: access to Advanced Placement classes. The distinguished panel included a national director of the AP testing program, two university presidents, and her fellow Dana Award-winner and ally, Uri Treisman. It was an energetic discussion, focused by data presented by Gary Hart's successor at the Institute for Education Reform.

The first day ended at 9 P.M. Mary Catherine stayed late, making sure everything was cleaned up for the meeting the next morning. Then she drove the hour-long journey home, only to get up the next morning at 4 A.M.

On Day 2, she attended staff-development sessions and site team meetings. She spent the day troubleshooting. There were dozens of complaints to handle: Rooms were too cold, too hot; chairs were too hard. She walked from meeting to meeting with a walkie talkie.

It was a roller-coaster ride. One moment she was dealing with huge global issues such as, "What needs to be done in education reform for the twenty-first century?" The next minute someone was crying, "The toilet backed up!" No sooner was this attended to than a teacher was gushing about the wonderfulness of being Mary Catherine Swanson.

At such moments, she wanted to tell people, *You know how I spent last weekend? Cutting my father's toenails and hair!*

But underneath, she understood the importance of personal contact. She was a symbol, a touchstone. Teachers who were now in the trenches were checking her out, up close, to see if she was pompous or full of herself. They needed to touch her arm, look into her eyes, silently asking: *Is she legitimate? Is she in touch with what I'm going through in my classroom? Or is she just a phony?*

These questions were on everybody's mind, but no one had the courage, or gracelessness, to speak of them openly. Somehow, AVID's integrity as an institution was bound up with her own personal integrity. This responsibility she bore willingly as a badge of honor. But when she was alone, the roller-coaster ride twisted her into knots.

— HERSTORY —

"Over 33 years, I have seen educational reform movements come and go. Some are benign. Some beneficial," Mrs. Swanson began, staring into the lights of the auditorium. "The reform movement is at it again. Promising the moon—and delivering lunacy? If we do not learn from history, we are doomed to repeat it. Let me tell you a story from a female teacher's perspective. Call it *herstory.*"

Mrs. Swanson took the audience back to 1980, when Clairemont High lost half its student body and 500 low-income students were bused in. The "old guard" saw the minority students as a threat, but an English teacher and her mentor saw an opportunity. It was unconscionable to place bright but poorly prepared students in remedial curriculum and doom their lives. It was a professional injustice to force highly motivated teachers to teach an unchallenging curriculum.

"Schools must see a reason to change," Mrs. Swanson explained. "Thus, AVID was born. Yet change caused misunderstandings. AVID students invited teachers to a meeting. This began a dialogue on learning that engaged highly motivated changemakers in the process of schoolwide change.

"These meetings became a hallmark of the school," she said. "Teachers and students felt good because they knew they were becoming effective. They were in control of their work, rather than being controlled by it. This group of changemakers called itself the AVID Site Team.

"By December of that first year, AVID students made a breakthrough, only to be accused of cheating. Their crime? They had earned As and Bs on the last exam. The English teacher was incredulous. She felt that not only had her students been falsely accused, but she, too, had been accused of devising some kind of cheating scheme. It stung, because the accuser had been a respected colleague and friend.

"The Inquisition forced the students to retake the test. After they correctly defined *ontogeny recapitulates phylogeny,* the students were exonerated. The biology teacher left the meeting with his head bowed and the English teacher felt emotionally drained.

"Unwittingly, and in a very painful way, the biology teacher precipitated a good thing," Mrs. Swanson told the audience. "The false and heartless assumptions caused the students and their teacher to rally round one another. The students learned two important lessons: They were stronger when they supported one another, and they could control their destinies rather than be victims."

Mrs. Swanson pointed to research showing that many students fail in school because they feel no sense of belonging and feel powerless to change their situation in school. Yet AVID students learned what it meant to belong to a positive group. They learned to defend themselves against prejudice and humiliation by wielding the shield of learning, not the dagger of violence or the excuse of victimhood.

"Schoolwide change must be focused on the needs of students," Mrs. Swanson said. "When teachers' beliefs that certain groups of students are bound to fail are proven wrong, both teachers and students see the unlimited possibilities to advance and achieve. Success breeds success.

"Yet success also provoked envy and bitter retaliation from within the district hierarchy. Administrators who had put their eggs in one basket—remediation—tried to crush AVID. The English teacher fought back by documenting results.

"Keep AVID students in the public eye," she advised the audience. "Collect and analyze all the data that you can possibly find on your students. When data reveals shortcomings, analyze the figures to discover what is—or is not—working. Ask: *What learning barriers are still in place? What needs to be done?*" Her voice dropped, causing people to lean forward to hear the most important point. "Accurate data is good data, *whatever* the results.

"The results were astounding. According to the district's own data, Clairemont High School, with the second lowest socioeconomic status of students in the district, surpassed the district's standardized test scores by 46.6 percent in language arts and 35 percent in mathematics. That year, 28 of the 30 AVID graduating seniors enrolled in four-year colleges and two enrolled in community colleges.

"Why were AVID students not surprised when teachers and administrators from around the district came to see their school?" Mrs. Swanson asked. "Why were Clairemont teachers not surprised when outsiders could not distinguish the Socratic Seminar sessions of the gifted students from those of the AVID students? Why were they not surprised when outsiders commented that so many ethnic groups worked together so well and there were few discipline or attendance problems on campus?

"In case it hasn't become apparent, I am that English teacher, and obviously I have lived to tell the story, not without a few bumps along the way," Mary Catherine confided. "What more powerful experience is there for a teacher than to see success in the eyes and in the work of her students? What more exhilarating professional experience is there than to be working collaboratively, determinedly, and effectively with one's colleagues?"

The teachers answered with their applause.

"That is why I am so proud to be a part of you," Mary Catherine said, embracing AVID colleagues with her outstretched arms. "We are professionals dedicated to our work, proud of our profession, yet humbled by our choice to be teachers, those who will most profoundly change the future. We have the tools and the vision of what our schools can be. We must have the will to make it happen, working together, step by step, discovery by discovery, victory by victory. This is no longer 'herstory,' or history, but *our story!*"

— ATTACK —

The speech was well received, but Mary Catherine felt increasingly worn out.

On Wednesday evening, she celebrated her son's birthday. He was helping train AVID tutors at the conference. After the day's debriefing, the staff developers sang "Happy Birthday" to him. He was embarrassed, but she was proud of her son. Tom was 27 today, the same age she was when she gave birth to him. Except for the year she had taken off after he was born, she had been working in education ever since. And now he was a teacher, who had his own ideas of how to teach.

Thursday, intense meetings and tense exchanges over policy issues did not leave her a moment to relax or catch her breath. She could not even go to the restroom.

That night, she felt ill. After eating a moderate amount at dinner, her belly was bloated. Pressure built up from her abdominal region to her lower back.

"Tom, did I overeat?" she asked.

He shook his head. "Is there something wrong?"

"No." She grit her teeth.

Over the next hour, the attack grew worse. She had never felt anything like it. What she did not know was that bile was trapped in her pancreas. The duct was blocked by particles, as fine as sand, called "sludge." The pancreas was swelling. She was suffering a gallbladder attack.

She stoically went about her business. She had more to worry about than her own pain. The closing luncheon was tomorrow, and she worried about her father attending. Would he become confused?

After three hours, the pain subsided.

Then came Friday.

— WHO IS THAT —
MAN WEARING
A FEDORA?

Mary Catherine's husband brought her father early, before the crowd scene. Edwin Jacobs came through the front doors of the convention hall in his navy blue suit and striped tie. He sported a Clark Gable mustache and his favorite fedora, checkered deep gray and brown. In contrast, his skin was ashen, his eyes dim, his step feeble. "Where can I put my hat?" he asked anxiously, fighting real fear.

Mary Catherine tried to calm him. This was a minor crisis every time they went to a public place. Newspapermen of his generation always wore hats. But hat racks had disappeared from the American landscape.

They finally found a place for his hat. He calmed a bit and looked around at the enormous banquet hall, which was the size of a football field. Round tables covered by white tablecloths sparkled with silver and glassware.

"Mighty big do," he said proudly, with a journalist's appraising eye.

Mary Catherine felt her father's gaze brushing her. Then he turned distractedly, and she was left smiling anxiously, standing there in her canary yellow jacket. That morning, Maria, the AVID comptroller, had rushed up to her with a surprise. "It's your special day," Maria had said, pinning a red and pink corsage on her yellow jacket. Mary Catherine thanked her friend and loyal colleague for thinking of her. Then her father had arrived and she had buzzed off nervously like a honey bee with rose pollen on her breast.

Mr. Jacobs was greeted frequently by strangers. He smiled. Only Mary Catherine knew that he was smiling because he didn't understand. Cataracts dimmed his vision and his hearing was bad.

"Please get him seated before the rush," she whispered to her son.

Tom maneuvered his grandfather to a seat at a table in front. Hatless, Ed Jacobs sat down and gazed around. The doors opened and hundreds of teachers poured into the room, chattering and dropping AVID notebooks on the floor with a steady series of concussions. It was the last day of the institute and they were both exhausted and exhilarated, their brains bursting and stomachs growling.

Mrs. Swanson stood by the door, greeting dignitaries. In 1980, she had no friends in high places, but today her guests included Gary Hart, the secretary of education; the chairs of education committees in both houses of the legislature; and the former chairwoman of the Carnegie Commission on Education.

Her family sat around the front table: Tommy, Tom, then her father. Mary Catherine sat beside them. A sunny face appeared at the table. It was Jerry Rosander, the retired county superintendent of education, and his wife. Dr. Rosander had dropped by Mrs. Swanson's office a few days ago, when he was visiting San Diego, and she had invited him to the banquet.

"Dad, I want you to say hello to Jerry Rosander."

Mr. Jacobs smiled that smile of confusion. "Oh, yes. You were superintendent here," he said.

Dr. Rosander shook his hand. From the look on her father's face, Mary Catherine doubted that he remembered Jerry as a boy sweeping up his office.

She sat between Dr. Rosander and her father. Next came Ron Ottinger and, beside him, Gary Hart. Her special student Clarence Fields sat smiling, dressed in a dark suit and bright tie; he was now a member of the AVID Center's board of directors.

The room was filled to capacity. Over 1,800 teachers came to hear the students and speakers at the send-off before returning to their school districts around the country and the world. They had grown closer during the week and there was a different feeling in the room now than there had been in the beginning. Mrs. Swanson was afraid to let herself feel it. She was too busy watching her guests. She could not enjoy the luncheon for its own sake. She could only try to make sure that everybody seemed to be happy.

At the next table sat a half dozen AVID students and their teachers. She recognized Sybil Beach and Claudio Fuentes, from Anaheim; Lynn Santamaria, a teacher from Glendale, California; and Lynn's student, Dolores Aguilar, whose stories would be told today.

Mrs. Swanson's responsibility was to see that the institute functioned smoothly, joining community and educators. She was one of them. She did not want to feel, in any way, apart from her colleagues. When it came down to it, teachers faced the same barriers as she had. Her experiences were only valuable in that they were universal, or nearly so, and this brought them all to this room. The rest of the year, they would be fighting for their students. Her father, her great supporter and comforter, was beside her again. But the years had turned the tables, and now he was helpless. She had to be strong.

Lynn was sitting almost elbow to elbow with Mrs. Swanson across the narrow space between tables. Seeing Mrs. Swanson's look of concern for her father, Lynn smiled sympathetically. Lynn's mother had died during summer institute last year, Mary Catherine remembered. Now Lynn was offering condolences for her mother. Mary Catherine smiled back. Lynn gently touched her elbow. Teacher to teacher, a touchstone.

Mrs. Swanson began the program by introducing guests. AVID now had many friends and supporters in high places. They were, nearly all of them, women who had championed children's causes and had risen in politics. But not all. Gary Hart in Sacramento and Ron Ottinger in San Diego were role models—men who took children and their needs seriously. The changes in the political world reflected the changes in America's leaders. Yet there was a generational lag between children attending school and the adults in power, whose decisions determined their future. AVID was, she hoped, preparing the next generation of leaders.

Until they came to power, it was good to have Gary Hart in Sacramento, she thought as she introduced him to the audience.

"I'd like to tell a story," she said, while the tall, sandy-haired man stood. "When I invited Secretary Hart to this luncheon, his assistant told me it was his birthday. I thought he would not be coming all the way down here to San Diego. But Gary said, 'There is nowhere I would rather spend my birthday than with the AVID family.'"

As Hart spoke, Mrs. Swanson looked around at the AVID family. She was not listening to his words, so much as absorbing their content. She was so caught up that, when he finished, she remembered that when she had introduced the elected officials, she had forgotten to mention the man who had helped her found the non-profit AVID Center. Ron Ottinger, AVID's national associate director, didn't need any introduction. He was at ease, funny, and warm. As school board president of the San Diego City Schools, he had rallied the voters of San Diego to pass a billion-dollar bond issue for school repairs. Yet there was more to him than the typical politician; he had heart. Without Ron, the AVID Center might never have been born.

— DUETS —

Now came the part of the presentation that Mrs. Swanson liked best—stories of students. They were the heart of the program. Two students and two teachers had written how AVID changed their lives; the essays were then taped and their pictures were projected on the screen. The real people sat at front tables while their images loomed above them.

"Think of these dialogues between students and their teachers as *duets,*" the speaker said, introducing them. As Lynn Santamaria heard her name, she proudly faced Dolores. Mary Catherine leaned forward, listening to Lynn tell her student's story.

Dolores

Dolores grew up in a Mexican immigrant family where the women stayed home and made tortillas while the men toiled in the fields. Yet she had found a teacher named Mrs. Santamaria who believed in her and helped her study and go to college. This was a tremendous opportunity but it was also a terrible conflict, because the higher she rose academically, the further she grew away from her roots in the soil.

Dolores graduated from college and began work toward a second degree at Stanford University. She told her teacher about a recent trip back to a family wedding in Mexico. The women made tortillas together and she quickly lost her feeling of estrangement and was laughing and listening to their stories. She was a part of these women who had flowered like the corn flower. And she had flowered at the university without losing her roots.

Listening to Dolores's story, Mrs. Swanson felt proud of this young woman. She reached across and touched Lynn's arm, communicating through touch: *You and Dolores are what AVID is all about.*

Claudio

The next duet was Claudio Fuentes and his teacher, Sybil Beach.

"Can an educational program targeted to help kids go to college affect an entire community?" the speaker asked the audience. "Ask Claudio Fuentes, the first kid in his barrio ever to attend the University of California."

Claudio grew up in the shadows of Disneyland. His immigrant parents crossed the Mexico border on the Fourth of July, seeking a better life in America. His father landed a job in the laundry at Disneyland. Claudio bawled to life back in 1978 at the UC Irvine Hospital in Orange County. The family crowded into a Spanish-speaking enclave that sprouted, literally, across the street from the Disneyland Hotel. The impoverished barrio was Disneyland's secret—no Mickey Mouse there.

The community called itself "Tijuanita," after the border town near San Diego. The savory odors of corn tortillas and *frijoles* wafted through its warren of apartments. The cramped, two-story, low-rent apartment buildings were hidden behind a wall, out of sight of

Disneyland Hotel guests. Pockets of Mexicans, Guatemalans, Salvadorans, and other ethnic groups dwelled in buildings. The whole community existed in an area that was four blocks long and one street wide. Forty apartment buildings, each with four to eight apartments: about 8,000 residents in a four-square-block area.

When Disneyland was founded in the early 1950s, it needed a work force of low-skilled, low-wage laborers. They needed to live close by, so entrepreneurs making a fast buck built cheap low-income housing.

The economic contrast between Disneyland and Tijuanita was stark. The Disney Empire is still one of the most successful entertainment corporations in the world, with billions of dollars in profits. Ironically, in 1999, the average income of a family in Tijuanita was $8,000.

The people who wash the sheets, fertilize the lawns, swab the toilets—the people without whom Disneyland could not function—were as far away from the American Dream as they were close to Fantasyland.

And, like many people who do the work yet reap few rewards, they were ambivalent. If it weren't for Disneyland and the tourist industry, many of them would not have had jobs—would not have been able to support their families. Yet for all Disney's hype about people existing in "One World," Tijuanita might be on the dark side of the moon.

Police say it is the most crime-ridden area in Anaheim.

Claudio's apartment house was right on the corner of Jeffrey Street, where members of a gang used to hang out. One night, the Fuentes family was preparing to go outside. Shots rang out.

They all froze inside the screen door.

Claudio was nine or ten at the time. Gazing through the wire-mesh door, he saw a car drive slowly in front of the building. He saw the guy who was driving. The driver stopped the car. He pointed a gun from the window. Sparks flashed from its barrel.

The *gang-bangers* ran toward Claudio. They dove for cover, hiding behind palm trees in the front yard of Claudio's building.

The gun kept firing.

A gang member fell to the ground. He screamed, clutching his leg. Blood oozed into a dark stain on his baggy trousers. The car screeched out of sight. Only then did the gang come back to their wounded friend. They carried their bleeding buddy away before the police arrived on the scene.

That was on a Friday night in Tijuanita. It did not make the news on the Disney Channel.

Claudio's family was strong, tenaciously protecting their children from the violence of the 'hood. Claudio's father worked hard so that his children could have opportunities. Although Claudio's parents had little formal schooling, they believed in education.

"A magnet elementary school opened in Anaheim. The students had to *want* to go to this school. There were no school buses, so Claudio's parents drove him back and forth to school. In the new school, Claudio found himself side by side with children of privilege. He was humble in appearance but, inside, he was proud of his Mexican background.

"In 1992, the AVID program was started at Loara High School in Anaheim. The teacher, Mrs. Beach, came to Claudio's middle school to interview students for the first AVID class. She was looking for kids whom other teachers thought had potential. Kids in the C range, whose parents had not gone to college, could go either way—toward college or toward crime in the streets.

"Claudio was already an A and B student, but his parents had no education and couldn't help him prepare for college. When Mrs. Beach met him, she saw that he had the potential to be a leader. In the new class, it was cool to study. Claudio lost friends from the barrio, who ridiculed him for studying hard. But he got a whole new set of friends in AVID.

"In 1992, Mrs. Beach started out with 30 AVID students. Four years later, only 14 AVID students remained.

"Claudio became a peer tutor for younger AVID students in his senior year. Before Claudio, nobody from Tijuanita had ever attended a four-year college. He is the first to graduate from high school and go to the prestigious University of California. Now, eight other kids from Tijuanita have joined AVID and are heading toward a university education.

Mrs. Swanson felt a lump in her throat. When she started AVID, she hoped to help 30 students. Now, in neighborhoods like Tijuanita, AVID was giving hope to a whole community.

As the lights of the banquet hall came on, the students and their teachers received a foot-pounding ovation. Mrs. Swanson clapped for Dolores and Lynn, for Sybil and Claudio, for students who had overcome incredible obstacles, for all the teachers who had changed students' lives. She clapped for the programs that had touched communities and for those AVID would touch in the future. The noisemakers from 13 states and 13 foreign countries broke the spell of Friday the thirteenth.

The duets rose in an AVID chorus, 2,000 voices strong.

— FULL CIRCLE —

I was in the audience on that day, the last Friday the thirteenth of the twentieth century, and I felt the incredible power of those students' stories. Two years had passed since I first saw the Wall of Fame mural; a year since I had begun interviewing Mary Catherine Swanson; months since I had met Clarence, Máximo, and other AVID students, past and present. I was halfway through my research and writing of this book and was trying to make sense of my journey. Now, the telling of Mary Catherine's story, from 1980 to 2000, had finally come full circle.

When the applause died down that afternoon, Mrs. Swanson called me up to the podium to speak. She introduced me to the audience, saying that I was writing a book about AVID, and she asked me to give a progress report.

"First, I'd like to share five lessons that I learned while researching this book on AVID," I said. "Finally, I want to share a private story about a certain woman in this room."

I felt a slight tremor in the audience. Or was it just in Mrs. Swanson's heart? Softly, Lynn Santamaria reached over and touched her arm.

"After a year of research, I believe that AVID comes down to two things—rigor and support," I said, emphasizing each concept by raising one hand and then the other. "You can't expect students to take rigorous classes unless you provide strong academic and social supports. And the reverse is also true: Teachers who give students lots of touchy-feely support but do not challenge them with rigorous curriculum do them no favors." Then I clasped my hands above my head. "AVID combines rigor *and* support.

"While on my journey, four news events shook the world." I counted off four fingers. "An American president was impeached by Congress and put on trial by the Senate. In a remote corner of the Balkans, the people of Kosovo were systematically terrorized, tortured, and chased out of their land. At the same time, two teenage boys at Columbine High School attacked their schoolmates with guns and bombs, leaving 13 dead. Finally, a revered president's son, who was flying his wife and sister-in-law in a small aircraft on a foggy night, suddenly plunged into the sea.

"These stories reflect four issues: integrity, tolerance, violence, and risk taking," I said. "AVID taught me lessons for each one. During the impeachment, people asked: 'How do we explain President Clinton's conduct to our children?' AVID teaches integrity. It helps kids connect their personal lives with their academic goals. AVID develops character—something our leaders need."

I raised a second finger: "Tolerance. The massacres in Kosovo and Rwanda underline the tragedy that inevitably occurs when neighbors hate and fear each other. Could this happen here? In many schools I visited, kids from different backgrounds hardly mix with each other. But in AVID, one sees African Americans, Latinos, Asians, and whites working on the same project. Group study is not voluntary. Students are *required* to exchange notebooks, quiz each other for exams—depend on one another. The curriculum that Mrs. Swanson designed for academic excellence has a social impact. AVID doesn't just preach tolerance, it builds lasting relationships."

I thought of Mrs. Swanson's relationships with Clarence and Máximo, Kuoang and Angelina; and with tutors Judy and Debbie. Many of her original students and tutors were still friends 20 years later. Judy Riffle had given up an executive position in banking to join the AVID Center. Every week, it seemed former students called up or dropped by. These were her most cherished moments.

I took a deep breath. "Now comes the part that no one wants to talk about. Violence in the schools. Every time there's a shooting, people ask: 'What can we do?'

"In April, I attended an AVID conference in Colorado. Educators from around the state were invited to hear about the AVID program. Students from the Cherry Creek School District gave testimonials, teachers described their experiences, and administrators advocated the usefulness of AVID. Someone said that AVID was especially effective in giving students a sense of belonging and purpose. Afterward, an educator from another school district west of Denver said that the program sounded good, but his budget was tight. He asked: 'How can my district justify spending on a program like AVID?'

"Three days later, he got his answer—the Columbine High School massacre. No one can say that AVID would have prevented the massacre, but I have a hard time believing that an AVID teacher would not have been aware of the anguish of those students and the danger they posed. We need to fight violence by building community within the schools."

Now teachers were applauding. Mary Catherine looked at her father. His face looked animated, pink, happy. Was he understanding what was being said?

"Finally, John Kennedy Jr.'s fatal airplane accident made us all think about risk taking," I said sadly. "Teens take risks. That's part of growing up. But what risks are worth taking? Remember what Jay Mathews said about making school 'scary'? It takes guts for C students from non-English-speaking families to take Advanced Placement classes, but real risks lead to real rewards, like college."

The audience had listened patiently to these lessons that I had learned from AVID teachers. Now it was my turn to give them something back.

"Now, I promised to tell you a personal story." I gestured to a front table where Mrs. Swanson was sitting and asked: "Who is this lady?"

There was an audible sigh as nearly 2,000 pairs of eyes turned toward Mrs. Swanson. In the semi-darkness, her shadowed face revealed no trace of emotion. Inside, she later told me, she worried how my remarks might affect her relationships with AVID educators, whom she considered her extended family.

Oblivious to her worries, I continued: "When I began my research, I wondered to myself: *Is she for real? Does she live by her principles?*"

My questions, apparently, struck a chord with the audience. After the presidential impeachment and the unmasking of private lives, Americans had grown cynical. Too many leaders had proved to be phonies, hypocrites, liars, thieves, scoundrels. Americans were looking for reputable leaders who had not lost touch with their constituencies and who led by example. *Was Mrs. Swanson such a leader?*

This was, I believed, the hidden question asked by every newcomer to AVID, by every school superintendent who considered adopting the program. The question of legitimacy. Teachers had sensitive antennae. Was she one of *them?* Did she really understand the problems? Were her methods relevant today? Could they trust AVID with the lives of their students? Darkly, some wondered: *Was Mrs. Swanson just another self-promoter? Was AVID a four-letter word for educational hype?* Teachers noticed that she dressed more like a successful businessperson than a social activist. These small details were petty, yet that is how the human psyche works. Judgments of character are not always rational, but they are necessary in order to make an informed choice. To take risks with children's lives, and their own careers, teachers needed to trust AVID.

Yet, for all her warmth in helping others, the founder and director of the program remained a private person, an enigma. Her public personae and family life were kept separate. She had trouble allowing her feelings to come out in public.

Now her family and colleagues were in the same room. I wondered what they were feeling, hoping they would not feel embarrassed or hurt. But I believed it was important for them to learn about the private woman I had come to know.

"This is a personal story," I confided to the audience. "In her talk, Mary Catherine outlined the lessons that she had learned as a young teacher at Clairemont High. But she left out the most personal part of her story, when her teaching career hit a brick wall and the program hung in the balance. At some point, every teacher reaches such a point, when there is a choice between sacrificing integrity or giving up. This story, I believe, reveals her character."

Mrs. Swanson stole an anxious glance at her father, who appeared to be listening intently.

"By 1986, AVID had decisively beaten the school district's remedial program in improving student performance," I said. "Yet she had alienated administrators who were defending the status quo. She could no longer stay at Clairemont High. She had to quit or find another home for AVID. A state grant, earmarked for preparing minority youth for college, could save the program. But first she needed the imprimatur of the County Office of Education. One day, the county superintendent made a visit to her classroom."

Mrs. Swanson turned to Jerry Rosander, who was sitting beside her. He had barely aged in the 13 years since he had visited her AVID classroom.

"Dr. Rosander came from immigrant Swedish stock, not unlike today's immigrants," I continued. "His parents' highest dream was for one of their nine children to graduate from high school. But this became a remote dream after Jerry's father died. Jerry had to support his mother and eight younger brothers."

Dr. Rosander winced at my mistake—he was the eldest brother of eight *sisters*, not brothers, he later told me. As Mrs. Swanson listened, she turned to her father. Alzheimer's disease had erased Jerry Rosander from Ed Jacobs's memory. In his 62 years as publisher of the *Kingsburg Recorder*—the longest career of any newspaper publisher in California—her father had probably mentored dozens of students. Dr. Rosander smiled at his old boss, and Mr. Jacobs smiled back at the stranger.

"The superintendent waited for the students to absorb his story," I continued. "Then Dr. Rosander turned to their teacher and revealed his secret: Because that publisher helped me learn to write and encouraged me to go to college, he told the students, I was able to become who I am today—the county superintendent of schools. As that newspaperman mentored me when I was your age, today his daughter, who is your teacher, is now mentoring *you* to go to college."

It took a moment for the realization to sink into the audience. As they grasped the significance of the two men's relationship, Mary Catherine felt nothing. She had repeated the story to herself too many times—usually, as an escape from the horrendous traffic jam on her commute home—to summon any emotion. Instead, she was frightened about how her grieving father, whose whole world had been torn from him, would react to being jolted back to his former life in Kingsburg.

A thunderclap shook the room. Ed Jacobs turned, as if hearing the report of a gun. His eyes blinked like a baby glimpsing a new world. A sea of faces seemed to be rising in a wave of applause that broke upon them. Her father was smiling with childlike joy. His mouth was clamped shut and his eyes were like black holes, but his lips curled up on the sides. To see her father smile gave Mary Catherine more pleasure than all the kudos.

Mary Catherine turned to Jerry Rosander. His eyes were shining and tears were running down his craggy cheeks.

"You could say this was a coincidence, or destiny," I said. "But Dr. Rosander supported her proposal, and Mrs. Swanson won a grant to replicate AVID throughout San Diego. Since that fateful meeting, AVID has not stopped growing."

Mary Catherine turned to Lynn Santamaria. Through Lynn's fingers, she could feel the impact of these personal connections on the teachers. Yet she still showed no emotion. She squeezed Lynn's hand, bracing herself, as I introduced her father.

"Today, at age 88, Mr. Ed Jacobs is attending his first AVID Institute," I said. "Joining him for the first time in nearly 50 years is Dr. Jerry Rosander. Without Jerry's support 13 years ago and the consistent backing of San Diego County Office of Education, AVID would have died long ago."

Then I introduced Mary Catherine's husband of 33 years, who had supported her every step of the way. And her son, Tom, a teacher of Advanced Placement American history. "Tom believes in access to Advanced Placement classes. Every student who wanted to take AP history was allowed to do so. This year, he taught 38 students; all 38 took the AP exam; 87 percent passed—an incredible record." The audience applauded and Tom bowed his head, embarrassed, but his mother's eyes shone with pride.

Across the table, Clarence was grinning at her like he'd just won another football championship. Through his eyes, she saw her original AVID class, and at the next table there were Claudio and Dolores, representing the new generation. Surrounding her from every direction were AVID teachers.

"AVID is truly family!"

As waves of applause crashed upon her loved ones, Mary Catherine was aware of everything, but felt only anxiety. She blocked out the din of thousands of hands clapping in a strange, Zen-like silence.

I've made it through another event, she thought. Tom got the car and took Ed home, leaving her to contend with departing guests. Next week, she had to face three grueling days of strategic planning. Then she would drive one last time to Kingsburg to pack her father's belongings and break up her childhood home. There was so much work to be done, she could not rest.

Yet the reaction of the teachers was different. They came up to her after the speech and told her how much it meant to them to hear her story. Something had changed in their attitude: a revelation of their own roles in the struggle? The world outside, she feared, was a dangerous school of hard knocks that demeaned students and burned out teachers, but this only made their commitment more vital. As they packed their bags and spread out into diaspora, the memory of this AVID family reunion flickered like an eternal light of hope.

— BRANCHES OF THE — AVID FAMILY TREE

A Jewish proverb says, "Life begins in the middle and ends there." Learning is also a never-ending journey toward the receding limits of knowledge. We like to think that, with graduation, loose ends are neatly tied up in a diploma, but life is never *solved*. Mrs. Swanson's original students are now in their mid-thirties and their lives have evolved in different directions; so, too, have the lives of their teachers and contemporary AVID students. What has happened to them?

AVID's 93 percent college-attendance rate has held up for 20 years. More specific data can be found in books and government reports, but AVID alumni are a growing repository of living data, with fascinating contradictions as individual as the lines on each human face. What of the anxious students we met on the bus in 1980? What about the children of despair and violence I observed in contemporary AVID classes and the teachers and families we have followed for 20 years? Did AVID's influence hold up on a personal level in their daily lives? Looking at this moving sequence of human "works in progress" recorded in Y2K, one must ask: *What might have happened to these people without AVID?*

The Students

Clarence Fields graduated from the University of Utah and is now a Production Solutions executive at the Xerox Corporation in San Diego. He is responsible for marketing high-speed documenting systems throughout Southern California, and he has won numerous President's Club Awards for top performers at Xerox, including number-one sales specialist in San Diego.

Clarence is the proud father of a five-year-old boy and attends all his son's sporting events—baseball, basketball, and soccer. "It's especially important to be there for my son," Clarence says, because his own father moved away when he was two years old. Clarence flashes a picture of his son printed on a Little League baseball card and the resemblance is remarkable.

Clarence is divorced and lives in suburban north San Diego County, far from the neighborhood where he grew up. He calls daily and frequently visits his mother. Advising her on decisions, he continues in his role as the man of the house. M'Dear has passed away, but her strong spirit abides in her grandson's memory.

Clarence is a member of the AVID Center's board of directors. With his athletic frame sheathed in a business suit, he often speaks about his AVID experiences to student groups, encouraging kids from similar backgrounds to shoot for the highest challenges and go to college.

Máximo Escobedo graduated from the Art Center College of Design in Pasadena and is a graphic designer at Miriello Grafico, a leading design studio in San Diego. He is art director for large projects for Fortune 500 companies, including Hewlett Packard, Gateway Computers, and Nissan Design International. He recently designed and produced a limited-edition book collecting the photographs of Bill Hewlett, co-founder of Hewlett Packard. The entire book was printed on HP's latest office-printing technology. Máximo is on the board of directors of the San Diego Chapter of the American Institute of Graphic Arts and is founding chair of the International Relations Committee. He receives great satisfaction from facilitating contact between the creative communities of San Diego and Baja California. Máximo created the concept and design of the cover for this book, *Wall of Fame,* using a photograph of his brother Javier. Máximo is married, with two daughters, and frequently gathers with his brothers and their families at his parents' home overlooking the freeway.

Máximo's brother Jaime graduated from the North American College at the Vatican, where Pope John Paul II blessed him and other honored deacons from around the world at a papal mass. Jaime is now a parish priest in San Diego County. In all, five Escobedo brothers graduated from AVID; all went on and graduated from college and one earned a Ph.D. They are now a graphic designer, a priest, a mechanical engineer, and a computer software engineer. Gustavo, who majored in political science, has earned a teaching credential and intends to teach high school. Their three older brothers, whose education predated AVID, took much longer to finish college, but made it nonetheless—a testament to the family's determination to prosper in America. Whoever believes that Hispanic immigrants must remain trapped in the cycle of poverty should behold the graduation portraits of eight Escobedo brothers hanging in this proud family's private "wall of fame."

Kuoang graduated from UCSD, *summa cum laude,* with a double major in mechanical engineering and physics. From there, he went directly to Cal Tech on a full fellowship for a Ph.D. degree in aeronautics, then immediately began work on the NASA Space Shuttle Program. After two shuttle launches, he confided to Mrs. Swanson, "Now that I've done this twice, it's boring." Kuoang joined a design team for the proposed Ground-Based Interceptor for NASA's "Star Wars" program. He took time to get married, "the best decision of my life," and traveled to Europe for a summer. But, ever restless, he went on to study business, graduating with an MBA from the Wharton School at the University of Pennsylvania. He is currently working in corporate finance for a major oil company, and writes: "Change is good and I am looking forward to new challenges."

Angelina graduated from San Diego State University with a degree in English, a major accomplishment for a Spanish-speaking immigrant who was once told that she was too ignorant to read a book. Angelina continued to support her younger sisters: one was involved in drugs and one had a child out of wedlock, but both completed college. Angelina became engaged to a man who was tragically killed in a train accident. She is involved in the abuse recovery movement and has written an unpublished autobiographical novel about her experiences.

Joe Canon graduated from San Diego State University and worked as an engineer in the Midwest. Following a lifelong dream, he studied to become an architect, and is designing homes in Arizona and running a small family business.

Joe followed up on his surprise call to Mary Catherine, which brightened her "Day of Hell," by lobbying his son's school district to adopt an AVID program. In February 2000, the superintendent and three principals from Joe's school district came to the AVID Awareness Seminar in San Diego. After the conference, they approached Mrs. Swanson. "We are so happy to meet you," the principal told her. "Joe Canon has been telling us about you and the program. We're going to implement AVID in three schools!"

Two days later, Mary Catherine got a call from Joe. "I have a problem," he said. "Because we didn't have AVID at my son's school last fall, I've been working at home with him on Cornell notes and other techniques you taught me. Now he's getting straight As. I'm afraid he won't qualify for AVID."

Bernice left the AVID program before graduating from high school. Mrs. Swanson has had no contact with her since and recognizes that, unfortunately, not all students respond to the AVID program.

Buay Tang has a presidential scholarship to Point Loma Nazarene College, and is majoring in chemistry and mathematics for a pre-med degree program. He is one of the few African-born students on campus, and remains in close contact with his brothers. Indefatigable, Buay Tang combines a scientific mind with a deep spiritual faith. He is grateful to his AVID teacher, Mr. Visconti, for seeing his potential, taking him out of remedial English, and challenging him to take advanced physics and calculus. He will never forget the suffering of his people, who are being massacred in a bloody civil war that persists to this day. His goal is to become a doctor in the United States and earn enough money to sponsor medical relief programs to save children in Sudan.

The Tutors

AVID tutors have all gone on to professional careers and three are actively associated with AVID:

James, the social sciences tutor, became a teacher in his own right, and today teaches history at Clairemont High School.

Nina, who introduced Cornell note-taking techniques to AVID, graduated from UCSD and is a legislative analyst in Minneapolis, Minnesota.

Judy graduated from UCSD with a degree in city planning and helped redevelop the center city area of San Diego, where she regularly took AVID students on field trips. Eventually she earned an MBA at UC Berkeley and today is the director of finance for the

AVID Center in San Diego, where she lives with her husband and young daughter.

Debbie graduated with a communications degree from UCSD, married, and has two children. She named her daughter after Mary Catherine and today manages an Advanced Placement curriculum project for the AVID Center.

Lisa, whose innocent enthusiasm landed AVID on the *11 O'Clock News*, graduated with a master of fine arts in theater management from the Yale School of Drama. She manages an Off Broadway theater in New York City and keeps in close contact with Mrs. Swanson.

The Teachers

Jim Grove retired from Clairemont High School in 1984 and, since that time, has been teaching freshman writing for the University of California, scoring Advanced Placement papers for the Educational Testing Service, and screening plays for the Old Globe Theater in San Diego. He and Mary Catherine are still in close contact.

Larry Visconti, the AVID teacher who created the actual Wall of Fame in his classroom, has achieved a perfect 1,000 batting average over the last five years, sending 123 AVID graduates to four-year universities. Recently, a group of principals associated with the Harvard University School of Education visited his AVID classroom. Larry grouped the principals with AVID students and gave them a practical lesson in creativity and teamwork. Each group was given an empty wine bottle with a cork lying inside; a handkerchief, tweezers, and two rubber bands. Their goal was to work together to extricate the cork from the bottle without smashing it. The team that won the contest—by what means remains a secret—was led by AVID students, who beat the principals. The principals admired the Wall of Fame, which now bears the names of 148 graduates. There is no longer room for any more names on the wall, so Larry is expanding the Wall of Fame to all four walls of his classroom. Mr. Visconti received a Five-Star AVID Award recognizing him for the fact that, over five years, 100 percent of his AVID seniors went on to attend four-year universities.

The Author

My journey through these extraordinary people's lives changed my own. During the two-year period when I wrote this book, my daughter graduated from high school and was accepted at Columbia, my son became a sophomore in high school and a member of the junior varsity lacrosse team. I remarried and my wife gave birth to a girl on April 1, 2000—one week after I finished the manuscript. Our newborn will be in the high-school class of 2018. Three years after first encountering the Wall of Fame in Mr. Visconti's classroom, I am returning to his class as a writing mentor.

The Family

Tom Swanson, as Mary Catherine's son is known to his colleagues, is a teacher of Advanced Placement American history in a high school in Cupertino, California. His credo is that every student who wants to take his AP class is welcome, a risk he shares with his students. If AP students score poorly, the teacher looks bad, which is why many AP teachers screen out all but the best students. But Tom's "unscreened" class performs brilliantly, which says important things about access, hard work, and Tom's extraordinary teaching skills. Despite his mother's influence in education, he has made it on his own, and does not teach AVID. Although he lives hundreds of miles away, he comes home regularly and takes good care of his grandfather.

Mrs. Swanson suffered a second gallbladder attack in the fall of 1999, yet ignored the warning. She was too busy putting out fires and was involved in strategic planning for the AVID Center. One Saturday, she was folding laundry when the third attack struck. The pain caused her to double over. Her pancreas had swollen to the size of a grapefruit, threatening to crush internal organs. She was rushed to the hospital.

Two days later, she had gallbladder surgery. She awoke in terrible pain, disoriented. Yet she never lost her determination. She was in her hospital bed receiving calls and handling AVID business. She could not afford to let people down who depended on her to keep things going. If she was to expect teachers and students to overcome obstacles, how could she do less?

As AVID prepared to celebrate its twentieth anniversary in the year 2000, she was in her thirty-fourth year in education, 20 in the classroom and 14 running a program. The teaching years were far more stimulating to her mind and satisfying to her soul than were all the kudos she received over the years. Yet the organization she created to replicate her principles and teaching techniques was, perhaps, her greatest achievement and arguably the most valuable legacy a classroom teacher has given to public education in recent times. AVID principles informed the national policy debate on educational reform. She could not rest until AVID Center had a solid financial foundation and was a recognized leader in the national education debate, and only then would she hand over her leadership role, which had never been her purpose in life.

Before she retires, Mrs. Swanson is determined to return to the classroom as an AVID teacher, preparing a new generation of leaders for the twenty-first century.

Rigor without support
is a prescription for failure.
Support without rigor
is a tragic waste of potential.

—Mary Catherine Swanson

EPILOGUE

VISION

TWENTY-FIRST CENTURY

— VISION —

It would be nice to believe that the cumulative efforts of educators like Mrs. Swanson over the past 20 years have made America a more hospitable place for children. But the reality visible in any inner city and in many suburbs and rural towns is that the conditions of life have grown worse for millions of America's children. If current income and education gaps continue to widen, it has been predicted that most students in America's public schools will be living in conditions that put them at risk of educational failure.

The problems that Mrs. Swanson faced at Clairemont High in 1980 are now being felt by teachers and students in America's heartland. It was not that AVID was ahead of its time, but that the times have caught up with it. As America's classrooms more closely resemble Mrs. Swanson's first AVID class, academic rigor and support have become national priorities.

"The changes in demographics we have observed coming for the past 20 years are juxtaposed against the educational needs of a postmodern country that is moving ever faster toward a high-tech, global economy," Mrs. Swanson wrote in an article, "Education for the New Millennium."

What is her vision of educational reform?

"I am not clairvoyant," Mrs. Swanson stressed at the dawn of the year 2000. "Having worked intensively on the issue of student achievement for the past 20 years, I can share with you what our educational system should look like in the year 2020, as the rest of the nation looks more and more like California, Florida, New York, and Texas."

To keep it simple, tomorrow's school should look more like an AVID classroom. More rigor. More support. Deeper relationships between students and teachers. Higher expectations for achievement. Greater tolerance.

AVID has grown from one classroom in one district in one state, to over 1,000 programs involving 50,000 students. Yet it still reaches only a tiny fraction of the "students in the middle." AVID Center has the know-how to expand exponentially, to truly become a nationwide program. But this should never be done at the expense of sacrificing quality.

AVID's principles and methods could be applied and modified within any school. The essence is to create an environment of academic rigor and support where powerful relationships can develop over time. The paradigm is one student, one teacher, and one class meeting for one period a day over the course of several years: *One to the Power of Four.*

The Dana Award citation said it eloquently, praising Mrs. Swanson for "innovative changes in the way the school day is structured." As the pace of change accelerates, education reform demands a change in the way time is structured in school. This might require extending the school day or rearranging schedules. The ingenuity of teachers, students, and parents working with administrators could create a wide variety of approaches. The key is to keep trying new ways until a problem is solved, then move on to the next one.

On a deeper level, the example of one teacher's struggle to improve the lives of her students has a significance beyond the program she created. It is an example of what individuals at the lower reaches of institutions, far from the levers of power, can do to change the conditions of people they care about and to improve their own jobs. Political platitudes and trendy reforms come and go, but enduring reforms come from teachers solving practical problems, one step at a time; people like those whose sagas are sung in this book.

There are no higher callings, Mrs. Swanson believes, than educating the young and healing the ill. Some of the fundamental principles involved in motivating students to succeed against all odds in school may be applied, she asserts, to help frustrated patients navigate through the health-care system. *Never think like a victim. Don't waste energy casting blame. Focus on the goal and work day by day to overcome the obstacles in your path. Ask for help when you need it, and help others when you can. Set expectations high. Accept no less than your best effort. And never give up.*

There will always be a need for people who mentor others, challenging them and supporting them. Just as a newspaper publisher helped a sweeper boy to go to college and become an educator, a county school superintendent helped the publisher's daughter, a teacher, help students become tutors mentoring younger students—an unending chain of mentoring that goes back before their birth and will lead beyond their deaths.

The significance of these myriad acts of mentorship that comprise AVID goes beyond the impact of this program.

AVID's story is a case study of what one teacher can do to help students overcome poverty and bigotry, while battling the system that places obstacles in her path. These portraits in academic courage reveal what extraordinary feats ordinary people can accomplish, if given rigorous goals and strong support.

There is an analogy between the challenges Mrs. Swanson overcame from 1980 to 1999 and the incredible challenges American public education must overcome if America is to survive as a democratic society in the twenty-first century. I wish I had 20/20 vision to predict how education reforms launched today will succeed or fail our children and grandchildren, but I do not.

Instead, I learned from Mrs. Swanson that expectations have the power to change lives and systems, if one is willing to keep trying new ways and never give up until the obstacles are overcome. Her expectation for America's public schools is to provide both rigorous curriculum and strong support for all students, not just those at the top or the bottom. Her expectation for America's teachers is to see that their job is not only to teach subject matter but to teach children, through personal example, to inquire and probe and never give up. Her expectation for students is to take difficult classes, work hard, believe in themselves, and get a college education. Her expectation for America is to stop the polarization of rich and poor and educate "children in the middle" to rise up and strengthen the middle class, upon which this country's survival as a land of opportunity and justice depends.

These expectations are not will o' the wisps, but reasonable expectations of what "we the people" can achieve: a renewal of public schools as the force driving new immigrants and the underprivileged to move into the middle class. To make education work, we must stop casting blame and acting like victims and set goals and a path to achieve them. If something doesn't work, try something else; if success causes jealousy from entrenched groups, fight for what is right—and keep a three-ring binder handy to organize it all.

AVID was born in a climate of conflict over desegregation and it thrives in today's diverse society. It made sense during the era of forced busing, and it makes sense for urban and suburban neighborhood schools; indeed, every school has children in the middle who can benefit from academic and social support. AVID helped students in the era of affirmative action, and now it prepares them to compete for college on an even playing field. It has survived political pendulum swings from left to right, and its balance of moral values and social activism makes it a winning policy for centrists. If the question is asked whether schools are better today than they were in 1980, many would say no. But students in AVID programs *are* better off today, and inculcating Mrs. Swanson's fundamentals—rigor and support—into the curricula for all students may be our best hope to save public schools.

*Any educational reform initiative that does not back up high stan-
dards with strong supports for both students and teachers is almost surely doomed to fail. But* failure *is not in Mrs. Swanson's vocabulary.*

Envision the day when a college-preparatory education is no
longer conducted within a Great Wall that keeps intruders out, but
rather in an inclusive classroom that teaches students from diverse
cultures the abiding disciplines of inquiry and determination so
that they, too, may cross the Great Divide. If we pass on these simple lessons, work hard together, and never give up, Mrs. Swanson's
expectations for her students will become the expectations of all
teachers for America's children—and millions of college-bound
graduates will inscribe their names on the Wall of Fame.

The perpetuation of democracy
and the long-term economic success
of the nation
in the twenty-first century
hinge on building an education system
to accommodate and prepare
all of our children.

—Mary Catherine Swanson

Author's Acknowledgments

Over two years, spanning three states, hundreds of people helped me create this book. I wish to thank AVID students who shared their lives; teachers who shared their experience; alumni who shared their stories; parents who shared their pride; administrators who shared their ideas; scholars who shared their research and critiques; staff who shared their enthusiasm; secretaries who shared their expertise, and Mary Catherine Swanson, who shared all of the above. This book could not have been written without you, the AVID family.

A journalist faces special difficulties in translating the immediacy of reportage into a lasting work of creative non-fiction. I thank my developmental editor, Debra Ginsberg, a writer in her own right, for giving this book a coherent structure and flowing narration; my friend, novelist Robert Harrington, for encouraging me to bring scenes to life; project manager and editor Stacy Moser-Simpson for masterminding publication; Freda Statom, an original AVID student, for tracking down alumni and teachers; and Máximo Escobedo, the AVID alumnus whose family saga graces these pages, for creating the visually arresting cover of this book.

I wish to thank the Charles A. Dana Foundation, for its generous financial support of the research and writing of this book, and Dana medalist Uri Treisman for his intellectual support. At a crucial stage, San Diego State University Press, under the direction of Harry Polkinhorn, became a collaborative partner with AVID Academic Press in bringing this book to a broader audience. Ron Ottinger, who opened the doors for me to teach in the San Diego City Schools in 1997, has supported this project from start to finish. Thanks to AVID teachers Rita Elwardi, Larry Visconti, Elizabeth Wosika, and Brett Weiss for trusting me to teach in your classrooms—and for bearing with my *faux pas*.

I especially thank America's public-school teachers, who perform daily miracles, and my students, who bear witness of their young heroic lives, for giving me hope.

This book is dedicated to you.

ABOUT THE AUTHOR

Jonathan Freedman has received many honors for his editorials and books, including a Pulitzer Prize for Distinguished Editorial Writing and the Distinguished Service Medal from the Society of Professional Journalists. *Esquire* magazine included Mr. Freedman in its special *Hero Nation* issue, honoring his work as a writing mentor of inner-city students.

Born in 1950, Mr. Freedman attended the Denver Public Schools and Phillips Exeter Academy. He graduated *cum laude* from Columbia College, where he was awarded the Cornell Woolrich Writing Award. The prize money launched his overland journey down the Pan American highway to South America. At age 23, he began his career as an Associated Press reporter in Brazil. In his thirties, he worked as an editorial writer and columnist for the *San Diego Tribune*. Freedman's Pulitzer Prize-winning editorials were instrumental in the passage of the U.S. Immigration Reform and Control Act of 1986, including an historic amnesty that brought more than two million undocumented workers out of hiding. He is the author of the critically acclaimed non-fiction book *From Cradle to Grave: The Human Face of Poverty in America,* and has published freelance columns in the *New York Times, Washington Post, Chicago Tribune, Los Angeles Times,* and *San Diego Union-Tribune*.

Mr. Freedman lives in La Jolla, California, with his children, Madigan and Nick, and his wife, Dr. Isabelle Rooney, a research scientist. The recent birth of their daughter, Genevieve, is contemporaneous with this book.

Copyright © 1998 Dave Gatley